Date Due

BC1 Feb 85		
BC 3 86		
Apr 19		

DISCARD

QUEEN CITY

Poems by Raymond Souster

Photographs by Bill Brooks

QUEEN CITY

Poems by Raymond Souster

Photographs by Bill Brooks

THE HATED CITY

We will go, you and I,
to the hated city.

Come in from the lake
over green-blue water,
slip between white beaches
and islands of willow,
see the morning sun
proudly striking her battlements.

We will lunch at the Savarin,
a little later sip wine
at a place no-one knows,
much later slowly stroll
under chestnut trees in blossom,
finally ride to our room
ten magic floors skyward,
with midnight long gone
and only the faint click
of lovers' heels over pavement
as we take our last look
at golden lights, shining lights
strung out everywhere
in twinkling fairy rows. . . .

We will go, you and I,
to the hated city.

FIRST SPRING DAY IN THE CANYONS

Christ, if I were dying
I'd have to get up if only for a minute
to stare down Bay Street this noon
of April First sunshine. Gape at all the girls
with their high-heel wiggles, their last-dollar
every-colour-of- the-rainbow coats and hats,
laugh at all the big shots
carrying their paunches out of exclusive clubs,
then waddling curb-side to cars
with the thick cigars of success slowly being chewed
    to death,
marvel at the store windows—cross-section
of all the useless baggage we burden our lives with
till they rebel (and rightly so)—finally drop a coin
in one of the many tin cups the armless the legless
    have ready,
that and their eyes, spring today bringing out the misfits
as well as the big and beautiful players
of this whirling game—life, did I hear someone say?

MARY ROSE VISITS THE
STOCK EXCHANGE

If the shouting bothers you
cover your ears, my lady,
if the disorder jars on you
reflect that in this disorder
there is strictest order.

Then, when you can't stand
any more of this interplay
of Commerce, why, move down
to the middle of the floor,
shake your hips a couple
of wonderful times and bring
this whole damn farce
to a paper-strewn halt.

MONEY TALKS

Money talks
so they say;

sometimes with the soft
persuasiveness of the pimp,
sometimes with the quick
deep cut of the lash,

but more often than not
when it's finally finished,
it really hasn't said
anything at all.

IS EVERYBODY HAPPY?

Doubt may exist, but evidence is everywhere at hand
to convince the most skeptical observer
of the kind efficiency of our civilization,
with nothing left to chance, everything provided
to make our stay on this earth a brief but happy interval.

For example, please enter the gates
of this modern mansion for the insane.
Observe the sweeping approaches, the simple but
    impressive architecture.
Come inside and walk the silent-tread corridors,
the miles of connecting tunnel. See how spotless
    everything is,
how skilfully the staff perform their duties.
Watch the happy faces of the patients all light up,
they thrive in this world of rest and sunshine.

(The bars on all the windows are unobtrusive.
The guards are efficient handlers.
The walls are well sound-proofed.
The patients are crazy anyway.)

Nothing's left to chance in our civilization, everything's
    provided,
and as further advances are made we can always
    build bigger, better, more efficient madhouses.

FOR THE STATUE OF QUEEN VICTORIA,
QUEEN'S PARK, TORONTO

The overnight snow
has given you a shiny white shawl
with headpiece to match,
but the passersby hardly notice,
your majesty escapes them completely.

During your reign
it was said the twentieth century
would belong to Canada.

Now it's 1978
but still we haven't yet begun
to take possession.

Perhaps even being second-rate
is almost too much for us,
keeps us all so busy
we have little time for anything,

especially statues of queens
who happened to live too long.

OLD ST. ANDREW'S

The soot of a hundred years water-pressured away,
she comes forth spanking clean, yellow-stone walls
    gleaming
in the morning sun that catches each peak, point and spire!

God's fortress of another time, solid, unassailable,
head high, resplendent, ready to chance
all change: the very stones about her shout it out
as uncertainty, bewilderment swirls all about her
and passes unnoticed; she is ageless, above and
    of the ages!

GIRDER GANG

You're monkeys, all of you,
sitting out at the end of a girder
fifteen floors up or more,
holding on with only your knees
because both hands are busy
signalling that crane from below
the exact spot to lower
the next girder into place beside you.

Or walking as if in the Yonge Street crowds
along narrow platforms,
tools flapping at your side.
No wonder you look down at lunch-time
and laugh as you spot us white-faced clerks
straining necks and tired eyes upward
to see what's going on,
then spit once to keep your luck,
(waiting for the pavement splash
that never comes all the way back?)
Monkeys no chain could ever hold.

JOHN STREET

I can't decide which will outlive the other—
the old men drooped on the steps of these run-down houses,
unshaved, unpaid, unloved,

or the buildings themselves, once proudly new and
    in fashion,
now breaking up, slow-rotting in their winter of time,
still stubborn like these old men right to the end—

but I'll bet the landlords know. . . .

ONE FACE OF TORONTO

The carved stone face
glaring down from the archway
of this bird-limed mausoleum,

looks quite a bit like
a one-faced cousin to Janus,
phoney leftover from Rome,

and badly needing by the look of him
a long weekend in Montreal,
where my good poet-friends
can no doubt arrange
to get him happy drunk
and have his ashes hauled,

then still get him back
bright and early Monday morning,
so he'll greet my arrival
in these downtown smog-lands
with a smile for a change
on his venerable kisser.

DOWNTOWN TRAIN

This morning my day's beginning could read like a hundred others—reluctant rising, kiss on the forehead of drowsing wife, gulped breakfast and a twelve-minute walk through shaded side-streets to Keele Station,

where a subway train rattles in on perfect time, where I take my window seat in the almost-empty car, where I make myself comfortable and doze off very soon after the trainman blows the second of two piercing blasts on his whistle and the coaches jerk forward,

to suddenly awaken, noticing with a start that I'm all alone in the long, beautifully air-conditioned car, that we don't slow down at all for approaching stations but flash right through—and, for that matter, why shouldn't we?—there's not a single soul waiting on any platform!

Still, the trainman's still aboard somewhere and of course the driver, so I'm not *all* alone—I hear his over-shrill whistle repeated with the same strength time and time again, though I can't tell exactly where he's stationed, and I wonder why he has to whistle at all now that the tunnel's pitch black with no red, green or yellow winking signal-lights ahead, now that we don't rush past station platforms any more, now that we're gathering more and more speed until it seems that the train won't be able to stay on the rails much longer, much longer. . . .

With all the time a warning sign above me flashing on flashing off FOREVER FOREVER FOREVER.

MEMORY OF BATHURST STREET

"Where are you, boy?"
my Aunt Maggie's calling,
but I can't hear her
in my attic eyrie,
where I watch the heat
swirl up from the tar roofs,
waiting for the cry
of the bearded rag-picker
down the lane from Ulster Street.

"Where are you, boy?"
my Uncle Jim's calling,
but I can't hear him
for the cooing of birds
inside this pigeon-coop
at the back of the garden,
where I scrape up the droppings
to earn my allowance.

"Where are you, boy?"
my Aunt Lizzie's calling,
but I can't hear her
from the upstairs sitting-room,
as I turn the pages
of my favourite book
where the Highlanders lie
in the blood of their death
on green Spion Kop.

CHASING THE PUCK

Viewing shoot-for-the-corner
slap-shot, drop-pass antics
of Hockey Night in Canada—
Leafs versus Red Wings
in Mr. Smythe's well heated ice-palace,

it's not hard to let the mind wander,
to put skates on twelve-year-old ankles,
to clear ice at Second Marsh and dodge
the tips of bullrushes sticking through;

to find one five-below morning
(spent under echo-bouncing curve
of Old Mill Bridge) my right foot
well frozen, and taking me
five-minutes' agony with snow
rubbed almost through the skin
to bring it redly back. . . .

To come to that afternoon
my shot caught their goalie on the eye,
and the game ruined, him turning
away from me after that. . . .

But now Gordie Howe
side-steps, fakes and moves in,
and I'm right there behind him
poised for the shot, the net-bulge, the electric roar!

OLD MILL BRIDGE

Under the arch of this bridge twenty years ago
I froze both feet playing hockey
on a five-below winter afternoon.

Now that bridge is still there, only older,
but I don't play hockey any more,
and we haven't had a real cold winter
since the second-last year of the War,
while my feet—they could still be frozen
for all they seem to lead me to. . . .

LAST BEER AT THE OXFORD HOTEL

We've drunk our last beer at the Ox, Don;
that old back room where once we drank out of steins
and had to shout to hear ourselves
above all the other shouting, is closed now,
there won't be any more nights like those we knew
before all the gang got killed off or married,
(or worse still, serious and old), when we'd come out
   the small side door
feeling high on two pints of beer,
and head up Bay for the Casino, more than ready
to laugh at the second-rate comics,
cheer and whistle as the strippers came slinking on. . . .

All I know is any beer we drink from here in
won't taste half as good, as honest or close again,
not because we've changed that much (we haven't,
   have we?),
but hell, our old backdrop's been shifted,
the familiar setting axed, and no other place
can ever be the same: we'll sit at a table somewhere else
and feel strange, the beer will somehow taste flat
and we'll wonder why—
                        then suddenly
look hard at each other and know.

SHAKE HANDS WITH THE HANGMAN

From Casa Loma looking down—
the City,
shower of lights at a roadside carnival.

It's cold in the streets, winter's coming.
The white whip of winter waits
to be swung with a crack
in our stupid, grinning faces.

The man selling flowers outside Child's
has the nervous, shifting eyes of the hunted.

Shake hands with the hangman.
Notice how steady those hands are
after such bloody work.

Shower of lights. . .
white whip of winter. . .
eyes of the hunted. . . .

Notice how steady those hands are
thick with the blood of this city.

HELL-FIRE ON YONGE STREET

Waiting patiently in the theatre lineup
for the nine-o'clock movie,
which coils, snake with no tail in sight,
round the corner of drab Shuter Street,

the young restless kids are amused
by a solitary man on the sidewalk
shouting at them above the noise of Yonge Street,
"You are all sinners, but you can be saved,
only don't wait until it's too late, too late forever. . . ."

Then he sees the taunting smiles on their faces,
these creatures with their cigarettes dangling
from their soft, lazy mouths, these punks
with their lip-smeared, eye-painted girls,

and he drowns in an ecstasy of rage
as he screams at them, "Laugh, go on, laugh,
we'll see how you laugh when they throw you
on the great fiery coals of hell. . . ."

BATTERED

My battered **Christ**
of Yonge Street,
now suddenly old,
more unwashed, more ragged than ever,

shaking so badly
you have to look **twice**
at the postcard he holds **out**
to decide it's the same **one**
he couldn't sell all last **week**.

THE CITY CALLED A QUEEN

How many poems have been smothered
by the tight strangle of buildings,
how many silenced effectively
in the crazed screech of traffic,
and how many more
broken cruelly at the touch
of that slow killer Boredom
(his curse a dark evil mist
over all this city) ?

Strange city,
cold, hateful city,
that I still celebrate and love
while out there somewhere
you are carefully working at my death. . . .

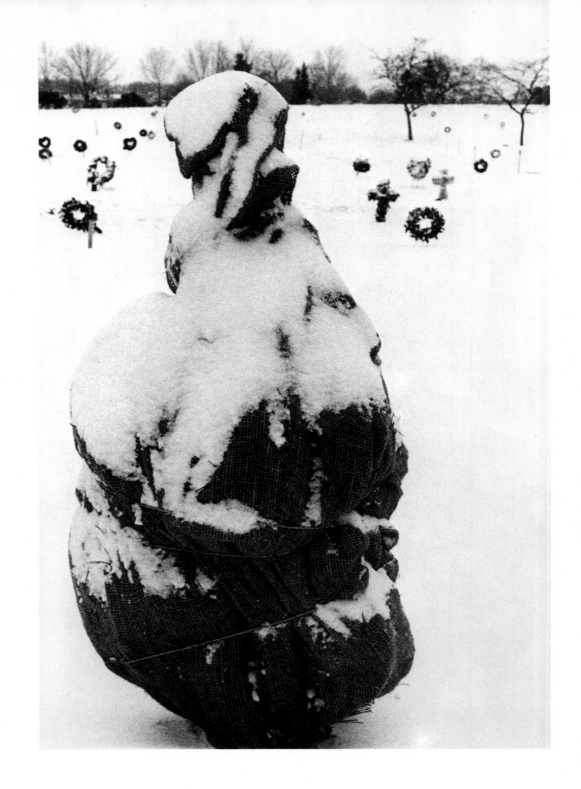

FUNERAL DIRECTOR

When the Reverend at graveside,
shouting over the wind,
reaches the appropriate words
on his flapping Bible page,

very deliberately your hand
sprinkles just the right amount
of fine brown sand
in the form of a cross
on the shiny coffin top,

then just as deliberately
returns to your leather glove,
before the January wind
now spearing the snow crust
turns and snaps your fingers off.

THE LECTURER

The blind—
leading the blind—
                    me here
at the end of the table
trying to tell young faces
about poetry:
                    when I don't know myself
which way to go:

while at forty the sound
of my own voice
is no reassurance

is no guarantee
I am even still alive.

POET OF THE VILLAGE

Arms bent back behind his head,
feet stretched full length,
his cigarette dangling.

Behold the artist at rest,
Poet of the Village
(Gerrard Street West, Toronto)
posing in his simple room.

What if he hasn't written
hardly any poems at all?

Hell, this is a magazine article,
and every Village has to have at least
someone who looks like a poet,
doesn't it?

THE ROOSTER IN THE CITY

Since he's moved to the city
this rooster's gone all to hell:
sleeps in until nine,
then out on the back fence
to face the east
and salute the dawn
three hours too late.

LAMBTON RIDING WOODS

Here where as children
we watched the proud riders go
up through the paths
on their strong-limbed horses,
chased the huge butterflies
over the meadows,
smelling of clover
and the burnt smell of hay:

here where we picked
the shy-eyed hepaticas,
hidden under the wet
sodden leaves on the wooded slopes,
here where we ran on
the partridge and drove it
crashing and stumbling
far away in the bushes,
here where red berries
stained all our faces,
stained all our hands
as we picked them like robbers:

here where we left
some part of our childhood,
left it in keeping
for some far tomorrow,
here where our lives
met a beauty so simple,
here where the world
was a palace of wonder—
they have cut down the trees,
ploughed the grasses under,
killed every flower. . . .

There are now rows of houses
on those hills, ugly houses
with bright, ugly colours,
even uglier fences;
all the roads are muddy
and twist like bewildered snakes,
with sewer-pipes waiting
to be buried deep under
the good clean earth
now dead forever.

And next spring more rows
of these squatting toads
with more obscene colours
to pollute the countryside,

with all beauty gone
from these hillsides forever,
the memories of childhood
come crashing down,

that world of wonder,
that world of wild roses
buried with the pipes
of next year's sewers.

No more the proud riders,
no more these children. . . .

NO ESCAPE

Even down in the subway
you can't escape it—
where to bank your money, what brassière
should cover your true love's breasts,
which cigarette to get lung cancer from. . . .

No escape
until each of our minds
is an endless, flashing billboard
plastered with a million catchwords,
ten million insidious slogans.

And look—up there in the sky
the Hand slowly scrawls
in spirals of smoke
DIE NOW AT HALF THE USUAL PRICE.

NO ESCAPE

Even down in the subway
you can't escape it—
where to bank your money, what brassière
should cover your true love's breasts,
which cigarette to get lung cancer from. . . .

No escape
until each of our minds
is an endless, flashing billboard
plastered with a million catchwords,
ten million insidious slogans.

And look—up there in the sky
the Hand slowly scrawls
in spirals of smoke
DIE NOW AT HALF THE USUAL PRICE.

THE IMMIGRANT

For Jozo

Each face has two ears
tuned up deaf to catch
each stumble of my speech,
two eyebrows to lift
at the clothing I wear,
two lips to form a sneer
at the house where I live.

Yet it's useless to hate
as my heart says it should,
for I must swallow pride
to ape everything they do,
somehow make myself over
into one of them,
or end up a nothingness,
not having learned
there's only one way up
for those such as me—

the death and burial
of the man I was:
only then will masks
lift, faces hold out their hands.

DUNDAS AND MONTROSE

Only the smallest of reminders
left now to give any hint
how many waves of people
have moved through these streets,
come and gone from these houses.

As in this grocery-store window
below the slightly torn awning
the words "Fruits and Vegetables"
(almost worn away now)
have become lower down
"Frutas & Vegetais,"

with a final "We deliver"
the perfect blending of it all.

CARIBANA PARADE, UNIVERSITY AVENUE

Don't be too surprised if, after this parade is over,
he suddenly feels the strength in these giant wings
to which he's attached himself, and with all the gods
    smiling,
propels his butterfly's body now here, now there
among the mouth-gaping crowd, then suddenly springs
and climbs upward, at last with his mind clear of earth
and her stay-at-home tyranny. Who knows how far
his dream may carry him, this brilliant-hued Icarus,
even if not as far south as his beloved Trinidad,
then perhaps to jewelled Jamaica, sparkling in the
    morning sun!

MILK-CHOCOLATE GIRL

By now it's a wonder
someone hasn't eaten you
ounce by delicious ounce,
milk-chocolate **girl**.

Taken already
in very small bites
the slightly snub nose,
the breasts still asleep,
the awakening hips,
the legs very firm.

We thank God you're still
very much in one piece,
to light up the darkness
of this lunch-hour for us
with a turn of your head,
a single flash from your eyes.

O easily the most
awkward (still charming) thing
you'll ever do in your life—
the way you're attacking
that slice of bread now!

KENSINGTON MARKET

Nothing here says
you must buy a dime's worth.

But even if you have to hold your nose,
shove your head
into the near-dark
of a few side-street stores:

examine fruits and vegetables
as you would the breasts
of a woman taken
to bed for the first time:

handle warily the yard-wide
caballero's hat—
the lining reads Madeira-made—
admit with a smile
that it hides too much of your eyes.

Above all, remember
each smell, each sensation
this hot day offers you,
how these people sweat to please.

And if you feel like a lie,
tell your friends: I had a squid
brained to order at Kensington—
they might almost believe you.

SHOPPING NOTES FROM CHINA VILLAGE

(For Ivy and Susannah)

People out in droves,
spilling out over the sidewalks;
weather spring-like for March
if the wind had been a little kinder.

Three or four of the market stores
had gleaming white buck-choy,
or if you prefer buck-choy-sum
with its lighter emerald leaves
and little yellow flower.

There were snow peas to make your mouth water,
sai yeung tsoi or watercress,
the white turnip called lo pak,
bean-sprouts, gai-lan or Chinese broccoli,
gou-toy looking like dark-green grasses,
the narrow shape of bitter melon
with its very rough scales,
yam-sweet potatoes and a gleaming purple vegetable
looking like a long, thin cucumber
too beautiful to cut up or peel.

So next time try to remember
to buy a few pastries at the Keefer Bakery,
somehow find out the names
of those barbecued delights
hooked up beside the gleaming glaze
of chicken bodies all in a row;

bring back with you, too, some of the smiles
on young, Saturday-happy faces,
the breathtaking serenity
of old eyes seen half-hidden under hats,
their feet very cautiously trying out the pavements,
not willing to be left behind
in this almost dragon-like procession
snaking east and west along Dundas Street.

COMPENSATION

For Victor and Elizabeth

We never did manage that corn-roast
on Ward's Island beach (my dream of it the lighthouse
on Eastern Gap's pier-end answering in flashes
red-orange magnificence
of our bonfire fanned by wind-bellows
and bent on shattering all darkness. . .).

But still we had that afternoon
of soft-shivering ferry floor under us;
of sailboats small and nervous
on big wind and chop of the bay;
of volleyball down at beach edge,
the girls eager, awkward prima donnas,
and that smash shot just out of reach;
of football on the sand, our winner
a six-year-old plunging fullback;

then a last dockside wait
(day's slowly sinking matador
taking one last bleeding wound
from the sharp-horned dig of the skyline);
with the island bedding down behind us
to twin songs of willow and water.

A DREAM OF HANLAN'S

(Southern England, 1945)

It's not homesickness, it's the thought of the morning sun
strong on the beach, warming the sand for the feet
of the young girl and boy I can almost see running
out the cottage door, down the walk, then free of the house
and anything holding them from the lake's tingling-cool
    water. . . .

And it isn't loneliness, it's just me imagining
the utter peace of mind, the quiet of those mornings,
when no aircraft roared off to bomb or to destroy,
no machine-guns, no cannon, shaking out sprays of death,
but with only the shouts of swimmers in the water,
the cries of children as the waves break on their impractical
castles of sand.
               It's nothing but desire to live again,
fresh from the beginning like a child.

A DREAM OF HANLAN'S

(Southern England, 1945)

It's not homesickness, it's the thought of the morning sun
strong on the beach, warming the sand for the feet
of the young girl and boy I can almost see running
out the cottage door, down the walk, then free of the house
and anything holding them from the lake's tingling-cool
    water. . . .

And it isn't loneliness, it's just me imagining
the utter peace of mind, the quiet of those mornings,
when no aircraft roared off to bomb or to destroy,
no machine-guns, no cannon, shaking out sprays of death,
but with only the shouts of swimmers in the water,
the cries of children as the waves break on their impractical
castles of sand.
                It's nothing but desire to live again,
fresh from the beginning like a child.

A SHADOW

A shadow should be
a comfort, a companion,
especially on cold winter nights.

Mine's neither,
being more of a nuisance,
either playing at stepping on my heels,
or making like terror, fond of showing
blackness so close behind
darker than anything I've seen
even deepest in myself.

ROOM AT THE TOP OF THE STAIRS

(For Margaret Avison)

Five-o'clock crowds,
policemen's whistles
whipping waves
of motors, lights
across
black intersections.

Noise grates,
rain mocks
these faces bleared
as never before. . . .

Then to come down
still street
to hid house,
climbing to a room
where the dim one light
breathes peace,
and the great untroubled
voice of poetry
is all.

MISTY MORNING, ASHBRIDGE'S BAY

The shoulders of the fog
take their last shrug,
begin to steal away.

Day will soon burn through.

It's a last chance
for birds and boats
to feel that strange
sweet-and-sour joy
that aloneness brings,

a final moment
hidden from the all-seeing
meddling eye of man.

FALLING OF THE ACORNS

Close together as one,
ears, eyes as one,
lying here in the matted sunshine
slipping down through the trees,
sliding down to the grass
with its litter of leaves,
golds, browns, yellows, crimsons.

Both of us nearly motionless
through the long voyage of the afternoon,
no word spoken, hardly a sound made between us,
everything said with a touch of fingers, press of lips,
so we hardly noticed the crashing partridge
who came on us suddenly in his blundering.

Bodies together as one,
ears, eyes as one,
listening with a patience born of long silence
for the deliberate, long-spaced falling of the acorns.

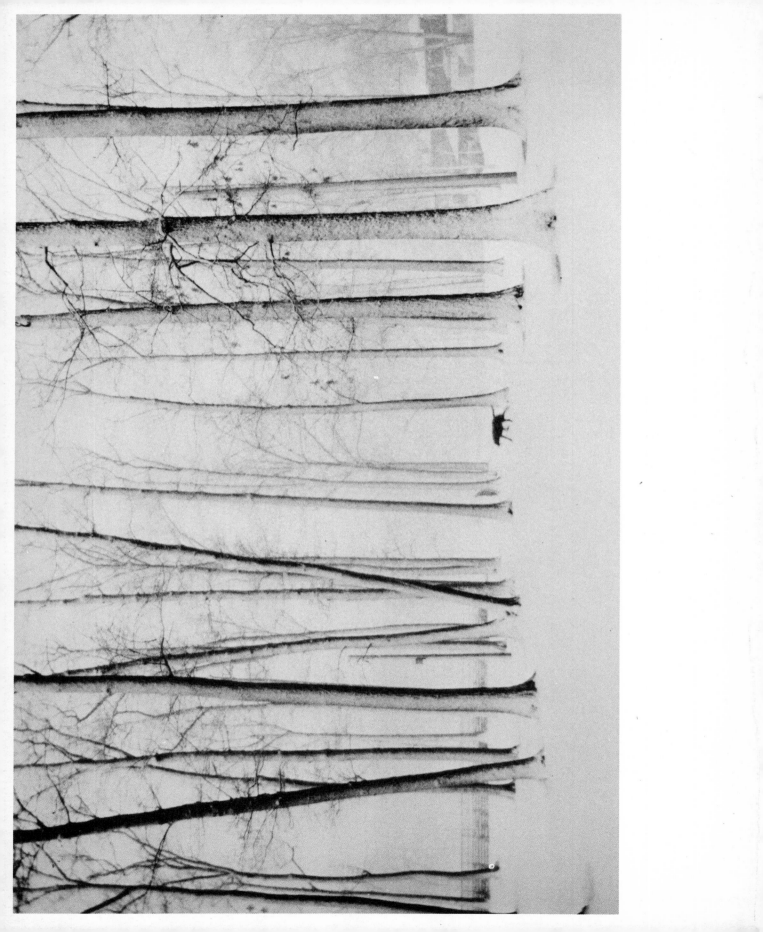

OUR WORLD IN WINTER

Darling, look at the snow
settling on our world out there,
sifted through the dark earth places
with the pureness of heaven.

Brushed against every tree,
its touch almost silk-like,
wrapping the last torn leaf
in the folds of compassion.

Covering the stiffened cold robin
morning left at our door
with such a fine grave-cloth
that death seems no evil,

only swift, incidental,
as snow shifting on the roof.

ISBN 0 88750 507 4

Typesetting and design by Michael Macklem

Printed in Canada

PUBLISHED IN CANADA BY OBERON PRESS

This book was published with the assistance of
a grant from the Toronto Sesquicentennial Board
in honour of the one hundred and fiftieth
anniversary of the City of Toronto.

Making Technology Investments Profitable

ROI Road Map from Business Case to Value Realization

Second Edition

JACK M. KEEN

WILEY

John Wiley & Sons, Inc.

658.4038
KEEN, J

Library of Congress Cataloging-in-Publication Data:

Keen, Jack M.
  Making technology investments profitable : ROI road map from business case to
value realization / Jack M. Keen. – 2nd ed.
      p. cm.
  Includes index.
  ISBN 978-0-470-19400-3 (hardback); ISBN 978-1-118-02858-2 (ebk);
  ISBN 978-1-118-02859-9 (ebk); ISBN 978-1-118-02860-5 (ebk)
  1. Information technology—Management.   2. Information technology—Economic
aspects.   I. Title.
  HD30.2.K427 2011
  004.068—dc22
                                                                    2010047241

Printed in the United States of America

10 9 8 7 6 5 4 3 2 1

To my family: Bonnie, Bryce, Mark, and Shanti, and to their families—for helping make this book possible in a hundred different ways.

Contents

Detailed Table of Contents

Preface to the Second Edition

Why a Second Edition?

Since publication of the first edition of this book eight years ago, the world, and management's response to it, has vastly changed. While the need to create trustworthy business cases, as emphasized in the first edition, remains as important as ever, executives are now also increasingly concerned about what do to *after* the business case gets the funding. How, they ask, can we be assured that the value promised in the business case actually gets realized? These leaders have learned the hard way that this task is tricky. They see firsthand how value leakage that begins as drips can quickly grow into torrents, leaving ROI-devastated solutions in their wake. Such disappointments disillusion stakeholders and discourage solution delivery people.

What management often doesn't see—and what this second edition explains—is that more often than not, the root cause of value shortfalls is management's inattention to value realization best practices. A modicum of management focus on value achievement discipline can help maximize ROI results.

Nature of the Advice

For the past decade, the author and his consulting colleagues have helped business transformation programs maximize ROI across four continents. In the process, many "value success" do's and don'ts have been identified, synthesized, and categorized. Some are obvious. Some are subtle. All are pragmatic. This second edition recaps these lessons, with an emphasis on how to quickly put them into action.

What's New in This Edition?

The guidance in this new edition takes into account several new realities related to IT-enabled investments: They are more important to enterprise success than ever before; they are more complex and costlier to implement; and they carry a high risk of failure, especially in terms of lost opportunity and time.

The first edition focused primarily on getting the business case right—the essential yet often misunderstood foundation for value achievement. This second edition extends that foundation to elaborate on what management can do to maximize ROI by detecting and eliminating large value leaks occurring throughout the design, development, launch, and operation of the proposed solution.

Seven new chapters are included in this new edition, dealing with:

- How to uncover ROI-draining value leaks that no one has noticed
- Steps for plugging those leaks and preventing similar ones from occurring in the future
- Management practices to put into place related to:
  - Business case creation and maintenance
  - Value measurements
  - Stakeholder accountability for value forecasts
  - Decision making to prioritize solution capabilities, requirements, and rollout sequencing
  - Benefits tracking
- Use of a new Value Practices Audit to make value leak detection and correction faster and easier.
- "Quick wins" to demonstrate the urgency and value of a more disciplined approach to value management

What has not changed from the first edition is a focus on simplicity and practicality. Getting value right is not a complex theory. It's a series of small but vital management-led steps for motivating everyone to be value thinkers, and value doers, 24/7.

Acknowledgments

Creating the second edition of this book, I benefited enormously from the guidance, expertise, and commitment of many Infosys colleagues, clients, friends, and associates.

Major thanks are due to Raj Joshi, cofounder and managing director of Infosys Consulting (IC), and to Sharad Elhence, Infosys's partner in IC's Core Process Excellence practice. Raj is widely recognized as the originator of many innovative value realization approaches that have been enthusiastically embraced by clients worldwide. Sharad is a master at thinking deeply about value realization, and driving the creation of new solutions that address a wide diversity of client needs. Both Raj and Sharad have been uncommonly generous in exchanging ideas with me about how to help clients "get value right."

Culture is crucial when it comes to creating value thinking (and "value doing") within a large organization. Special recognition is given here to key Infosys leaders who have been profoundly committed to creating an Infosys-wide culture where "client value success" is a deeply engrained commitment. Several Infosys leaders have been especially instrumental in making this happen. In addition to Raj and Sharad mentioned above, a great debt of thanks goes to value culture creators Steve Pratt, CEO of Infosys Consulting; Ming Tsai, IC managing director; N. R. Narayana Murthy, Infosys's cofounder, chairman of the board, and chief mentor; Nandan Nilekani, cofounder and former CEO of Infosys Technologies, Ltd.; Kris Gopalakrishnan, Infosys's CEO and MD; and K. Dinesh, Infosys's director and head of quality.

Additional thanks are also due to other Infosys colleagues who have contributed, over many years, a constant stream of ideas and sustained passion to help create and implement innovative value realization solutions. These Infosys people include: Saurabh Agrawal, Joe Attia, Arindom Basu, Brandon Bichler, Joshua Biggins, Amar Chhatwal, Andre DuPlessis, Raul Fabre, Shweta Gupta, Cesar Jelvez, Ash Joshi, Sandeep Kumar, Steven Lambert, Heidi Lamberts, Eric Librea, Peter Maloof, Jeremy

Milward, Nitin Pradhan, Mahesh Raghavan, Surabhi Sah, Bibhash Shah, Lars Skari, Chris Spangler, Manu Tyagi, Vivek, and many others too numerous to mention here.

This second edition, like the first edition, would never have happened with the sustained enthusiasm and dogged determination of my editor, Tim Burgard, at John Wiley & Sons. He somehow manages to uniquely combine extreme patience (while I searched for scarce writing time) with a firmness about deadlines and a flexibility to account for unexpected twists and turns. Tim's team, especially Laura Cherkas and Helen Cho, were likewise exceedingly helpful while still reminding me when completion dates were looming.

Intellectually, Dr. Robert Benson, adjunct professor at Washington University in St. Louis, Missouri, greatly influenced my thinking with his pioneering information economics research in the late 1980s. His writings (see the Bibliography) were seminal in turning my career, from the early 1990s onward, to "all ROI, all the time."

An important debt is owed to Professor Warren McFarlan of Harvard Business School. His unique insights through the decades have helped all of us make sense of the always-expanding yet easily fumbled role of technology in business success. Warren's classes, publications, presentations, and conversations have unerringly pointed the way to astute business management of technology, thus helping managers of all types and sizes to "get it." A McFarlan exposition of any kind is an important intellectual (as well as entertaining) opportunity not to be missed.

Several colleagues of mine outside of Infosys have also been very helpful in enabling me to solidify ideas related to maximizing ROI. Thanks especially to Ron Barbaree. Heartfelt thanks also to the brothers Sherman (Craig and Randy), as well as to Christine Comaford, Peter Cunningham, Karl Drexhage, Janine Haines, Beth Holtz, the late Jackie Kessel, Jan McDaniel, Teresa Pahl, Rich Peterson, Jewel Savadelis, and Bob Vizza.

Lastly, I'd like to thank the hundreds of savvy business and IT leaders who have been my clients for value realization–focused engagements. Because these global leaders believed in a vision of better value results, they invited my colleagues and me in the door to team with them to launch value realization best practices that truly made a difference. Not only their ideas, but also their pragmatism as well as the diversity of their industries, sizes, and locations around the world helped me distill universal truths and best practices that have become the core of this book.

Thanks to everyone for contributing to the understanding that while being "on-time" and "on-budget" is a good thing, being "on-value" is the ultimate measure of our success.

Jack Keen
JackMKeen@gmail.com
Basking Ridge, New Jersey

Introduction

Price is what you pay. Value is what you get.
    —Warren Buffett, 1930– , American investment entrepreneur

What This Book Is About

Ultimately management exists to maximize value. All else is a means to that end. Thus, it's surprising that three-quarters[1] of IT-enabled investments still do not deliver their expected value. Why is management allowing this to happen? Based on extensive field experience over the past decade, this book explains why value leaks still persist in gusher-size proportions, and what management can do to stop them.

This book's central thesis is that while dangerous value leaks are prevalent, they are quite preventable. The key is for senior and operational management to discard their ad hoc approach to value assurance and replace it with pragmatic, disciplined practices that create a value-focused culture that is both broad and deep.

The widespread lack of management attention to value-enhancing practices usually exists because decision makers:

- Underestimate the huge value penalty of current management practices, and/or
- Are unsure about the most effective ways to get value back on track, and/or
- Misjudge the centrality of their role in value success.

---

1. Standish Group Survey, "The Chaos Report" (2009).

The chapters that follow discuss ways to locate and then fix existing leaks, as well as identify management practices to prevent future ones. Included are explanations of how to spot warning signs of value trouble, such as:

- *Missing or flawed business cases.*[2] Experience indicates that over 50 percent of funded IT projects still use no formal ROI guidance. Over 80 percent of the business cases the author has seen are flawed in overt or subtle ways. Shiny shoes, a tap dance, and a few discreet, offline conversations continue to grease the skids for approvals of favored projects. Political influence lurks at every turn to trump objectivity.
- *Shallow and/or ambiguous accountability.* "One hundred percent of our executives have bought into the program's benefit goals" is not a statement of assurance. The key question is: Will they and their key subordinates be accountable for benefits realization at bonus time? If all managers and staff who can directly influence value realization do not truly believe in and are not formally accountable for their share of an investment's value success, the program is flying on a wing and a prayer.
- *Value-blind design decisions.* A solution's design is the result of hundreds, if not thousands, of design decisions related to capabilities, requirements, and functionality. If these design choices are not primarily selected based on "contribution to value," then the solution itself cannot hope to be an ROI triumph.
- *Value-flawed prioritization decisions.* Decisions related to prioritization choices, such as when to customize packages, how to sequence rollouts, and resolution of scope control issues, can easily subvert ROI if they are not value guided.
- *Loosely disciplined benefits tracking.* Benefits tracking that is ad hoc or has little management discipline for continuous review and resolution will leave stakeholders wondering, "Was the investment really worth it?" Solutions with ambiguous benefits leave stakeholders questioning the credibility of everyone associated with their design and implementation.

From these insights comes the conclusion that the single most important ingredient for value success is senior management's willingness to champion a better value management process—clearly, loudly, and often.

---

2. For the purposes of this book, a *business case* is defined as an analysis describing the business reasons why a specific investment option should or should not be selected.

For these reasons, this book's mantra is that value is maximized only when programs are completed not only "on-time" and "on-budget," but most importantly, "on-value."

When such management commitment to and discipline for being on-value is in place, many advantages accrue, including:

- A higher likelihood that forecasted investment returns will be realized, making all stakeholders more satisfied in the present and more supportive of other investments in the future
- Greater assurance that program costs won't go out of control due to lack of consensus on where the value lies and what is driving it
- Increased buy-in to management's investment decisions, due to a more open, objective, and value-focused process of selection, design, and implementation
- Reduced political friction due to a stronger, shared sense that chosen investments are appropriate, objective, and fair
- Decreased time and effort in evaluating and prioritizing projects for funding
- A higher likelihood that the funded project will be completed on-time and on-budget, due to more streamlined, value-based design and implementation decisions
- More confident and inspired program sponsors, developers, implementers, and solution users

What Makes This Book Unique

Distinctive characteristics of this book include:

- *New wisdom on how to shape compelling business cases.* Good ROI is more about conversations than calculations. More about psychology and politics than percentages. More about logic and wisdom than tons of numbers. More about the visibility of intangible (nonmonetary) benefits than obsessive focus on "hard" money payoffs. More about a life-cycle-enduring spotlight on managing value than a "get the funding and run" mind-set.
- *How to begin, not end, value achievement with a strong business case.* Turning value forecasts into value attainment demands that a reliable and continuously updated business case serve as the foundation for value management decisions and monitoring during every step of the project's lifetime.
- *Field experience holds center stage.* Every observation and recommendation in this book reflects the experiences of thousands of IT-enabled programs from dozens of industries worldwide.

- *Real-life cases and stories are plentiful.* Vignettes, both short and long, help readers quickly "get it" by showing how key concepts and principles relate to the real world.
- *Inclusion of a self-guided Value Practices Audit (VPA) with step-by-step procedures.* This easily applied assessment tool shows readers how to quickly determine the existence of value leaks and their likely causes.
- *Focus on immediately useful tools, techniques and tips.* "Usable tomorrow morning" is the theme song for the abundance of methods explained in this book.
- *Emphasis on "quick wins."* Over 30 "see results fast" approaches are presented.
- *A complete best-practice ROI business case example.* The Appendix contains a full-featured sample ROI business case that incorporates the reliable methods and principles advocated in this book.
- *Balanced discussion concerning "What," "Why," and "How."* It takes all three to get it right.
- *A concise, "nugget"-oriented writing style.* Points are succinct. Paragraphs are intentionally short. Visuals are abundant. Helps drive quick comprehension and ease of reference.

Audience

This book is primarily for managers and staff, from boards and CxOs down to first-level supervisors, who have the interest and power to improve management practices to increase technology investment payoffs.

Other readers, such as advisors, trainers, industry analysts, academics, and students, will benefit from this succinct overview of technology value creation methods and "how-to" approaches.

Origins of the Author's Views and Methods

The contents of this book are the results of the author's and his colleagues' combined experience of hundreds of years in the information technology industry. Specific to the topics within this book, a major information source has been the knowledge gleaned during the past 20 years from the author's completion of over 200 value realization–oriented consulting assignments in more than 15 countries worldwide. These engagements include global business transformation programs, often representing the biggest IT investment bets a firm has ever made. Also influencing this book's content are experiences with smaller projects, measured in person-months of effort, but nevertheless important to the enterprise's business success. Over 10,000 people on the world's major continents have been trained on various combinations of the methods outlined in the chapters that follow.

From this rich base of "the school of hard knocks" content, the author uncovers root causes of technology payoff challenges and then establishes practices and methods to avoid or mitigate such problems. From those experiences the author has distilled for this book a variety of pragmatic, commonsense audits, guides, procedures, and tools.

Scope and Content Focus

This book focuses on how to prevent, detect, and stop value leaks in order to maximize value realization from information technology investments of all types. Examples include:

- **Global business transformation programs,** such as those involving enterprise resource planning (order to cash, finance, human resources, legal, IT, etc.), plus customer relationship management and more
- **Applications and infrastructure software,** such as customer-facing, back office, data warehousing, and middleware solutions, as well as technology research and development programs
- **Internet and digital media,** including eCommerce, social networking, and self-service programs
- **Systems investments,** such as hardware, software, and services
- **Platforms** involving Internet, Intranet, mainframe, client-server, PC, terminal, and mobile components
- **Process improvement projects,** such as business process reengineering, as well as methods, standards, and policies adoption
- **Business process outsourcing, applications maintenance, and testing**
- **Operations options** such as outsourcing, IT group centralization or decentralization, and training

Whether you are seeking entirely new initiatives, prototype development, or maintenance and upgrades for existing investments, if the funding is significant and value success requires the buy-in and focused support of a variety of important stakeholders, then the methods in this book are needed to help maximize value realization.

Although this book focuses on IT-enabled programs, most of the principles and methods discussed can also be applied to many other non-IT related investment decisions, such as business strategy choices (e.g., whether to enter a new market), capital equipment options (e.g., whether to boost truck fleet capacity by 50 percent), or departmental budgeting options (e.g., whether to invest more in advertising, or elsewhere).

The principles, concepts, and examples discussed are applicable across all industry and economic sectors, including both for-profit businesses and nonprofit entities, such as education and government.

Better ROI-enhancing methods explained here complement and reinforce several powerful business practices, such as:

- **Balanced Scorecards**: Kaplan and Norton's globally popular strategic analysis and performance measurement methodology.[3] Business cases can gain clarity via usage of Balanced Scorecard value categories. Balanced Scorecard users can benefit from a more reliable business case process for identifying the true business value of strategies the Scorecard is helping to support.
- **IT portfolio management**: a methodology for optimizing IT investment value by selecting and managing multiple IT projects for the greater good of the entire enterprise. Business cases are more effective when they incorporate portfolio management concepts. IT portfolio management proponents will find that stronger management focus on value-based decision making for implementation life cycle options and follow-up benefits tracking will help ensure that expected value becomes actual value.
- **Performance management**: the typical HR-driven management practice of measuring and rewarding managers and staff, based on contributions to business success. The value realization approaches in this book strongly emphasize stakeholder accountability—a focus that directly intersects with performance management practices.
- **Lean Six Sigma and Six Sigma**: methods for finding and eliminating errors in processes and operations, using analytical assessments and quantified targets. Many value improvement practices discussed in this book reinforce as well as augment Six Sigma principles. For example, a business case can embody those Six Sigma targets relevant to a given solution being justified. Stakeholder accountability, value-based design, and benefits tracking can use the areas and targets identified by Six Sigma. Similarly, Six Sigma efforts can gain from leveraging many of the value practices discussed in the chapters which follow.

Fortunately, the road to achieving more payoffs from technology-driven investments is more about learning and discipline than about big chunks of decision process reengineering. A simple belief in the power of

---

3. Examples of business cases employing Balanced Scorecard principles are found in Chapter 10 and the Appendix.

a few key principles and an unswerving commitment to apply them can bring big results faster than expected.

I'm looking forward to hearing of your experiences with the approaches outlined here. Drop me an e-mail with your questions, comments, successes, suggestions and/or challenges. Maximizing value is a continuous learning affair for all of us.

Jack Keen
JackMKeen@gmail.com
Basking Ridge, New Jersey

PART ONE

Understanding Value Leaks: Major Threats to Program Success

A strong passion for any object will ensure success, for the desire of the end will point out the means.
—William Hazlitt, 1778–1830, English writer

Theme

Value leaks are big deals. Preventing and controlling them can make or break value success.

Jerry Kaplan was perplexed. Twenty minutes ago he had entered the boardroom in an upbeat mood, exuding self-confidence and ready to give his CIO a report on the status of the global ERP program.

He proudly reported that the rollout of the firm's largest IT-enabled program was fully on-schedule and on-budget. Jerry was surprised when his audience became upset, even antagonistic.

The problem, they told him was that although his program was hitting schedule and timeline milestones, it was not on-value. And value was the only thing they ultimately cared about.

(continued)

> Of course, they didn't use words like "on-value." They said things like "not worth it," "too much pain," "too expensive," and "I've got a business to run." But Jerry knew it meant the same thing.
>
> Jerry was concerned. What's the problem? he asked himself. They had funded this initiative because of an impressive business case. Every capability they requested was now installed. No time or budget target was missed. Sure, a few business disruptions had occurred, but that is always the case.
>
> Now Jerry faced a challenge. The whole cadre of senior management was questioning whether the program was "worth it." Jerry was convinced the program was transformational. But now he had to figure out how to explain this to his leaders and peers. He had very little time to devise the best way to do this, and thus get the program's stakeholders back on his side. Also gnawing at the back of his mind was the question of whether the stakeholders of his other 15 important in-flight programs were also going to ask if their programs were "on-value." If they did, what was he going to tell them?

Jerry, in the midst of his typical 12-hour workday, forgot that ultimately, it's all about the value. Even if key stakeholders don't say "on-value" out loud, it's what they really want. Making sure programs are on-value (and communicating it) is a major management challenge. This is especially true since many senior leaders lack a understanding of the seriousness of value leaks, why they happen, and what to do to prevent or fix them.

A value leak is a benefit opportunity that could have been realized, but wasn't, because of avoidable missteps by management. These threats to return on investment lurk at every step of the implementation cycle. Some examples are:

- Hidden benefits never discovered when building the business case
- Compelling benefits discarded by hyperconservative managers who misunderstand enterprise needs
- Valid benefits rejected due to poor explanations in the business case
- Omission of crucial intangible (nonmonetary) benefits that can make or break an investment's appeal
- Value that never sees the light of day because no one is held accountable to make it happen
- Design decisions that unintentionally optimize low value capabilities

- Scope control decisions that ignore the value implications of choices available
- Rollout priorities that disregard impacts on value achievement

The nature and timing of these value leaks, and the impediments to resolving them, are discussed in Chapter 1, with special attention given to value leaks triggered by business case shortcomings. Chapter 2 recaps why value leaks persist and outlines the central importance of "Being On-Value." Part Two ("Flushing Out Value Leaks: A Guided Journey") provides direction on how to locate these often elusive value destroyers. Part Three ("Plugging Value Leaks: Success Begins Here") suggests actions for stopping these leaks. The final section, Part Four ("Getting the Business Case Right") provides a deeper look into how to create more trustworthy business cases, the foundation from which all value results spring.

CHAPTER 1

Why Value Leaks Torpedo Program Success

A small leak will sink a great ship.

> —Benjamin Franklin, 1706–1790,
> American politician, inventor, and scientist

Theme

Value leaks, like water seeping through a dike, can become catastrophic.

When IT Program Problems Are Really Value Leakage Problems

More than 76 percent of all information technology (IT) program investments fail to meet their economic goals.[1] This is a sobering finding for IT—the biggest single usage of capital investment funds. For example, at this rate a $100 million public firm could boost its share price 3 percent annually by reducing this failure rate by 40 percentage points.[2] An organization with 1 percent of its expenses in IT programs could increase

---

1. Standish Group Survey, *The Chaos Report* (2009).
2. Calculation assumes the firm has, before the failure rate improvement, a 10 percent profit after taxes, 10 million shares outstanding, an EPS of $1.00, and a P/E ratio of 10.

its operating margins by 3 percent.[3] The opportunity costs of IT program shortfalls can be even greater, reshaping the character and destiny of both firms and industries. Some examples:

- For an enterprise, needed market share gains are undermined by disappointing customer relationship management (CRM) system upgrades. Massive defections of key customers are triggered by fumbled Web-based customer service implementations.
- For an industry, entrenched leaders can fall to new entrants. For example, a lack of IT vision and commitment hastened the forfeiture of many retailers' leading market positions to IT-empowered Wal-Mart.

Attempts by management to halt IT investment hemorrhaging have brought mixed results. Popular remedies, such as tighter program management controls, better training, and more senior management oversight, can reduce, but seldom eliminate, IT program shortfalls.

How Value Leakage Problems Torpedo IT Success

Very often IT program problems are actually symptoms of deeper, hidden value leakage–related problems of which decision makers are only vaguely aware.

Being conscious of value leaks can be especially tricky because at first glance, the analytical shine of a promised return on investment (ROI) seems reassuring. A ROI of 125 percent looks better than one of 35 percent. However, behind this seemingly impressive financial facade may reside erroneous assumptions, overlooked inconsistencies, and/or unreliable data. On top of that, during the actual building of the solution and rolling it out to the field, a lack of a disciplined focus on value management can result in major benefit shortfalls that could have been prevented. These flaws may not be intentional, but nevertheless they can threaten the very foundations of IT investment payoffs. Consequently, decision makers may be falsely guided to:

- Approve IT programs that should have been rejected
- Reject IT programs that should have been approved
- Overlook program opportunities that should have been proposed
- Approve good programs that fail during implementation

---

3. Calculation assumes the firm has, before the failure rate, a 10 percent profit before taxes.

Top Ten Danger Areas for Value Leaks

Because the link between IT success and value leaks is often misunderstood, attempts to avoid these implementation disappointments often misfire. For example:

- Program cost overruns are thought to be due to poor expense control during implementation. In reality, overruns may be the consequence of a deeper problem, such as misstated cost assumptions in the business case during approval of program funding.
- Missed program deadlines are said to result from unexpected expansion of the program's scope, which in turn is attributed to lax enforcement of agreed-upon program boundaries. Deeper analysis indicates, however, that the real root cause is the fuzzy program boundaries that were allowed to slip by in the original cost-benefit justification.
- Slower than expected field adoption rates for a new initiative are blamed on technology hiccups. Closer assessments uncover that field management hesitated to embrace the new solution due to lack of buy-in to the business value touted by senior leaders.
- Lower than expected worker productivity increases are thought to stem from inadequate training on new systems. A more thorough investigation shows that the real problem is lack of management and worker motivation. The business case never identified "What's in it for me?" for these key stakeholders during the program's initial approval.

There are certain times between a solution's proposal and its implementation when it is especially vulnerable to value leakage. These benefit-draining danger spots are frequently found in 10 areas (see Exhibit 1.1), all related to management decision making.

The remainder of this book expands upon how to detect obvious as well as subtle value leakages in these areas.

The Business Case: The High Cost of Not Getting It Right

While there can be multiple causes of value misfires occurring when passing through these top 10 danger areas, the leading (and foundational) culprit in these ROI-related deficiencies is the *business case*. Rather than being the accurate explanation of the true business value potential of a program, the business case can have unrealized shortcomings that can greatly misrepresent value, thus threatening program investment decisions.

EXHIBIT 1.1. Top Ten Danger Areas for Value Leakage

Solution Approval
1. Project funding
Solution Shaping
2. Capabilities prioritization
3. Requirements prioritization
4. Package selection
5. Customization decisions
6. Scope control decisions
Implementation Rollout
7. Project sequencing
8. Project prioritization
Accountability
9. Assigning value responsibility
10. Tracking value results

In addition, an untrustworthy business case can undermine the assignment of value accountability, design targets, and benefits tracking. For these reasons, is it crucial that the business case be "right."

Exhibit 1.2 illustrates several examples where business case problems were the unexpected root cause of IT program difficulties.

The Business Case: Flawed Afterthought or IT Value Star?

The business case is one of the most important, yet misunderstood and underutilized, resources in the entire IT program management process. For the purposes of this book, a business case is:

> *A document written for executive decision makers, assessing the present and future business value and risks related to a current IT-enabled investment opportunity. The purpose of a business case is to guide management in making the investment decision, from a business value point of view. A business case primarily consists of cost and benefit calculations, assumptions, rationale, evidence, and support—all recapped into a narrative "value story."*

Perceived Problem	Cost Overrun	Delivery Delay	Worker Productivity Shortfalls	Missing Key Functionality	Mid-Program Cancellation
Assumed Cause	Poor cost control	Mismanaged tasks	Inadequate and/or improper user training	Lack of program team resources to implement	Program management problems
	⬇	⬇	⬇	⬇	⬇
Actual Contributing Cause	Erroneous cost estimates	Program scope creep	Lack of user motivation to make the system successful	No value analysis of dropped features	Newly involved executives lack awareness of program's business value
	⬇	⬇	⬇	⬇	⬇
Root Cause Related to the Business Case	Undetected omissions in the business case	Fuzzy program boundaries in the business case	No personal value for workers in the business case	Lack of post-funding use of the business case	Lack of post-funding use of the business case

EXHIBIT 1.2 Business Case–Based Causes of IT Program Problems

For all its good intentions, however, too often a business case is revealed to be an unintended cauldron of half-truths, glaring analysis gaps, convoluted conclusions and so many numbers that even an accountant would choke.

Spotting Business Case Defects

Recognizing potentially misleading business cases is not hard. Common warning signs include: terminology confusion, content defects, and role restrictions.

TERMINOLOGY CONFUSION: WHEN YOUR ROI IS NOT MY ROI The confusion over return on investment begins with the excessive variety of meanings used for the term *ROI*. In the pantheon of abused phrases, ROI stands tall.

EXHIBIT 1.3 Multiple Meanings for the Term "ROI"

When someone mentions "ROI," she or he could actually mean ...
...a formula called:
Return on Investment (ROI) (which different people may calculate in different ways*)
...or a document, which someone else might call a:
• Business case
• Cost-benefit justification
• Benefit analysis
• Benefits realization
• ROI analysis
• Value analysis
...or a process, which someone else might call:
• Value management
• Benefits determination

*The Glossary shows the formula mostly commonly used for return on investment. However, there are many variations of this formula.

Try asking half a dozen program stakeholders for their definition of ROI. If two or more answers are the same, that is rare.

Exhibit 1.3 lists a few examples of the different meanings of ROI.

Failure to be precise concerning what is meant by ROI can lead to erroneous investment decisions and/or undertaking tasks that under- or overaddress management's expectations.

CONTENT DEFECTS: CURVE BALLS FROM EVERYWHERE Many business case curve balls are traceable to flaws in the document's content. Overlooked costs and benefits, misdirected payoffs, and misunderstood enterprise issues are but a few. Exhibit 1.4 outlines common failures of this type, with cross-references to chapters discussing their detection and resolution.

ROLE MYOPIA: BEWARE THE ONE-TRICK PONY A good business case is more than a free pass through the Program Funding Police. Once a program has

EXHIBIT 1.4 Examples of Common Business Case Errors

Missed Benefits and Costs

ROI-Related Problem	Example of Error	Cause of Problem	Consequences of Error	Details
Overlooked key benefits	*"Improved quality of decision-making due to better data not included."*	Lack of understanding by business case creators of the area being automated.	Understated program value. Risk of funding rejection.	Chapter 10
Overlooked key costs	*"Retraining costs due to normal employee turnover."*	Weak understanding of the full spectrum of costs.	Loss of credibility: mis-set ROI expectations.	Chapters 10–11
Lack of use of intangible benefits	*"Only hard money tangibles will be used in this program justification."*	Lack of awareness of the central role in intangibles in informed decisions.	Important decision factors unaddressed.	Chapter 14
Inability to quantify important benefits	*"Biggest value, better worker morale, not computed."*	No training on converting intangibles to tangibles.	Understated program value. Risk of funding rejection.	Chapter 14

Weak Link to Strategic Issues

No linkage to enterprise vision-value-goals	*"Strategic goal of better market share not included."*	Lack of awareness by business case creators.	Understated program value. Risk of funding rejection.	Chapter 10
Business risks inadequately identified	*"Risks of investment are outside scope of analysis."*	Lack of management directives; low business knowledge.	Program shortfalls—no risk reduction plans.	Chapter 10
Assumes better data is a direct business benefit	*"The primary value of the program is better data integration."*	Business case creators lack insights into how data helps business success.	Understated program value. Risk of funding rejection.	Chapter 10

(continued)

11

EXHIBIT 1.4 Examples of Common Business Case Errors *(Continued)*

Weakened Credibility

ROI-Related Problem	Example of Error	Cause of Problem	Consequences of Error	Details
Nonverifiable references to support claims	*"According to industry experts, 20% can be saved."*	No "credibility" guidelines for business case creators.	Erroneous payoffs accepted at face value; valid payoffs rejected.	Chapter 11
Lack of evidence and support of calculations	*"Annual $1 million savings in data entry time."*	Lack of knowledge of how to develop credible evidence.	Erroneous payoffs accepted at face value; valid payoffs rejected.	Chapter 11
Inappropriate degrees of precision	*"This program will save $1,232,657.74 annually."*	No understanding of realistic levels of precision.	Loss of business case credibility.	Chapter 11

Low Audience Appeal

Concerns of all key decision influencers not addressed	*Financial systems justification overlooks impacts on nonfinancial users.*	Lack of awareness of all decision influencers, such as HR, field management, etc.	Risk of funding rejection; implementation resistance.	Chapter 10
Excessive length, no executive summary	*50-page business case with no summaries.*	No management guidelines on content, format, size.	Erroneous conclusions due to hasty skimming by decision makers.	Chapter 12

Economic Logic Issues

No cost avoidance analysis	*"Excludes $2,000,000 savings from future hiring."*	Valid cost avoidance savings are not carefully justified.	Risk of funding rejection.	Chapter 11
Incremental labor savings are rejected	*"Excludes $2 million savings cut in labor for transaction processing."*	Management disallowed labor savings based on one-hour reduction per person (i.e., lack of immediate headcount reduction).	Valid savings ignored due to not considering cost avoidance of future hiring.	Chapter 11

received investment go-ahead, the business case's purpose should change from being the value forecaster to the value enabler. This new purpose requires the business case to star as management's value insurance policy throughout the program's lifetime.

Eight Ways Good Business Cases Shape Program Success

Exhibit 1.5 profiles the multiple, important roles that a business case plays during a program's lifetime.

EXHIBIT 1.5 Eight Roles of a Business Case During a Program's Lifetime

---

During Funding

Role #1: "Money Magnet": A business case's most common role: Get the financial support for the program by telling a believable story of sufficient future riches to gain the backing of funding decision makers.

During Implementation

Role #2: "Crowd Convincer": In this role a business case helps win the crucial support of reluctant end users of the new system who were excluded from the program justification loop. The business case becomes a crowd-pleaser by explaining how the new system overcomes pressing problems they care about. Benefits are explained in end-user language, devoid of executive-ese (e.g., not "enhance our firm's competitive advantage," but rather "you will receive fewer irate customer calls").

Role #3: "Accountability Agent": Value results are solely dependent upon the willingness and ability of myriad stakeholders to make often far-reaching changes in processes, procedures, policies, and organizations. The business case provides the agreed-upon benefit targets for measuring and tracking their success.

Role #4: "Gyroscope": Gyroscopes stabilize ships during stormy seas and guide them to safe harbor. A business case plays a similar role when program scope extensions threaten to add extra time and effort. By highlighting the value of the program's original boundaries, the business case keeps the program focused on the original plan and thus staying the course towards an on-time/on-budget/ on-value arrival at the planned destination.

Role #5: "Team Cheerleader": Like our bodies, programs have biorhythms. The program team's "high" during early stages typically plummets as midprogram challenges surface. Unexpected obstacles, schedule slippages, and unwelcome overtime drain energy from the team. The business case's cheerleader role keeps teams motivated by emphasizing their crucial role in making program payoffs a reality.

(continued)

EXHIBIT 1.5 (Continued)

Role #6: "Designer's Best Friend": The key value expectations defined by the business case are a crucial input to the work of process designers and system configurers. By "designing to value," these experts can be assured that their creative work is appreciated as a crucial driver of the solution's ROI success.

Role #7: "Executive Reminder": Programs need continuous executive support. Original sponsors often become distracted with other tasks, or replaced by less-committed managers. Sooner or later someone with authority will ask "Why are we spending all this money and time on this program? Aren't there better uses for these resources?" At this point, the executive reminder role of the business case enters to explain to management doubters why this program is so vitally important to business success.

During a System's Operational Lifetime

Role #8: "Value Progress Tracker": The business case should be the foundation of a feedback loop for measuring value creation progress. The money magnet role forecasts value. The value progress tracker role reports if the forecast is becoming a reality.

Overcoming ROI defects and positioning investment results for stardom are not rocket science. A dose of management commitment and "structured common sense" will do the trick.

As with any search for a solution to an important business challenge, finding the real root cause of the problem is a vital first step. The next chapter begins that inquiry.

CHAPTER 2

Being "On-Value"

The Essential Third Pillar of Investment Success

Things only have the value that we give to them.

—Molière, 1622–1673,
French actor and playwright

Theme

Programs are truly successful to stakeholders only when their investments are on-time, on-budget, and most importantly, on-value.

If value leakage is to be consistently stopped, we need to fully understand why these threats spring up in the first place and then devise a workable strategy to either avoid or plug them.

Why Value Leaks Persist: Finding the Root Cause

The reason value leaks persist is because leaders have not made plugging them a priority. Establishing the management practices and discipline to prevent return on investment (ROI) drainage is relatively simple. The critical success factor is to "just do it."

Four common reasons why smart managers give short shrift to providing an intentional, high-visibility focus on value realization are:

1. **Lack of awareness** of the seriousness of value leaks to ROI success
2. **Misperceptions** about why these leaks occur

3. **Lack of consensus** on the best way to find and plug the leaks
4. **Lack of commitment to leading the organization** to stop them

The following 10 myths about value contribute to management's lack of action.

Myth #1: "Value" is simple. Everyone understands it. There's no need for a lot of special attention from management.

Reality: Value is an elusive, highly personal, moving target. Value means different things to different people and even to the same people at different times. Since it takes many teams (with diverse points of view) to successfully design and implement an IT-enabled solution, steps must be taken to ensure that all stakeholders are marching toward the same value goal.

Myth #2: A business case's most important role is to get the funding.

Reality: Funding only ensures that the implementation can begin. A business case's most important contribution to value success occurs after funding, when it becomes the foundation for value understanding, accountability, and tracking.

Myth #3: If the value of an initiative is obvious, we don't need to do a business case or its related measuring and tracking mechanisms.

Reality: Business cases flush out inevitable value misunderstandings and bring a broad range of diverse stakeholders to a common consensus on value expectations, and what must be done, by whom, to ensure that value happens.

Myth #4: Investment returns are automatically maximized if programs are closely managed to time and budget.

Reality: Value inevitably dissipates unless management overtly makes value achievements as important as time and budget success.

Myth #5: Formally assigning ownership to value expectations is overkill.

Reality: Value that is not owned by individuals is never maximized. Value results are often different from traditional performance measurement targets, thus requiring their own analysis and assignment.

Myth #6: Solution designs by talented technicians automatically generate optimal business value.

Reality: Too often talented technical experts put their focus on designing to experience. Because management does not emphasize designing to value, designers will create results reflecting their individual interpretations of the world.

Myth #7: Formalized value tracking complicates program management and prolongs implementation completion.

Reality: Value tracking is a low-cost insurance policy for seeing value expectations become value realization. If important value shortfalls are caught early, fixing them will be less expensive and time consuming than corrections that are applied later.

Myth #8: Comparing value achieved with value expected is a waste of time—too many nonprogram factors influence actual value realized.

Reality: Few measurement situations in business life have a 100 percent direct cause and effect. Meeting sales quotas and budget targets are examples of cases when people are willingly held accountable for results over which they have some, but not 100 percent, control. Being accountable for value should be no different.

Myth #9: We're okay since we already do business cases and track value realization.

Reality: It is tricky to determine whether you are just doing these activities, or doing them well. The distinction can make a big difference in value results.

Myth #10: Everyone knows value is important. Getting more of it is mainly a matter of senior management edicts.

Reality: Value's elusiveness requires not just edicts but senior leadership's strong commitment to installing management practices that make achieving it an everyday way of doing business.

Managing to "On-Value": The Ultimate Success Measure

After a program has been implemented, even if it was on-time and on-budget, key stakeholders will not be truly satisfied, unless they know for sure that the value they signed up for is actually happening.

Consider this assessment from the president of a Latin American manufacturing division of a global firm.

We finished the ERP implementation on-time and on-budget. But not without much blood, sweat, and tears. Nevertheless, I was grateful my handpicked Program Manager from the U.S. had pulled it off. But as I watched his airplane rise into the sky above São Paulo, heading back to the U.S. for his next assignment, I thought to myself, "Now what? Where's the value? We installed the system. But why did we do it? What's different now that's really important to the business?" It spooked me that I could not be sure it was all worth it. We spend a ton of money. It all boiled down to gut feel. But I couldn't prove it to anyone. So when a peer of mine, with responsibility for Western Europe, sought my advice on

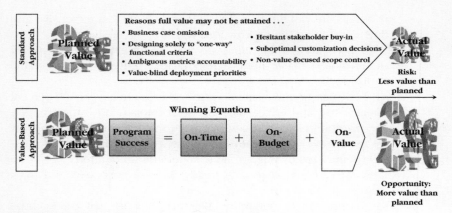

EXHIBIT 2.1 Realizing More Returns through On-Value Management

whether to do a similar program, I could only truthfully say about my own experience "I think so, but I'm not sure. Maybe we should have used that money to build another manufacturing plant closer to our customers."

No senior leader wants a legacy of consistently delivering on-time and on-budget programs that are of uncertain value.

For this reason, astute managers are now realizing they need to manage toward being on-value as intentionally and visibly as they manage toward being on-time and on-budget.

The essence of the choice regarding whether or not to manage programs to be on-value is distilled in Exhibit 2.1.

The traditional approach of on-time and on-budget management in the top half of Exhibit 2.1 runs a major risk that unaddressed value leaks will significantly undermine the inherent ROI that could have been delivered. In contrast, with the approach shown in the bottom half of the exhibit, managing all three aspects of success—on-time, on-budget, and on-value—provides the opportunity to achieve or exceed expected value—the sure path to creating happy stakeholders.

To put on-value management into practice, a clear path is needed to find and plug existing leaks and to avoid future ones. Such a path is outlined in the chapters that follow. Thus, Part Two focuses on finding existing leaks and understanding their root causes so they can be plugged. Part Three outlines some specific actions for getting started without delay. Part Four elaborates on how to ensure that the most important part of an on-value approach—getting the business case right—is correct.

Flushing Out Value Leaks: A Guided Journey

All that I say is, examine, inquire. Look into the nature of things. Search out the grounds of your opinions, the for and against. Know why you believe, understand what you believe, and possess a reason for the faith that is in you.
—Frances Wright, 1795–1852, Scottish-born lecturer and author

Theme

Eight key areas harbor the most serious value leaks. The Value Practices Audit tells you where to look.

Part One described the nature and impact of value leaks, the biggest threat to an initiative's ultimate success. The four chapters of Part Two introduce the concept of a "Value Improvement Strategy" for quickly assessing the seriousness of value leaks via a simple, pragmatic Value Practices Audit.

Chapter 3, "Avoiding Half-Right 'Fixes,'" outlines common strategies that seem right but contain subtle, costly shortfalls.

Chapter 4, "Introducing the Value Practices Audit," outlines a pragmatic, scoring-based approach for quickly assessing whether value leaks are a serious issue within an enterprise.

Chapter 5, "Evaluating Value Practice Areas," explains the nature and importance of seven of the eight areas audited and offers improvement tips.

Chapter 6, "Shifting the Mind-Sets of Management: A Key Fix for Value Leaks," explains the eighth Value Practice Area, often the ultimate root cause of all other identified value leaks. The chapter includes a story about a group of executives who were surprised to discover significant value leaks, and the actions they took to resolve these threats to ROI success.

CHAPTER 3

Avoiding Half-Right "Fixes"

Be sure you put your feet in the right place, then stand firm.
—Abraham Lincoln, 1809–1865,
American president

Theme

Value is maximized when it becomes inherent in "how we do business."

Need for a Value Improvement Strategy

Major value leaks don't have to be tolerated as "just the way it is." Value returns from key IT-enabled initiatives can be maximized with a targeted "find and fix" strategy involving highly visible management commitment and implementation of proven management practices. The imperative is to create a strategy that not only sounds right, but *is* right.

Half-Right Value Strategies

Rare is the C-level executive who doesn't profess to have practices in place for maximizing value from investments. Often these practices are shiny on the surface and contain useful elements. Unfortunately, they also can harbor serious shortcomings that undercut value results.

We call these "half-right strategies." Here are some examples:

BUSINESS CASE CONTENT

Strategy Element	**Having a standard template for business case submissions**
Advantage	Consistent content, look, and feel
Typical Shortfall	Insufficient guidelines for defining key content, such as rationale and sources of value claims
Result of Shortfall	*Value leaks due to missed or misleading benefit claims*

BUSINESS CASE DURABILITY

Strategy Element	**Having strong and enforced standards for creating business case content**
Advantage	Building a credible business case that rightly gets the funding
Typical Shortfall	Discarding the business case after funding is achieved; no referral or content refreshing after funding
Result of Shortfall	*Value leaks due to lack of stakeholder accountability for results and out-of-date value targets for design and implementation decisions*

BUSINESS CASE CREATORS

Strategy Element	**Senior leaders are actively involved in creating the business case**
Advantage	Communicates importance of the business case; helps ensure buy-in at the top
Typical Shortfall	Senior executives set value improvement goals without field input
Result of Shortfall	*Low buy-in from field-based stakeholders, threatening the rate of solution adoption and hence speed and size of ROI achievement*

ACCOUNTABILITY

Strategy Element	**Demanding stakeholders have accountability for results**
Advantage	Senior leaders are assigned value realization targets
Typical Shortfall	No cascading of accountability down to the field level
Result of Shortfall	*Value leaks at field level due to insufficient buy-in or unresolved conflicts in priorities*

PRIORITIZATION DECISIONS

Strategy Element	A systematic process for prioritizing capabilities, requirements, and road map sequencing
Advantage	A rational, logical prioritization approach
Typical Shortfall	Little or no usage of "business value" as a key criteria for prioritization
Result of Shortfall	*Value leaks due to solution designs and launch priorities that unintentionally emphasize low, not high, value areas*

BENEFITS TRACKING

Strategy Element	Tracking and reporting on value results
Advantage	Process established for benefits tracking
Typical Shortfall	Lack of senior leadership review of tracked results and initiation of corrective action
Result of Shortfall	*Value leaks due to insufficient and/or delayed organizational focus on remediation*

Whenever these half-right strategies exist, there's a major opportunity for management to upgrade its commitment to value by converting these approaches into fully effective, best practices–driven Value Improvement Strategies.

Characteristics of an Effective Value Improvement Strategy

Maximizing value is inevitably a tricky undertaking because value is a very subjective concept. Different people have different attitudes about what value means to their groups and themselves. To compound the challenge, value's meaning often changes due to time and circumstances. And yet getting value right is at the heart of making the enterprise successful. For these reasons, an effective Value Improvement Strategy needs the following characteristics:

- **A common language** for value-related terms and concepts. Otherwise, teams can never direct their actions towards a central, agreed-upon goal. For example, if one group assumes product returns are excluded from the definition of "sales," but another group doesn't, erroneous decisions could easily be made when comparing the magnitude of "sales" across different market segments.

- **A common best-practices method** for value realization components, such as creating business cases, allocating metrics for stakeholder accountability, making program decisions based on value, and tracking value results. Without this, people waste their scarce time trying to reinvent the wheel and risk producing substandard outcomes.
- **Highly visual explanations** of value, in order to accelerate understanding and buy-in among a large and diverse set of stakeholders.
- **A framework** for integrating a mutually reinforcing set of management tools, templates, best practices, policies, and procedures for dealing with value leaks. Above all, the framework must be simple and pragmatic. Such integration enhances productivity and helps enforce consistency among all those involved.
- **A value knowledge repository** to help people learn and become more productive, faster, with their value activities. Most of the value methods, practices, and tools will be reusable by other business units, and thus should be readily accessible from this repository.
- **A value governance function** to make sure that (1) a given program truly focuses on value (rather than just offering lip service), and (2) value focus becomes a part of the DNA of every employee's activities and decisions.
- **Integration with existing management processes** in order to provide smooth and mutually reinforcing inputs and outputs. Typical integrations relate to performance management, balanced scorecards, budgeting, and strategic planning processes.

Given the characteristics of an effective Value Improvement Strategy identified above, the next question is, "How are we doing right now?" The next chapter, "Introducing the Value Practices Audit," provides an approach for answering that question.

CHAPTER 4

Introducing the Value Practices Audit

It is better to know some of the questions than all of the answers.
—James Thurber, 1894–1961,
American author

Theme

To plug a serious value leak, you first must find it.

Why a Value Practices Audit?

Dangerous value leaks won't be plugged if no one knows where they lurk. The Value Practices Audit (VPA), introduced and explained in this chapter, is a relatively quick and pragmatic way to flush them out into the open.

This chapter explains the scope of and approach for using this audit. Chapters 5 and 6 outline in more detail how to conduct the audit and explain the nature and potential impact of any leaks discovered.

Where Leaks Typically Hang Out

Big, insidious value leaks are often found in the following areas:

- **Within a business case:** Value scope and expectations should be set here for the program's lifetime. (Leakage threats include false logic, overlooked benefits, foggy assumptions, unquantified benefits, and failure to use the business case to guide implementation decisions.)

- **In visual communications**: When stakeholders reach consensus on a value story in a visual way, they are more likely to endorse it. (Leakage threats include lack of clear visual value explanations, shaky cause-and-effect, and fuzzy links to business strategy.)

- **When establishing stakeholder accountability**: Assigning responsibility for making value happen is crucial to ROI success. (Leakage threats include ambiguous accountability, lack of accountability below senior managers, no formula tracking of results, and few consequences for shortfalls.)

- **Program decision making**: Even a small initiative can require over 100 management decisions that impact the solution's ultimate value. Examples of such decisions are program capabilities, requirements, functionality, rollout sequence, and scope control. (Leakage threats include absence or minimal usage of business case–determined value expectations as a prioritization decision criterion.)

- **Value-based design**: Building a solution that maximizes value, not techno/function desires, is a crucial design practice. (Leakage threats include no assigned value targets for level 2, 3, or 4 process designs, designer's lack of awareness or buy-in to value targets, and little or no review to confirm that designs reflect value goals.)

- **Benefits tracking**: Monitoring value's emergence (or lack thereof) and taking early action to overcome shortfalls is management's last chance to "get ROI right." (Leakage threats include ad hoc tracking processes that miss crucial shortfalls, lack of formal corrective action, and minimal interest from senior leaders.)

- **Value governance**: Value is maximized when it is continuously at the center of program management. (Leakage threats include fading of value focus as program evolves, lack of education of program contributors concerning the what and why of value governance, and infrequent value progress reports to senior management.)

- **Management mind-sets**: Ensuring management leadership is visibly and fully committed to best practices for boosting value results is a hugely important success factor. (Leakage threats include senior executives underestimating the importance of plugging major value leaks and not taking highly visible roles in eliminating or minimizing such gushers.)

Overview of the Value Practices Audit

Scope of the Audit

The audit's focus is on individual initiatives (programs) that comprise the portfolio of an organization. The audit poses questions whose answers are relatively easy to determine.

The scoring of the audit (see below) is based on the experienced judgment of key managers and/or staff.

Final scores should be viewed as indicative, not precise. Consider viewing them as within a confidence range of roughly plus or minus 25 percent. A combined score of 80, for example, should be viewed as likely reflecting a score within the range of 60 to 100.

Guiding Principles for the Audit's Design

The VPA is based on experience gained from hundreds of value realization assessments for medium- and large-scale enterprises, both national and global, over the past 15 years. This know-how has been distilled into the following key principles, which have guided the audit's design:

- Audit actions are relatively easy to conduct
- Focus is on common sources of major value leaks
- Audit focus is on easily observable characteristics
- Scoring technique (1–5–10) is simple to understand
- Management judgments are used for scoring, giving indicative, not precise, results

Effort and Duration of the Audit

Recommended resources and level of effort for conducting the full audit include a couple of knowledgeable managerial and organizational people, for a total of five to ten person-days, over a period of a few weeks.

A faster option is also available. When time and/or resources for the audit are limited, a "Quick Look Tip" approach can be used, which is described in the Value Audit Profile for each area (see Chapters 5 and 6). These tips serve as proxies for a more detailed evaluation.

Using Audit Results

Once the audit is completed and the score is tallied, comparison can be made to the scoring guidelines provided in the "Instructions" section below. If the score indicates value leakage to be a potentially important or even an urgent matter, then management is advised to immediately put remedies into place.

Relationship of the Value Practices Audit to "Quick Audits" Found Elsewhere in This Book

In addition to the Value Practices Audit, this book also contains five "Quick Audits" (see the Index for their locations). These audits are designed to complement the Value Practices Audit by looking into more detail within specific areas. By conducting the Quick Audit related to a given Value Practice Area, the auditor of the VPA can get specific characteristics of what constitutes a best practice. For example, when doing a VPA for business cases (Chapter 5), Quick Audit 1 will provide insight into specific aspects of business cases which, if not present, can be sources of value leakage. By way of illustration, in this Quick Audit, question 9 asks if the business case under examination "clearly shows how system features directly link to enterprise goals." If the answer is "Little" or "Some," then one aspect of value leakage is known to be present. This provides guidance for the auditor's overall scoring on the VPA for the business case area.

Typically each Quick Audit has 10 or more questions. The five Quick Audits' titles and locations are:

1. *Seven C's content audit tool for business cases (Chapter 8, Exhibit 8.3)*
2. *Process audit tool for value realization (Chapter 9, Exhibit 9.5)*
3. *Seven tests for alignment (Chapter 10, Exhibit 10.11)*
4. *IT -enabled project selection process audit tool (Chapter 16, Exhibit 16.3)*
5. *IT benefits realization process audit tool (Chapter 17, Exhibit 17.3)*

How to Apply the Value Practices Audit

Exhibit 4.1 below outlines the steps for completing the Value Practices Audit. The eight key assessment areas of the VPA are shown in Exhibit 4.2.

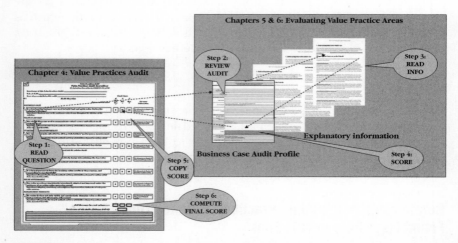

EXHIBIT 4.1 Steps and Information Flow for the Value Practices Audit

EXHIBIT 4.2 Value Practices Audit Scoresheet

Value Practices Audit Scoresheet
(See Instructions, Steps, and Scoring in Exhibits 4.1 and 4.3)

Name/scope of this Value Practices Audit: _____
Date of Audit: _____
Name of person(s) doing this Audit: _____

ID #	Audit Question	Circle Score			For more information
	Extent of Fit >>>>>	**A** Little or None	**B** Some	**C** Much	

A. BUSINESS CASE

| 1 | Is a trustworthy business case used to both justify funding and serve as the visible source of value targets during the solution's lifetime? | 0 | 15 | 30 | *See discussion in Chapter 5, Business Case section* |

Importance: Business case is the continuous value beacon throughout the lifetime of the solution.

B. VALUE FLOW MAP

| 2 | Are visual diagrams used to communicate value's cause and effect to all stakeholders? | 0 | 5 | 10 | *See discussion in Chapter 5, Value Flow Map section* |

Importance: Measured value targets motivate and keep stakeholders focused on actions that drive important benefits.

C. STAKEHOLDER ACCOUNTABILITY

| 3 | Are measurable metrics targets embedded in annual performance plans of all key stakeholders, including field managers? | 0 | 5 | 10 | *See discussion in Chapter 5, Stakeholder Accountability section* |

Importance: Measured value targets motivate and keep stakeholders focused on actions that drive important benefits.

D. PROGRAM DECISION MAKING

| 4 | Is an objective, value-based scoring method used to prioritize the solution's key design characteristics? | 0 | 5 | 10 | *See discussion in Chapter 5, Decision Making section* |

Importance: Top value targets must be designed into the solution itself.

E. VALUE-BASED DESIGN

| 5 | Do designers fully understand and are they actively designing solutions to address the key value areas of a program? | 0 | 5 | 10 | *See discussion in Chapter 5, Value-Based Design section* |

Importance: Value measurement targets motivate stakeholders and keep them focused on actions for driving key benefits.

F. BENEFITS TRACKING

| 6 | Is a formal process in force for (1) tracking value results as they emerge, and (2) responding to any shortfalls? | 0 | 5 | 10 | *See discussion in Chapter 5, Benefits Tracking section* |

Importance: Measured value targets motivate and keep stakeholders focused on actions that drive important benefits.

G. VALUE GOVERNANCE

| 7 | Are value practices consistently introduced, adopted, and enforced under the close guidance of a program management group? | 0 | 5 | 10 | *See discussion in Chapter 5, Value Governance section* |

Importance: Adoption, consistency, and continuous improvement are hallmarks of enterprise value success.

H. MANAGEMENT MIND-SETS

| 8 | Are senior leaders visibly and convincingly championing value realization best practices, as well as requiring adherence? | 0 | 5 | 10 | *See discussion in Chapter 6, Management Mind-Sets* |

Importance: Major opportunities to maximize value are undermined if senior leaders underestimate the discipline needed to make them happen.

Add the score for each column > > > [____] + [____] + [____]

Total score of this Audit (Columns A+B+C) = [_____]

Comments
_____
_____
_____

Each addresses a single Value Practice Area scoresheet category, such as Business Case, Value Flow Map, Stakeholder Accountability, and so on. More information on conducting the audit for each area is found in Chapters 5 and 6.

Explanation of steps circled in Exhibit 4.1:

Step 1—Select one of the eight areas to audit (listed in Exhibit 4.2).

Step 2—Review the corresponding Value Audit Profile: Turn to the relevant Value Audit Profile (either in Chapter 5 or Chapter 6) and review the information regarding the nature and impact of the Value Practice Area being examined.

Step 3—Read explanations: Review the pages immediately following the Value Audit Profile. They discuss the nature of the Value Practice Area, including characteristics and challenges.

Step 4—Score: Decide on the score in response to the analysis completed on the audit question. As mentioned previously, completing a relevant Quick Audit can provide important input to the scoring decision. Write down the score in the relevant field on the Value Audit Profile.

Step 5—Copy the score: Circle the score from step 4 on the Value Practices Audit (Exhibit 4.2) where you started in step 1 above. Include helpful comments to explain the score.

Step 6—Compute final score: Once the scores for all the questions in the Value Practices Audit in Exhibit 4.2 have been finalized and tallied, the Scoring Table in Exhibit 4.3 can provide guidance on how the score compares with industry experience.

EXHIBIT 4.3 Scoring Table for the Value Practices Audit

SCORING TABLE
(maximum possible score = 100)

---

70 or over: VERY GOOD: This scoring range suggests that the Value Practice Areas audited have a high proportion of best practices for minimizing value leaks. While value leaks may not be gushing on average over all the areas surveyed, any individual area which scored 5 or less (or under 15 for the Business Case question) may have noticeable value leaks and thus should be reviewed in more detail.

55 to 70: ADEQUATE: This scoring range indicates that the threat of significant value leaks, *on average*, is relatively moderate. However, any individual Value Practice Area scoring less than a 5 (or under 15 for the Business Case question) could be an important value leakage area, and thus should be examined in more detail. This

EXHIBIT 4.3 (Continued)

is especially true of the Business Case area, since it has so many far-reaching impacts on value responsibility assignment and tracking during the lifetime of the initiative.

Under 55: WEAK—AT RISK: This scoring range is considered "at risk" since it is an average across all Value Practice Areas. It is recommended that immediate action be taken on the firm's value realization processes, as outlined throughout this book. Note that Chapter 7 includes a number of Quick Wins for making immediate progress.

Once the Value Practices Audit Scoresheet has been completed, then a reading of Chapter 7 ("Getting Going") and subsequent chapters is recommended.

CHAPTER 5

Evaluating Value Practice Areas

I conceive that the great part of the miseries of mankind are brought upon them by false estimates they have made on the value of things.
—Benjamin Franklin, 1706–1790,
American politician, inventor, and scientist

Theme

Value leaks should be carefully scrutinized within every phase of the implementation life cycle.

Understanding and Using the Value Practices Audit

This chapter explains where to look within your organization for the first seven of the eight common value leak areas (listed in Exhibit 4.2 and categorized in Exhibit 5.1) and how to interpret what is discovered. The eighth value leak area, management mind-sets, is described in Chapter 6. Because experience has shown that management mind-sets are most often the ultimate root cause of value leaks, they are discussed in greater depth.

Each section of this chapter contains:

- An **Audit Profile**, which provides step-by-step guidance regarding what is being audited, why, and where to go for additional explanations.
- **A discussion of the nature and importance** of this Value Practice Area to solution success.

33

EXHIBIT 5.1 Areas Contained in the Value Practices Audit

Section	Value Audited Area
A.	**Business Case:** Must be the guiding beacon for value focus during the program's lifetime. But is it?
B.	**Value Flow Map:** How visual is your value? If it isn't explained in images, misinterpretation is highly likely.
C.	**Stakeholder Accountability:** The big risk is that too few are held accountable.
D.	**Program Decision Making:** Hundreds of management choices need, but often lack, a value focus.
E.	**Value-Based Design:** Building a solution that addresses the largest value areas.
F.	**Benefits Tracking:** Measuring progress and taking early action to overcome shortfalls.
G.	**Value Governance:** Activities for ensuring value enhancement policies, procedures, and tools are used when and where they are most relevant. An audit is needed. Also included is an area for scoring and commenting.
H.	**Management Mind-Sets:** Ensuring management leadership for implementing proven best practices for boosting value results.

- **Tips** for quickly understanding examples of what is good and/or bad about areas examined.

Audit scores from each section should be rolled up into the Value Practices Audit Scoresheet in Chapter 4 (Exhibit 4.2), in order to compute an overall audit score. This score will provide a rough indication of the seriousness of any leaks found. This chapter, as well as Chapter 6, suggests dozens of action steps to either avoid or plug these leaks.

Section A. Auditing the Business Case

Audit Question 1

Is a trustworthy business case used to both justify funding and guide value during the solution's lifetime?

A trustworthy business case is the must-have management tool for ensuring value success. This crucial document describes the value possibilities so that the solution can be justified and therefore funded. The business case must also become the guiding beacon for assessing value progress during the program's entire lifetime. Therefore it must endure beyond the funding gate.

Unfortunately, while it often seems satisfying to have a business case, a business case's findings can easily be misleading. For example, a million dollars of labor savings might be proclaimed, yet subsequent closer examination could reveal neither a reliable rationale nor reliable data to support the claim. If this misstep is not caught, the wrong programs can get funded, suboptimal design and rollout decisions can be approved, accountability for value achievement can be misplaced, and benefits tracking can be incorrect.

1. Value Practices Audit Profile for the Business Case

Instructions: Use Exhibit 5.2 to follow the four steps (2.a, 2.b, 2.c, and 2.d) for auditing the specified area. Once step 2.d has been completed, copy that information to the Value Practices Audit Scoresheet (Exhibit 4.2).

2. Nature and Importance of the Business Case

Experience suggests that half or more of all the value leaks are traceable to business case issues. For this reason Part Four of this book, "Getting the Business Case Right," focuses in detail on how to diagnose and resolve business case problems, as well as how to avoid the occurrence of such issues in the first place. The remainder of Section A summarizes many of the lessons explained in more detail in Part Four.

Of all the Value Practice Areas, the business case has the most interrelationships with other components. For example:

- The **Value Flow Map (VFM)** can be an input to and/or an output from the business case. The VFM should be done in parallel with creation of a business case, as it helps to visually clarify what business changes the business case should focus on.
- For the **Stakeholder Accountability** component, the business case inputs the most important metrics to assign to relevant people for ownership of results.
- The **Program Decision Making** component receives value areas from the business case that go into the scoring matrix that is at the heart of the prioritization process.
- **Value-Based Design** uses value targets from the business case to guide process designers and those doing system configuration.

EXHIBIT 5.2 Value Practices Audit Profile for the Business Case

STEP 2.a: BEGIN WITH THIS AUDIT QUESTION	
i. Audit area	A. BUSINESS CASE
ii. Audit question #1	Is a trustworthy business case used to both justify funding and serve as the visible source of value targets during the solution's lifetime?
iii. Description	"Trustworthy" means a business case that thoroughly and convincingly explains relevant benefits and costs, with clear explanations, reasonable assumptions, and carefully documented sources and rationale.
iv. "Quick Look" tip	Ask when the last refresh date was for the business cases of the three most important programs currently in flight.

STEP 2.b: REVIEW AUDIT CHARACTERISTICS	
i. Why audit this area?	Business cases are a major driver of buy-in for key stakeholders. Business cases set the foundation for stakeholder accountability, program decision-making, and benefits tracking. Business cases are typically the largest source of value leaks among the eight Value Practice Areas.
ii. Typical value leaks	Overlooked benefit areas, incorrect costs, unclear linkage of benefits to business strategy, ambiguous sources of claims, fuzzy rationale, false assumptions, intangible benefits that could be tangible, insufficient identification of key intangible payoffs, lack of explanations told in a storytelling mode, not all key stakeholders are aware of its contents, no updating once implementation gets underway.
iii. Early warning signs an audit is needed	Business case does not exist for an important initiative; existing business case not being refreshed as the implementation undergoes value changes; business case is only known to a few stakeholders.

STEP 2.c: REVIEW FURTHER EXPLANATIONS	
i. Explanation in this section	Ch. 5.A.2 (Nature and Importance of the Business Case); Ch. 5.A.3 (Tips for Recognizing the Trustworthiness of a Business Case)
ii. Explanations in other chapters	Chapters 8 through 17

STEP 2.d: DO SCORING	*Definition of scores*
Score = 0	Doesn't exist, or exists but has only a few of the needed characteristics
Score = 5	Exists, with important pluses and minuses
Score = 10	Exists and is applied thoroughly and in a trustworthy manner
i. Score selected	
ii. Comments	
iii. Name(s) of scorer(s)	
iv. Date of scoring	

- The **Benefits Tracking** component monitors business case value to be sure it is realized as the solution goes operational. The tracking itself is based on changes in metrics that were defined in the Stakeholder Accountability component, which in turn was shaped by the business case.
- The **Value Governance** component's entire focus stems from the value expectations set by the business case.

In turn, any of these components should also provide new information back to the business case in order to keep its value forecasts up to date. For example, during Value-Based Design, an unforeseen opportunity to boost value beyond expectations may warrant an update to the business case.

3. Tips for Recognizing the Trustworthiness of a Business Case

There are times when seemingly appealing business cases bear false gifts. The following list gives 11 examples.

1. *"False value" business case.* This type of business case claims interesting value, but unintentionally harbors misleading or outright untrue benefit claims within supposedly tangible payoffs. The cause is often erroneous assumptions, invalid rationale, and/or incorrect data, all of which were left unchallenged by business case reviewers.

   Resolution: Be as tough on the rigor of explanations within a business case as is demanded with other important areas of analysis and conclusions, such as strategic plan development or budget forecasts.

2. *"Soft benefits not allowed" business case.* Business cases devoid of soft benefits (i.e., ones for which monetary measures are not applied) are misleading. Decades of research on the realities of executive decision making point to the centrality of soft (often called "intangible") benefits as essential ingredients in effective business choices. (See Chapter 14, "Handling Intangibles: The Emotional Enigma of Value Realization," for more specifics.)

   Resolution: Encourage a balance of tangibles and intangibles in a business case. Just be sure they are labeled as such.

3. *"Value missing" business case.* In this type of business case, hidden value was never unearthed.

   Resolution: Review Chapter 13 ("Finding Hidden Value That Others Miss"). It describes 20 of the most common areas where hidden value may be lurking, such as in the value of improved decisions due to better data from the new solution. In addition, tips are given on where to find such elusive benefits.

4. *"Here today, gone tomorrow" business case.* Even if the business case is a rock-solid analysis and triggered the desired funding, if the document was placed on the proverbial dusty bookshelf and thus forgotten, value loss can be serious. If you do not embed value goals into stakeholder accountability and solution design decision making, and do not monitor if/how such actual value emerges (or doesn't), the program's eventual ROI success is seriously at risk.

   Resolution: Position the continuously updated business case deeply into program governance so that the entire implementation and management team can focus on being on-value, as well as on-time and on-budget.

5. *"Smoke-filled back room" business case.* This type of business case is rapidly created, in good faith, by a few senior executives, with minimal input or buy-in from other key managers. The document looks good on paper to these leaders, since they are mostly talking to themselves. However, their business case lacks believability at the field level, and most likely detailed rationale. These are potentially fatal flaws when it comes time for dozens, hundreds, or even thousands of stakeholders to fully buy in to the business case's vision and thus willingly support such change and enthusiastically revise their ways for the new tomorrow.

   Resolution: Educate the offenders, such as suggested in Chapter 6 ("Shifting the Mind-Sets of Management: The Key Fix for Value Leaks").

6. *"Let sleeping dogs lie" business case.* In this situation, the program is in-flight and key stakeholders are relatively happy with progress to date. However, no one appears to be using, much less paying attention to, any known business case.

   Resolution: Bring this discovery to the attention of senior leaders for this program. Educate them on the known risks to value underachievement, such as the lack of business case–driven benefits accountability.

7. *"Thanks but no thanks" (aka "Who needs it?") business case.* This is the most dangerous business case of all—the one that never existed. It typically is not present because key stakeholders believe the value is obvious. Everyone is anxious to start implementing the solution and not waste time. Solution investments especially susceptible to this misstep are those for catching up with competition or responding to regulatory demands.

   Resolution: Point out that the risk of ROI disappointment is high because there is no value focus on the volumes of crucial design and implementation decisions and no quantified accountability for results. Identify the business implications of such a shortfall.

8. *"It's not my business case" business case.* It takes a team to make a complex implementation successful. If any key stakeholder groups,

including the all-important "users," can't find value in the business case that directly appeals to them, then their wholehearted support is often lacking. This subverts adoption.

Resolution: Rigorously identify all types of key stakeholder groups (usually five or six) and be sure what is important to them is an integral part of the value of the solution.

9. *"Out in left field" business case.* To paraphrase a popular 1930s song, "It Don't Mean a Thing (If It Ain't Got That [Business] Swing)." A business case that doesn't clearly show the cause-and-effect alignment from the solution's functionality all the way up to key enterprise strategy goals is at risk of becoming misleading to investment decision makers and solution designers.

Resolution: Use a Value Flow Map to dramatize how lower-level business improvements from the solution in turn trigger higher-level benefits, which ultimately link to the most important strategic goals of the enterprise.

10. *"Risk-free" business case.* A business case that does not discuss risk and its mitigations in great detail is a fantasy. Risk abounds in the real world in the best of circumstances. Thus it must be an integral part of the business case.

Resolution: Thoroughly and accurately identify risk, along with workable strategies for avoiding or overcoming it.

11. *"Storyless" business case:* Business cases that are mostly computations are killers. Conversations, not calculations, are the ultimate way by which stakeholders understand and thus buy in to a business case.

Resolution: Express all the analytical findings in clear and compelling narratives about how the future will be better with the proposed investment.

Section B: Auditing the Value Flow Map

Audit Question 2

Are visual diagrams used to actively communicate value's cause and effect to all stakeholders?

Value doesn't exist if no one understands it. When the drivers of value (i.e., the reasons why value emerges and from where) can be shown visually, then comprehension jumps and commitment can soar. The Value Flow Map (VFM) is a diagramming method for visually showing stakeholders the entire Value Story of the proposed initiative. These diagrams can take many forms and shapes. What's important is that they exist and are accurate and clear.

1. Value Practices Audit Profile for the Value Flow Map

Instructions: Use Exhibit 5.3 to follow the four steps (2.a, 2.b, 2.c, and 2.d) for auditing the area specified. Once step 2.d has been completed, copy that information to the Value Practices Audit Scoresheet (Exhibit 4.2).

2. Nature and Importance of a Value Flow Map

A Value Flow Map is designed to tell a visually compelling yet straight-forward story explaining value from multiple points of view. Exhibit 5.4 shows an example.

To quickly see the power of visual representation, consider the partial equivalent in text here. While the information is almost identical, the ability to comprehend it rapidly and thoroughly is greatly enhanced by using the Value Flow Map.

How to Read the Value Flow Map in Exhibit 5.4

What is the value of an investment in an expanded online learning program for key employees of ABC Corporation? For the corporate training director, value is in terms of more effective and efficient learning. To the HR director, that is only a means to an end. That person considers value to be the ability to cut turnover and have employees be more excited about doing higher value work. The value perspective for the executive running the firm's business unit is to perform more dependably (i.e., predictably) via managers who have better knowledge to make more effective decisions. The CEO is looking for stronger overall enterprise results. All of these benefits form a cause-and-effect chain from bottom to top.

Each of the stakeholder groups has a different value point of view, but they reinforce one another. Thus, the Value Flow Map presents a single, integrated value story with appeal across all key stakeholder groups.

EXHIBIT 5.3 Value Practices Audit Profile for the Value Flow Map

STEP 2.a: BEGIN WITH THIS AUDIT QUESTION	
i. Audit area	**B. VALUE FLOW MAP**
ii. Audit question #2	Are visual diagrams used to communicate value's cause and effect to all stakeholders?
iii. Description	The Value Flow Map is a visual diagram showing, typically on one poster, how the solution improves both tactical and strategic value levers of the business, of interest to every key stakeholder.
iv. "Quick Look" tip	Request to review any visual explanations that exist of the value expected (or being realized) from a key initiative.

STEP 2.b: REVIEW AUDIT CHARACTERISTICS	
i. Why audit this area?	People absorb complex information in different ways. Some best understand text, some want numbers, others relate best to drawings and diagrams. It's best to use all three information types to communicate the value potential of an important initiative. If key stakeholders don't fully appreciate the value potential of an IT-enabled investment, their support and enthusiasm is liable to be lacking.
ii. Typical value leaks	Lack of Value Flow Maps of any type; lack of visual links from the solution to enterprise goals; visual diagrams that are too detailed and confuse and/or overwhelm their intended audiences.
iii. Early warning signs an audit is needed	Value seems strong to some key stakeholders, but vague to others; complete lack of any visual displays of value alignment.

STEP 2.c: REVIEW FURTHER EXPLANATIONS	
i. Explanation in this section	Ch. 5.B.2 (Nature and Importance of the Value Flow Map); Ch. 5.B.3 (Tips for Building a Highly Effective Value Flow Map)
ii. Explanations in other chapters	Chapter 10, Step 3: ALIGN (Connect the Dots)

STEP 2.d: DO SCORING	*Definition of scores*
Score = 0	Doesn't exist, or exists but has only a few of the needed characteristics
Score = 5	Exists, with important pluses and minuses
Score = 10	Exists; is well done: complete, accurate, and clear
i. Score selected	
ii. Comments	
iii. Name(s) of scorer(s)	
iv. Date of scoring	

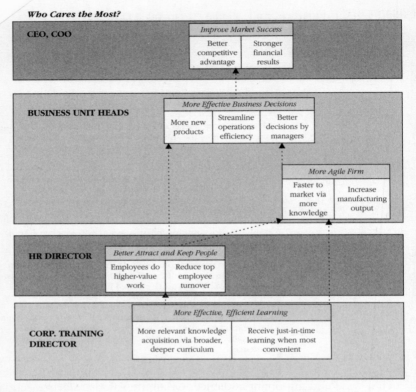

EXHIBIT 5.4 Value Flow Map Example: Online Employee Learning

When such a Value Flow Map also shows the business case benefit calculations, the viewers can see the monetary as well as the tactical and strategic payoffs that are possible.

WHAT A COMPLETED GOOD VALUE FLOW MAP TELLS US   Once constructed, and paired with a business case that quantifies relevant value, an effective VFM answers the following questions:

- Is the value broad enough and deep enough to justify investing in this solution? By seeing the pattern of value, stakeholders can judge its worthiness.
- Where does the most value reside? Does this make intuitive sense? Is it too focused, or too scattered? This tells us where we need to focus our management attention.
- What must change in order for expected value to be realized, or what do we need to manage to be sure this value comes true?

ADVANTAGES OF THE PROCESS OF CREATING THE VALUE FLOW MAP Much like strategic planning or budgeting, the process of creating a VFM can be as valuable as its final result. For example, VFM creators and viewers will:

- *Deepen their own understanding of what value is,* and upon what it depends. From this can emerge the most accurate expectations and a fuller appreciation of the management actions that will be necessary to achieve the value desired.
- *Better understand the full enterprise value* for the solution in question, thus potentially encouraging individual stakeholder groups to become more supportive of the entire initiative.
- Gain insights into what *management strategies and actions will be required* to realize the value.
- Become more aware of the *breadth and depth of change the initiative will trigger.* This awareness can improve implementation preparedness, thus enhancing the likelihood of success.
- Enable technical people with minimal business involvement and business people with minimal IT understanding to see the *interdependencies of each other's* value impact. This insight enhances cooperation.

VFM'S RELATIONSHIP TO OTHER VALUE PRACTICES AUDIT COMPONENTS A VFM can be created before, while, or after a business case is developed. Experience indicates that the sooner a VFM is created, the better. No other single tool provides such a clear picture of value expectations and drivers to such a wide and important audience. Of all the value artifacts discussed in this book, the Value Flow Map typically has the most instant and enduring appeal, especially to senior managers.

3. Tips for Building a Highly Effective Value Flow Map

Actively and frequently use the Value Flow Map to enhance understanding of value and thus boost buy-in. For example, show it to:

- Get buy-in from key stakeholders for funding approval
- Get buy-in from key stakeholders whose support during implementation is vital to success
- Boost understanding and encourage rapid adoption by the solution users
- Motivate all concerned regarding the solution's enterprise impact
- Improve training effectiveness by helping participants understand how their actions impact the enterprise's success

Carefully select the scope of the VFM. Should it be enterprise, group, department, or other? Pick the boundary that includes all key stakeholder groups whose buy-in is needed for ROI success. Ambiguities can discourage stakeholders from accepting its value messages.

Include benefits that personally appeal to every stakeholder group to whom the VFM is directed.

Keep the benefits boxes to 20 or less (to prevent clutter).

Represent all stakeholder groups. Typically, the VFM should include groups who will (1) approve funding, (2) provide resources for the implementation, (3) be significantly impacted by change the solution brings, and (4) be users of the solution. A useful rule of thumb is to add one stakeholder group higher in the organization than conventional wisdom says is necessary. More often than not, business case decisions for important investments are reviewed at higher levels than typically advertised. For example, if knowledgeable people proclaim that the vice president of human resources will be approving a major human resources solution investment, then also include the vice president's boss, such as the COO or the CEO, as a stakeholder group, and represent her or his interests on the Value Flow Map.

Section C. Auditing Stakeholder Accountability

Audit Question 3

Are measureable value targets embedded in all key stakeholders' annual performance measurement plans, including those of field managers?

Stakeholder accountability is the Achilles heel of value realization. The main problem is not that responsibilities for achieving targeted value are never assigned. The challenge is being sure stakeholder accountability is monitored in a way that motivates and guides the people who can most influence value achievement. More often than not, savvy managers underestimate the breadth and depth of rigor in order to manage the accountability needed to squeeze out all the value a solution can provide.

1. Value Practices Audit Profile for Stakeholder Accountability

Instructions: Use Exhibit 5.5 to follow the four steps (2.a, 2.b, 2.c, and 2.d) for auditing the area specified. Once step 2.d has been completed, copy that information to the Value Practices Audit Scoresheet (Exhibit 4.2).

EXHIBIT 5.5 Value Practices Audit Profile for Stakeholder Accountability

STEP 2.a: BEGIN WITH THIS AUDIT QUESTION	
i. Audit area	C. STAKEHOLDER ACCOUNTABILITY
ii. Audit question #3	Are measurable metrics targets embedded in annual performance plans of all key stakeholders, including field managers?
iii. Description	Assignment of ownership for the realization of every key improvement area identified in the business case. Such assignments are to be embedded in annual performance measurement plans so they become an integral part of the personal "Strategic Agenda" of each key stakeholder.
iv. "Quick Look" tip	Ask a mid-level manager with responsibility for an important value area of the business case what his/her annual performance goal related to the initiative is, and whether it will be formally reviewed at year end.

STEP 2.b: REVIEW AUDIT CHARACTERISTICS	
i. Why audit this area?	Lack of assigned ownership for benefits realization means insufficient management attention and resources may be applied to manage the significant amount of change to be incurred.
ii. Typical value leaks	Performance measures do not use specific value targets, but instead focus on standard business metrics, which can be different; no measureable targets between senior executive and mid- and first-level managers in the field; metrics data not accurate and/or timely; measureable targets but little management oversight to see if they are being met.
iii. Early warning signs an audit is needed	Known lack of performance measures that tie directly back to value areas of the business case; disappointing support for the initiative from key stakeholders.

STEP 2.c: REVIEW FURTHER EXPLANATIONS	
i. Explanation in this section	Ch. 5.C.2 (Nature and Importance of Stakeholder Accountability); Ch. 5.C.3 (Tips for Addressing Stakeholder Accountability)
ii. Explanations in other chapters	Ch. 17 ("Tracking: Making Sure Benefits Get Realized")

STEP 2.d: DO SCORING	*Definition of scores*
Score = 0	Doesn't exist, or exists but has only a few of the needed characteristics
Score = 5	Exists, with important pluses and minuses
Score = 10	Exists; is well done: complete, accurate, and clear
i. Score selected	
ii. Comments	
iii. Name(s) of scorer(s)	
iv. Date of scoring	

RELATIONSHIP OF STAKEHOLDER ACCOUNTABILITY TO OTHER VALUE PRACTICE AREAS The starting point for deciding what metrics to use for stakeholder accountability is to look at the business case. The metrics that are used for computing the key benefits in that document are the natural candidates for beginning the process of decomposing metrics into units that can be appropriately assigned to relevant stakeholders.

For example, if global inventory is expected to be reduced by 10 percent and will be measured by the metric called "global inventory turns," then that metric can be assigned to the global owner of that inventory. However, a subset of that metric called "Americas warehoused inventory" can be assigned to the inventory manager for North and South America. This method of breaking broad-based metrics down into smaller and smaller components is called the Metrics Structuring. This Metrics Structure can be input into Program Decision Making, in order to prioritize the solution's capabilities, requirements, functionality, and implementation sequence.

Metrics Structure also supports Value-Based Design by decomposing value measures to be used as design guides for process levels L1, L2, L3, and L4.

2. The Nature and Importance of Stakeholder Accountability

Value expected from an initiative never becomes real without significant management focus and effort. The key is to hold a wide and deep set of stakeholders personally responsible for achieving value from areas over which they have some control. The best way to do this is to identify relevant metrics that measure this value, and then assign such metrics to the appropriate stakeholder owners across the enterprise.

From a value realization viewpoint, metrics are sets of measurements reflecting the financial worth the solution is expected to deliver. Widely used measures, such as milestone metrics, tell us if the program is on-time, for example. Other metrics tell us if budgets are under control. Too often what is missing, however, is a dependable set of value metrics that fairly measure the worth of the initiative to business success. A gleaming new inventory system may be on-time and on-budget, but did it really increase inventory turnover by the expected 25 percent? The revamped CRM program may have been delivered two months early and below budget, but has it increased sales productivity by 15 percent as promised?

Value metrics help us answer the question "Is our program on-value?" Too often, the answer is "We don't know." For those investments, maximizing ROI is unlikely, regardless of whether the programs are on-time and/or on-budget.

3. Tips for Addressing Stakeholder Accountability

Stay on the lookout for these common value metrics practices shortfalls, which threaten value loss:

- Using too few metrics
- Using too many metrics
- Applying the wrong metrics
- Using metrics that are not well understood and/or supported
- Lack of good baseline and/or future-state data, or educated estimates
- Lack of alignment of metrics to enterprise goals
- Lack of highly visible accountability

Use a systematic approach to selecting relevant metrics (i.e., key performance indicators). Here is a brief description of three useful steps.

STEP 1: ASSESS WHAT'S HAPPENING NOW How ready is the organization for a value metrics approach, and to what extent do needed measures, data, and structure already exist? Questions to ask include:

- What metrics are currently used that can relate to value goals from the business case?
- To what extent is data available and easily accessible for these metrics?
- How strong is the organization's performance measurement culture? Will it tend to embrace or resist the Metrics Structure approach?
- How are current metrics governed? Are people held accountable at strategic, operational, and tactical levels? Are performance results highly visible at the corporate level?

STEP 2: IDENTIFY KEY PERFORMANCE INDICATORS Key performance indicators (KPIs) are metrics that count. For a given value area, they are the single measure that is the most reliable gauge of success. A KPI for customer satisfaction might be "customer turnover" or "annual percent increase in goods purchased per household." A KPI for reduction in invoice processing costs could be "number of errors per 100 invoices" or "number of person-hours per invoice produced."

Questions to ask for identifying the most relevant KPIs include:

- What KPIs will most fairly measure the process improvements driven by the solution?
- What KPIs will most fairly measure the business improvements driven by process improvements?

EXHIBIT 5.6 Characteristics of an Effective KPI

Specific
- Clearly defined and valid across the organization
- An agreed-upon baseline across units and regions

Measurable
- Linked to quantitative targets (overall, units and regions)
- A specific formula for calculation (including critical assumptions, submetrics, etc.)
- Data sources consistently available across units and regions

Achievable
- Realistic
- Estimated cost of measurement (in personnel hours per year, system cost per year, etc.) is not higher than the benefit
- Has both an owner and a provider (responsible for acting on metric and collecting data metrics, respectively)

Relevant
- Establishes a threshold value (when it should be considered a significant problem)
- Sets an expected "life" of metric (when this metric will be reviewed for relevance/target adjustment)
- Addresses a specific area of the strategic agenda or value area
- Can be complementary or additive to other KPIs but should not conflict with other KPIs or be redundant

Timely
- Well-defined frequency of measurement
- Measures impact across the optimal duration of the underlying project/operation
- Clearly stated frequency of reporting

- What KPIs measure shareholder value (which is the ultimate payoff from the investment at hand)?
- Which KPIs have the key characteristics identified in Exhibit 5.6?
- What is the smallest list of KPIs that will effectively measure the value of the solution?

STEP 3: ESTABLISH KPI OWNERSHIP, HIERARCHY, AND GOVERNANCE Embed KPI measures in the strategic, operational, and tactical fabric of the business.
Questions to ask include:

- For each KPI, what are its definition, scope, boundary, data elements, calculations, and sources?
- How can a KPI best be decomposed so that it addresses all four levels of measurement, as outlined in Exhibit 5.7?

Performance measures should be multilayered, scalable, integrated, and matched to the appropriate reporting forums.

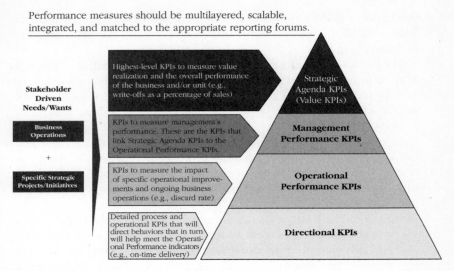

EXHIBIT 5.7 KPIs Address Four Levels of Business Activity

- How can KPIs best be matched as value targets for process design occurring from L1 to L4?
- To whom should ownership of KPI results be assigned?
- Can KPIs be embedded into each owner's performance measures? If so, what is the best way of doing this?
- What is the best way to ensure close, ongoing governance for the value KPIs?

Use both leading and lagging indicators. Leading indicators deal with measurements that suggest a future result; for example, sales of a new product during the first three months of launch (predictor of sales in first year) or lipstick sales (predictor of market downturns!). Lagging indicators deal with results that have already occurred. Examples include number of invoices with errors or number of hits per web site page.

Be prepared for pushback on using value metrics. A typical response is "We already have metrics. We don't need any more." The first statement is likely 100 percent factual. The second assertion can be 100 percent wrong if the solution involved has important business payoffs. Three reasons for this are:

1. Standard performance measurements, such as those used to judge general business performance, usually do not have a value viewpoint. Thus, only a subset of value metrics would already be part of a performance measurement program. Example: The VP for Supply Chain

may have a goal of reducing inventory costs. However, she may not have a KPI for a key aspect of the business case, namely "reducing inventory turns."

2. Value metrics may exist at senior management level, but not below. It is risky to not have ownership of value results that cascades down to middle and even supervisory levels in the organization. Otherwise, the source of shortfalls may be hard to catch in time to insert effective remedies.

3. Lack of reliable baseline data for KPIs. It is possible that data exists, but key people are simply unaware of it. Some creative sleuthing can quickly uncover this. If hard-core financial statement baseline data truly is not available, then multiple alternatives exist for obtaining information:

First, it could be extrapolated from related data. For example, if sales are known in 60 percent of all regions, a useful sales figure for 100 percent could be extrapolated and used, along with a well-documented rationale.

Second, if sales of product X are aggregated into a larger bundle, a subject-matter expert can be asked to apply his or her best judgment as to what the sales of X might be.

Third, if related data does not exist, then the baseline might be "grossed up" from "sample" observations obtained by interviewing numerous people who have partial views of the topic.

Fourth, external benchmarks can be evaluated for relevance. Locating metrics related to similar situations from other enterprises can provide general guidance (not precision) for bracketing a likely baseline. By estimating the maturity in this area of the firm versus the benchmarked one, an adjustment factor can be applied.

Section D. Auditing Program Decision Making

Audit Question 4

Is an objective, value-based scoring method used to prioritize the solution's key design characteristics?

Implementation value success means correctly navigating stakeholders and program teams through hundreds of decisions related to solution capabilities, requirements, and functionality characteristics, not to mention timing and rollout priorities. Rarely will more than a fraction of the people involved have the same opinion on which direction to take at each fork in the road. Yet an incorrect (value-wise) choice at any point can undermine, if not sabotage, value creation.

Think of the damage of dropping functionality that later proves to be crucial to countering a major competitive threat. What if the solution targets the needs of market segment X when in reality market segment Y is a bigger value producer for the firm? Or what if the solution emphasizes a reduction of billing errors (who doesn't want error-free bills?), when greater value is realized by getting invoices out faster? Only when the sources of top value, as articulated in the business case and Value Flow Map, are embedded in the program decision-making process will the best solution be created for bringing that value home. This area of the Value Practices Audit assesses how well these crucial decisions are based on business-case value targets.

1. Value Practices Audit Profile for Program Decision Making

Instructions: Use Exhibit 5.8 to follow the four steps (2.a, 2.b, 2.c, and 2.d) for auditing the area specified. Once step 2.d has been completed, copy that information to the Value Practices Audit Scoresheet (Exhibit 4.2).

2. Nature and Importance of Value-Directed Decision Making

Experience indicates that as much as 40 percent of an investment's value can be gained or lost based on decisions made during the design stage. In contrast to simpler, less integrated systems in the past, today's programs are more complex, more interrelated, and more important to the business. If these solutions are not carefully constructed with close attention to what creates value, they will become significant ROI disappointments. What good to a stakeholder is a system that is on-time and on-budget, but off-value?

TYPES OF DECISIONS NEEDING VALUE DIRECTION   Following are seven decision types that, if they don't have business case–derived goals embedded in their selection criteria, could jeopardize the program's ultimate value success.

Solution Design Decisions

1. *Prioritization of capabilities, requirements, and functionality.* For example, should Requirement X really edge out Requirement Y to be in the top 10 design goals, if it turns out that Requirement Y produces three times the business value of X?
2. *Process and system configuration design.* For example, what is the value penalty if analyst Joe Smith designs his processes to

EXHIBIT 5.8 Value Practices Audit Profile for Program Decision Making

STEP 2.a: BEGIN WITH THIS AUDIT QUESTION	
i. Audit area	D. PROGRAM DECISION MAKING
ii. Audit question #4	Is an objective, value-based scoring method used to prioritize the solution's key design characteristics?
iii. Description	Solution design requires that hundreds of choices be made regarding capabilities, business and technical requirements, and functionality. When dealing with package software, additional decisions are needed related to customization of code. Furthermore, choices must be made related to rollout priorities. Using a weighting- and rating-based scoring system to prioritize these solution aspects helps reduce the emotions and politics that otherwise can tilt decisions in directions that produce lesser value.
iv. "Quick Look" tip	See if minutes exist from the most recent capabilities prioritization session. Review for HOW the prioritization was done. Was a scoring method used? Did it include business value as a key criteria category? Did the participants feel the process was objective and fair?

STEP 2.b: REVIEW AUDIT CHARACTERISTICS	
i. Why audit this area?	Wrong choices about program characteristics can doom the implementation to major value disappointments. In addition, important stakeholders can be alienated if they feel that the capabilities selection process is unduly political and/or arbitrary.
ii. Typical value leaks	Suboptimal capabilities are designed into the solution; key capabilities, in terms of value creation, are missing; solutions undergo major, avoidable rewriting costs due to lack of a disciplined value process for making design choices.
iii. Early warning signs an audit is needed	No evidence of an objective prioritizaton approach; grumblings from key stakeholders unhappy with capabilities being selected; prioritization process is very opaque.

STEP 2.c: REVIEW FURTHER EXPLANATIONS	
i. Explanation in this section	Ch. 5.D.2 (Nature and Importance of Program Decision Making); Ch. 5.D.3 (Tips for Effective Program Decision Making)
ii. Explanations in other chapters	Ch. 16 ("Selecting: Prioritizing Programs with Confidence and Ease")

STEP 2.d: DO SCORING	*Definition of scores*
Score = 0	Doesn't exist, or exists but has only a few of the needed characteristics
Score = 5	Exists, with important pluses and minuses
Score = 10	Exists; is well done: complete, accurate, and clear
i. Score selected	
ii. Comments	
iii. Name(s) of scorer(s)	
iv. Date of scoring	

reduce labor costs, because no one has told him that the business case emphasizes that eliminating errors provides twice the business value?

3. *Scope control.* For example, how can our governance committee know if we should allow or reject Scope Change Request A, if we have no clue of its business value impact versus other requests?

Solution Vendor Decisions

4. *Package vendor selections.* For example, even though Vendor B looks better than Vendor A, how can we be sure if no value-focused way has been established to compare them?

5. *Custom development vendor selections.* For example, is Vendor C better than Vendor A or B just because their price is lower? What about the likelihood their solution will be on-value versus their competitor's?

Solution Rollout Decisions

6. *Rollout priorities.* For example, is it better to give Europe top priority for rollout if we don't know the business value advantages or penalties that occur by assigning the Americas as second priority?

7. *Rollout sequencing.* For example, should Western Europe be implemented prior to Southern Europe if we don't know whether one region has business value realization dependencies upon the other?

3. Tips for Effective Program Decision Making

The primary difference between value-directed decision making and other types of decisions is that the former overtly includes decision criteria related to the business value of the items being prioritized. A powerful, but simple approach for doing this is to use a scoring sheet, such as shown in Exhibit 5.9.

The seven-step approach for establishing a value-based scoring table, such as shown in Exhibit 5.9, is as follows.

1. Establish agreed-upon decision criteria along two major dimensions, such as Business Value and Ease of Implementation (Arrow 1).
2. Identify decision criteria for each category (Arrow 2). No more than 10 criteria, and preferably fewer, are recommended.
3. Assign weights to each of the criteria (Arrow 3). Guideline: 50 to 75 percent of weights go to Business Value and the remaining 25 to 50 percent goes to Ease of Implementation.
4. Establish rating scores for each of the criteria (not shown), such as from 1 to 5, with 1 being lowest fit and 5 being highest fit.
5. Score each option against the criteria.
6. Prioritize options based on total scores.
7. Use Step 6 results to guide, not dictate, final prioritization decisions.

Creating the Decision-Making Framework

Get input from leaders representing the enterprise strategy; they can articulate factors to be considered when making decisions:

- Scoring weight of "Business Value" (Increase Revenue, Decrease Costs, Reduce Working Capital) versus "Ease of Implementation"
- Decompose the Business Value section into the most important value levers from the Value Flow Map. Do the same for Ease of Implementation. Weight the criteria selected by their importance to organizational strategic goals as defined in the business case.

Business Value (75%)						
Criteria	Improve Customer Experience	Increase Sales Productivity	Reduce Time to Market (Products)	Optimize Pricing	Decrease Revenue Leakage	Improve Marketing Efficiency	Increase Alternate Channel Sales
Weight	25%	15%	10%	10%	5%	5%	5%

Ease of Implementation (25%)		
Criteria	Implementation Risk	Implementation Simplicity	Speed of Implementation
Weight		25%	
Report usage by customer		8 (Easy to implement)	

EXHIBIT 5.9 Value-Based Scoring for Prioritizing Proposed Design Requirements and Functionality

Some critical success factors for prioritization are the following:

- Criteria and weights should be selected by representatives of every key stakeholder group.
- Stakeholders should be heavily involved: As Program Decision Making is a consensus-driven process, transparency, and thus stakeholder buy-in, is paramount. Decision categories, criteria, weights, and rating scales should be agreed upon by key stakeholders. The process of guiding them toward consensus will help them to both understand the process and feel themselves to be a part of it.
- Scoring transparency: Once decision criteria, weights, and rating scales are established, then a small number of carefully chosen people should do the scoring. These scorers should be politically acceptable to the key stakeholders.
- General guideline: Keep key stakeholders continuously in the loop. In addition to having them validate the construction of the decision matrix, provide them with a look at preliminary and final results. Ask for their acceptance. If they don't agree with the results, make adjustments to accommodate them, if possible.

Remember that the decision framework, such as shown above in Exhibit 5.9, even when completely scored is still only an indicative input to the final decision. A good decision approach, such as outlined here, will increase the confidence of decision makers and key stakeholders. However, the final decision will likely involve other factors that cannot be easily scored, such as experience and judgment.

Section E. Auditing Value-Based Design

Audit Question 5

Do designers fully understand and are they actively designing into their solution the key value areas of a program?

An often overlooked area for plugging value leaks is in solution design. Even with the discipline of a trustworthy business case, and the rigor of assigning value accountability to a wide set of stakeholders, rarely are value targets proactively used to guide the design of the final work product. Solution architects, process designers, and configuration analysts frequently are allowed to make their design decisions with little or no formal understanding of where the value is expected to come from. This ROI-destroying practice is the issue the Value Practices Audit has been created to detect and assess.

1. Value Practices Audit Profile for Value-Based Design

Instructions: Use Exhibit 5.10 to follow the four steps (2.a, 2.b, 2.c, and 2.d) for auditing the area specified. Once step 2.d has been completed, copy that information to the Value Practices Audit Scoresheet (Exhibit 4.2).

2. Nature and Importance of Value-Based Design

Too often detailed design decisions are made without any explicit link to measurable value targets that were identified when the initiative was approved. Design at the analyst level is considered to be much art and some science. Who decides whether a process, say invoicing, is optimized for labor costs, cycle time, or error reduction? Just because the business case focuses on labor cost reduction, it doesn't mean every process should be optimized for that result. What if a given process is creating so many errors that the labor cost of fixing them is three times the cost of producing more correct invoices? Might not it provide more value to the overall solution if invoicing processes were designed to reduce errors, even at the cost of added labor? Who knows? Who will check to see if value-based design is happening or not?

Reasons why these value-free design situations occur include:

- Business case development is disconnected from design and build activities. Too often the business case gets shelved after funding is received.
- Stakeholders are not held accountable for value success.
- Since many process analysts consider themselves artists, they are often resistant to suggestions on how to do their "creative" work. Thus, better approaches are rarely sought.
- Design decisions are often limited to process design and frequently don't include the full scope of solution design needed for program success, such as policy changes, resource allocation, skills definition, role definition, and so forth.
- Process work is not held to a consistent standard of quality. Often the unspoken criteria for process design success are that it works and it's on time. The fact that the invoicing process design creatively minimizes labor, when errors are the bigger economic cost, never gets considered.

EXHIBIT 5.10 Value Practices Audit Profile for Value-Based Design

STEP 2.a: BEGIN WITH THIS AUDIT QUESTION	
i. Audit area	E. VALUE-BASED DESIGN
ii. Audit question #5	Do designers fully understand and are they actively designing solutions to address the key value areas of a program?
iii. Description	Designers have multiple choices regarding how they design processes and systems and how they configure package solutions. Value-based design is the approach by which top value areas from the business case are decomposed and assigned to processes in a manner that enables the designers to guide their work to maximize such value.
iv. "Quick Look" tip	At the next designer team meeting, ask for a show of hands of people who know the top five value areas of the business case solution for which they are designing.

STEP 2.b: REVIEW AUDIT CHARACTERISTICS	
i. Why audit this area?	Solutions designed independently of value goals for the program are not likely to produce the benefits that are expected to justify the program in the beginning. In addition, designers often are not held accountable for their design choices, so their inclination will be to design the way they feel most comfortable.
ii. Typical value leaks	Processes designed to reduce "X," instead of increase "Y" (e.g., using a design that will reduce labor costs of a process, a minor value area, rather than one that will speed up the transaction cycle, a major value area).
iii. Early warning signs an audit is needed	Designers' lack of awareness of top value areas of the business case for the program they are working on. Stakeholders complain that solution doesn't overcome major problem areas they originally cited.

STEP 2.c: REVIEW FURTHER EXPLANATIONS	
i. Explanation in this section	Ch. 5.E.2 (Nature and Importance of Value-Based Design); Ch. 5.E.3 (Tips for Doing Value-Based Design)
ii. Explanations in other chapters	Ch. 7 ("Finding the Best Quick Wins")

STEP 2.d: DO SCORING	*Definition of scores*
Score = 0	Doesn't exist, or exists but has only a few of the needed characteristics
Score = 5	Exists, with important pluses and minuses
Score = 10	Exists; is well done: complete, accurate, and clear
i. Score selected	
ii. Comments	
iii. Name(s) of scorer(s)	
iv. Date of scoring	

3. Tips for Doing Value-Based Design

- Establish value target goals as design guidelines.
- Decompose metrics targets and align them to L1, L2, L3, and L4 processes.
- Make process analysis more transparent.
- Focus on value-based design of the most important processes. Do not get bogged down in areas that contribute only marginal value, no matter which way they are designed.
- Apply consistent standards of quality to designing solutions and business processes.

Section F. Auditing Benefits Tracking

Audit Question 6

Is a formal process in force for (1) tracking value results as they emerge and (2) responding to any shortfalls?

The roles of benefits tracking are to (1) detect if value forecast by the business case is being realized as planned, (2) compare value realization results to expectations, and (3) trigger remedial action if reality is falling short of value promises.

1. Value Practices Audit Profile for Benefits Tracking

Instructions: Use Exhibit 5.11 to follow the four steps (2.a, 2.b, 2.c, and 2.d) for auditing the area specified. Once step 2.d has been completed, copy that information to the Value Practices Audit Scoresheet (Exhibit 4.2).

2. Nature and Importance of Benefits Tracking

It is not unheard of for an entire global program to be shut down in-flight, or at least retooled at considerable cost and loss of time, due to a failure to track expected program benefits and report them reliably and frequently to all stakeholders. Especially during "go live" implementations, stakeholders may see large amounts of business disruption, employee confusion, and slippage of customer service levels. Knowledge that expected benefits

EXHIBIT 5.11 Value Practices Audit Profile for Benefits Tracking

STEP 2.a: BEGIN WITH THIS AUDIT QUESTION	
i. Audit area	**F. BENEFITS TRACKING**
ii. Audit question #6	**Is a formal process in force for (1) tracking value results as they emerge, and (2) responding to any shortfalls?**
iii. Description	**A value tracking process continuously monitors the extent to which expected benefits are actually being realized. In addition, management processes are in place that provide for frequent monitoring and rapid response to any value surprises that are uncovered.**
iv. "Quick Look" tip	**If a benefit tracking process is said to currently exist, ask for a copy of the latest business case and a copy of the latest benefit tracking report. Compare the two documents to see if the tracking report is based on the latest business case. Ask for the date of the most recent management meeting when the tracking report was discussed and action was taken.**
STEP 2.b: REVIEW AUDIT CHARACTERISTICS	
i. Why audit this area?	**Benefit results can rarely be convincingly discussed with stakeholders unless an objective process exists to measure actual value achieved. Benefits tracking is typically not a highly mature process, and thus likely could use some upgrading, even if in place. Value shortfalls caught early can be more easily corrected, and at less cost.**
ii. Typical value leaks	**Not all key value areas from the business case are being tracked; key value areas are being tracked, but are less than expected; there is no disciplined plan for resolving any benefits shortfall; benefits tracking exists but management reviews and responses are infrequent.**
iii. Early warning signs an audit is needed	**Benefits tracking plan is not included in the implementation plan; benefits tracking is rarely, if ever, discussed in management meetings.**
STEP 2.c: REVIEW FURTHER EXPLANATIONS	
i. Explanation in this section	**Ch. 5.F.2 (Nature and Importance of Benefits Tracking)**
ii. Explanations in other chapters	**Ch. 17 ("Tracking: Making Sure Benefits Get Realized")**
STEP 2.d: DO SCORING	*Definition of scores*
Score = 0	**Doesn't exist, or exists but has only a few of the needed characteristics**
Score = 5	**Exists, with important pluses and minuses**
Score = 10	**Exists; is well done: complete, accurate, and clear**
i. Score selected	
ii. Comments	
iii. Name(s) of scorer(s)	
iv. Date of scoring	

are beginning to appear, as planned, on the horizon can give them hope that the program is under effective management control, and thus provide the confidence to stay the course.

The benefits tracking reporting tool, often called a dashboard, should not be confused with a CEO dashboard. The former focuses on value harvesting areas for a specific investment, whereas the latter tracks business results more closely related to the firm's official financial statements. The benefits tracking dashboard and the CEO dashboard should be kept separate, but closely aligned.

3. Tips for Effective Benefits Tracking

Quick wins are important for stakeholder morale and for boosting credibility of program management. Build several of them into the benefits tracking process.

Make certain that data crucial to benefits reporting (such as baseline numbers, as well as improvement results) are readily available for timely and cost-effective reporting and analysis.

Check that senior leader oversight groups, such as program steering committees, participate in creation of the benefits tracking process, as well as receive information from it.

Establish monthly reviews of benefit realization results by the program steering committee, as well as by the enterprise's executive committee.

See Chapter 17 ("Tracking: Making Sure Benefits Get Realized") for a more detailed discussion of the nature and characteristics of benefits tracking, as well as additional tips and keys to success.

Section G. Auditing Value Governance

Audit Question 7

Are value practices continuously introduced, adopted, and enforced under the close guidance of a program management group?

Detecting and plugging the value leaks in audit areas 1 through 6 discussed above will contribute much to boosting value results for key IT-enabled investments. The Program Management group is the logical and most effective place for establishing value maximization, and thus ensuring their active and effective use throughout a program's lifetime.

EXHIBIT 5.12 Value Practices Audit Profile for Value Governance

STEP 2.a: BEGIN WITH THIS AUDIT QUESTION	
i. Audit area	**G. VALUE GOVERNANCE**
ii. Audit question #7	**Are value practices consistently introduced, adopted, and enforced under the close guidance of a program management group?**
iii. Description	**Value maximization practices include the business case, Value Flow Map, stakeholder accounting, program decision making, value-based design, benefits tracking, and shifting of management mind-sets. Plans for their staffing, approach, tools usage, and progress reporting must all be put into place, and then tracked closely.**
iv. "Quick Look" tip	**Ask to review the current program management plan in place for a key initiative now in flight. Examine it for evidence that value practices are thoroughly defined and managed.**

STEP 2.b: REVIEW AUDIT CHARACTERISTICS	
i. Why audit this area?	**Given the complexity, time pressures, and resource constraints of important program initiatives, it is easy for the "value focus" to get lost if program management does not provide close oversight on activities that are key to being on-value.**
ii. Typical value leaks	**Value practices are defined, but not actively put into play; value practices are actively reviewed, but little or no action is taken on plan slippages; value practices slippages are not visible to senior management; value practices shortfalls are not a formal part of weekly and monthly program management status reports to senior management.**
iii. Early warning signs an audit is needed	**No evidence of value practices activities tracking in regular program management status reports. No Value Practice Areas except the business case are watched by program management.**

STEP 2.c: REVIEW FURTHER EXPLANATIONS	
i. Explanation in this section	**Ch. 5.F.2 (Nature and Importance of Benefits Tracking); Ch. 5.F.3 (Tips for Effective Value Governance)**
ii. Explanations in other chapters	**Ch. 3 ("Avoiding Half-Right Fixes"); Ch. 4 ("Introducing the Value Practices Audit")**

STEP 2.d: DO SCORING	*Definition of scores*
Score = 0	**Doesn't exist, or exists but has only a few of the needed characteristics**
Score = 5	**Exists, with important pluses and minuses**
Score = 10	**Exists; is well done: complete, accurate, and clear**
i. Score selected	
ii. Comments	
iii. Name(s) of scorer(s)	
iv. Date of scoring	

1. Value Practices Audit Profile for Value Governance

Instructions: Use Exhibit 5.12 to follow the four steps (2.a, 2.b, 2.c, and 2.d) for auditing the area specified. Once step 2.d has been completed, copy that information to the Value Practices Audit Scoresheet (Exhibit 4.2).

2. Nature and Importance of Value Governance

Value governance can make or break value realization success. Promised value will typically not appear to the degree expected unless the Value Practice Areas activities are established and closely managed by a central program management group.

3. Tips for Effective Value Governance

Create a special section in the weekly/monthly program management status report for updates on Value Practice Areas as outlined in this book.

For major programs, create a single position of responsibility and contact for value realization. The person holding this role should report directly to the program's full-time executive manager.

Ascertain that those people responsible for value practices activities are sufficiently trained, equipped, and motivated to perform their duties, many of which may be new to the organization.

CHAPTER 6

Shifting the Mind-Sets of Management

The Key Fix for Value Leaks

For having lived long, I have experienced many instances of being obliged, by better information or fuller consideration, to change opinions, even on important subjects, which I once thought right but found to be otherwise.
—Benjamin Franklin, 1706–1790,
American politician, inventor, and scientist

Theme

Senior management leadership is the key to overcoming significant value leaks.

The ultimate root cause of value shortfalls can be found in senior management's personal views and actions (or lack thereof) related to value realization practices. It is only via strong, visible, and frequent executive management advocacy for the adoption of required value realization best practices and disciplines that such an important change in enterprise behavior will occur. This chapter addresses the issue of how to determine whether key leaders of a firm "get it," and provides approaches for encouraging them to take needed action.

The Value Practices Audit introduced in Chapters 4 and 5 is provided below related to management mind-sets. After reviewing the Audit Profile in the following sections and scoring your firm, take time to read the story titled "Management Mind-Sets Shifting at GEI." It narrates typical problems encountered in making this shift and suggests over 20 pragmatic "Quick Wins" for getting senior leaders on board to maximize value.

Section H: Management Mind-Sets

Audit Question 8

Are senior leaders visibly and convincingly championing value realization best practices, as well as requiring adherence?

1. Value Practices Audit Profile for Management Mind-Sets

Instructions: Use Exhibit 6.1 to follow the four steps (2.a, 2.b, 2.c, and 2.d) for auditing the area specified. Once step 2.d has been completed, copy that information to the Value Practices Audit Scoresheet (Exhibit 4.2).

2. Nature and Importance of Management Mind-Set Shifts

Many senior managers believe that value will be created almost automatically when new business initiative implementation teams are put in place. Overcoming this misplaced mind-set myopia is essential to widespread value improvement success.

Senior leadership's championship of a Value Improvement Strategy is essential. Management must spearhead doing things differently. The way tasks were performed to date is ingrained in the enterprise. Changing people's view of the world can be a challenging task. Senior management must take charge and:

- State how the new initiative will change the way business is conducted
- Specify improved methods for more accurately discovering value potential, designing value into the solution, and tracking value results
- Outline who will be made accountable for what value results and when
- Articulate their own role in making certain that value-thinking is engrained in everything dealing with IT-enabled solution selection, implementation, and operation.

EXHIBIT 6.1 Value Practices Audit Profile for Management Mind-Sets

STEP 2.a: BEGIN WITH THIS AUDIT QUESTION	
i. Audit area	H. MANAGEMENT MIND-SETS
ii. Audit question #8	Are senior leaders visibly and convincingly championing value realization best practices, as well as requiring adherence?
iii. Description	CxOs (i.e., CEOs, COOs, CIOs, CTOs, CFOs, CMOs, SVPs, Group VPs, and CEOs' direct reports) can have enormous influence on the speed of acceptance of value practices by the remainder of the firm. They must be believers in the value focus, and loudly proclaim so. They also must establish a culture of value performance measurement and accountability.
iv. "Quick Look" tip	Review executive leadership's most recent meeting agenda. Is "on-value" a frequent, actively discussed topic?

STEP 2.b: REVIEW AUDIT CHARACTERISTICS	
i. Why audit this area?	Changing leaders' mind-sets to proactively manage to "on-value" is crucial to long-term value maximization.
ii. Typical value leaks	Low-value initiatives are unwittingly funded instead of high-value ones; adoption rate for major programs is slower than desired; key stakeholders withhold their support, thus prolonging achievement of expected benefits.
iii. Early warning signs an audit is needed	Leaders accept business cases and value progress reports at face value, rarely questioning their rationale, evidence, or conclusions, nor are they actively involved in overseeing major programs. Key stakeholders are not fully committed to critical program initiatives.

STEP 2.c: REVIEW FURTHER EXPLANATIONS	
i. Explanation in this section	Ch. 6.H.2 (Nature and Importance of Management Mind-Set Shifts); Ch. 6.H.3 (Tips for Shifting Management Mind-Sets)
ii. Explanations in other chapters	Ch. 4 ("Introducing the Value Practices Audit"); Ch. 7 ("Finding the Best Quick Wins")

STEP 2.d: DO SCORING	*Definition of scores*
Score = 0	Doesn't exist, or exists but has only a few of the needed characteristics
Score = 5	Exists, with important pluses and minuses
Score = 10	Exists; is well done: complete, accurate, and clear
i. Score selected	
ii. Comments	
iii. Name(s) of scorer(s)	
iv. Date of scoring	

EXHIBIT 6.2 Management's Mind-Set Shifts for Boosting Value Realization

---

For CIOs: *A shift from* MILESTONE TRACKING *to* VALUE ASSURANCE
For CFOs: *A shift from* NUMBER OBSESSION *to* VALUE STORYTELLING
For CEOs: *A shift from* SPORADIC ATTENTION *to* VISIBLE LEADERSHIP
For VPs of Business Units: *A shift from* ASSUMED VALUE *to* MANAGED VALUE
For Steering Committees: *A shift from* VALUE CASUALNESS *to* VALUE RESOLVE
For Program Directors: *A shift from* ON-TIME AND ON-BUDGET *to* ON-VALUE

These activities must all be done in a motivated, coordinated approach. Only senior leadership has the authority and visibility to make this happen.

Lack of focus on value management endures because key leaders unconsciously endorse common myths about value, such as:

- Value leaks are not that big a deal.
- Value automatically occurs when a firm is on-time and on-budget.
- The need for value is self-evident, and thus requires little additional management attention.
- Existing performance management processes ensure value focus.
- Value success is the program director's job.

In yesterday's world, when program complexity and business impact were smaller, these mind-sets could persist without incurring serious penalties. However, in today's world, transformation programs can make or break enterprise success. Unattended value leakage can be the death knell of program victory.

To get management focused on plugging value leaks, mind-set shifts are needed from those senior managers responsible for key business areas. As shown in Exhibit 6.2, typically there are six key leadership groups where this shift is vitally important.

Shifting mind-sets is never easy, especially those of key leaders. However, it is by no means impossible. Very frequently, accomplished managers will change their views once they see compelling evidence for the need and clarity about their role in the solution.

3. Tips for Shifting Management Mind-Sets

Understand the nature of the task. A *mind-set* is a world view that is deeply believed, is rarely questioned, and contains a strong propensity to maintain prior conclusions. When thinking about shifting the "how IT-enabled value is created and destroyed" mind-sets of senior leaders who by definition are powerful and self-assured, understanding what works, as outlined below, can be very helpful.

Identify a management leader known to be open to new ideas. It might be you. It might be someone you have a solid relationship with. It might be someone you know who knows someone else with this characteristic. In any case, find a way to approach a leader who is predisposed to self-examination and always alert to innovative ways to help the enterprise become more successful.

Educate and motivate. Help this selected leader quickly understand the nature and importance of the issue (value leakage), and its consequences. Once he or she is convinced that value leakage is a potentially significant issue for the firm, ask for guidance on next best steps. It could be conducting a Value Practices Audit (Chapters 4, 5, and 6). It could be having discussions with that person's peers and/or boss.

Ask for involvement. Boosting program ROI by getting value leakage under control requires senior leaders to take action. Request that the leader identified above help lead the charge to uncover and fix areas that undermine the ROI potential of important programs.

Establish a pilot project to demonstrate the opportunity. Select a program or area for applying the approaches outlined in this book. Pick one that is important to the firm, yet not so complex that determining a "quick win" would not be possible.

Stay alert for examples and analogies. Shifting the mind-sets of enterprise leaders is a journey, not a quick fix. Be constantly on the lookout for new examples and situations that senior managers can relate to.

Read and understand the GEI story. Presented next, this story indicates how, in the face of a major but preventable crisis of program buy-in, an organization's top management rallied to the challenge.

Management Mind-Sets Shifting at GEI (A Story)

The following story is a composite of multiple true life experiences. Using fictional names for the firm and its employees, this narrative recounts ways to redirect management views toward a more emphatic focus on actions that plug value leaks and thus boost a program's value success.

Mind-Set Shifting at GEI

Global Enterprises, Inc. (GEI) is a well-respected, brand-name, worldwide manufacturing firm. GEI's most pressing challenge is to ensure that its industry leadership is maintained despite turbulent times. To this end, nine months ago the board launched the biggest ERP-based transformation program ("Synergy") in its history. When Marv Chen, GEI's CEO, announced Synergy's funding to employees and the financial community 12 months ago, he emphasized that its main goal was to ". . . enable our far-flung business units to discard their silo mentality and work in a common manner. From this, significant efficiency and productivity will follow. This in turn provides the drivers for GEI to keep its industry leadership intact."

To ensure that Synergy was a success, Marv set up a special Synergy Management Steering Committee (SMSC).

A. CIO's Mind-Set Shift: From MILESTONE TRACKING to VALUE ASSURANCE

Two months ago, at the Executive Operations Group (EOG) meeting, it seemed like smooth sailing. CIO Jeff Brown had launched the first installation of Synergy in North America. He announced that once this, GEI's largest region, was up and running, the rest of the regions would easily follow. At last month's EOG meeting Jeff proudly reported that Synergy was 100 percent on schedule and, to the CFO's delight, 7 percent under budget.

But as today's EOG gathering progressed, Jeff soon realized something was going horribly wrong. Two of the three North American vice presidents were up in arms. The disruption to their business from Synergy's introduction was intolerable, they told Marv Chen. Bill Smith, vice president of eastern operations, pointed out that weekly shipments were down 30 percent and delivery errors were up 75 percent, making major customers livid. Several long-time employees, who prided themselves on providing outstanding customer service, were demanding a return to business as usual. "To add insult to injury," Bill said, "the program didn't even address the most important aspect of my operations—more rapid customization of products for my top 10 customers. Synergy's solution has optimized labor costs, not customization and speed." Bill continued, "The business case for Jeff's program is a joke. I have no idea what its real value is supposed to be—but whatever it is, it's not worth it. My legacy systems were doing just fine, for the most part. I say kill Synergy before it takes us completely under."

Maria Gonzales, western operations VP, chimed in. "Why did North America get chosen for the initial rollout? I would have thought you would pick some small region where mistakes would not be so far-reaching. Also," she added, "how is all this cost-cutting via Synergy going to improve my sales, when the system is all about back-office support?"

After listening to several additional blistering condemnations of Synergy's first installation, Jeff asked the group to give him a week to get to the heart of the problem and propose a solution. They agreed.

The next morning, Jeff quickly assembled a cross-business task force. He told them, "I want to find out the root causes of this installation catastrophe. Then I want to know what we must do to fix it."

Six days later, having closely studied the analysis that his task force had provided to him, Jeff concluded that as a senior leader he had made four crucial mistakes:

Mistake 1. The business disruptions were expected to be temporary and were within Jeff's range of expectations. However, this expectation had not been communicated well to the field.

Mistake 2. The regional VPs didn't believe in the business case. In order to "not bother them," little input had been requested from them. Nor had they reviewed the conclusions. Thus they had no strong value vision to offset the temporary chaos of Synergy's first installation.

Mistake 3. Synergy had not been adequately designed to reflect Bill's need for speedier product customization in the North American eastern region. Since the primary reason for the program was announced as increased efficiency and productivity, this was the benefit focus for over 200 key design decisions made prior to first launch. Jeff realized he had neither probed the field for other value targets nor asked his designers to be alert to them.

Mistake 4. Field execs didn't have ownership of implementation success. It was "Jeff's systems conversion," not theirs. Thus, with their "wake me when it's over" mentality, they did not put their best people on the project, were not personally overseeing progress, and were resisting business changes that would enable GEI to operate in a globally consistent manner. Jeff realized that allowing Synergy to be positioned as an IT program seriously undermined the field's commitment to it, and thus the program's ultimate success.

Reflecting on how these problems could have slipped past him, Jeff realized his mind-set had been focused on what had always

(continued)

brought him success in the past—relentless focus on meeting time and schedule milestones. Now, seeing how value could bleed away in spite of milestone success, he became determined to start focusing on value assurance. To this end, he made some brief notes on six quick wins (Exhibit 6.3) that he would champion to help get his mind-set, and the mind-sets of the executive team, focused on preventing these very serious, yet avoidable value leaks.

EXHIBIT 6.3 Jeff Brown's Notes on CIO Quick Wins for Value Success

Quick Win #1: Position Synergy as a business transformation program, not an IS upgrade.

Problem: Field managers believe Synergy is a plug-and-play systems replacement, and thus not their responsibility. They expected changes to their business operations to be minimal.

Solution: The reality of Synergy is that to obtain global business consistency, field leaders must adjust many of their regional process differences to a common, worldwide approach. Field leaders need to buy into the "what" and especially the "why" of business change. Needed is a CEO-led directive to this effect, plus continuous reinforcement by the entire executive team. Draft the directive and ask Marv to send it out under his name.

Quick Win #2: Get the business case right, from the field's point of view.

Problem: The sole purpose of the original business case was to get funding for Synergy. It was created by senior headquarters and staff managers. Once completed, the justification's distribution was narrowly restricted to the board, the CEO, and his direct reports. Field leaders were in the dark about the value of making proposed major changes.

Solution: Work closely with the CFO and key field leaders to revalidate the business case. Head off common business case pitfalls by following business case best practices, tools, templates, and training.

Quick Win #3: Get stakeholder ownership for achieving Synergy results.

The problem: Even if stakeholders help create a solid business case, achieving the expected value depends upon hundreds of people doing new things the right way. This doesn't happen automatically.

The solution: Decompose the ownership of benefits realization down to first-line supervisors, if relevant. Identify by name exactly who is responsible to deliver what value, by when. IT is to set the example by establishing multilevel value ownership for all benefits 100 percent driven by IT.

Quick Win #4: Prioritize solution decisions based on value.

The problem: Value won't be maximized if requirements and customization prioritization, rollout sequencing, and scope control decisions are made without considering value impact.

The solution: Create a decision framework to score and rank these factors based on (a) contribution to business value and (b) ease of implementation. CIO is to champion this approach, and demonstrate examples to accelerate stakeholder buy-in.

Quick Win #5: Make solution design decisions based on value impact.

Problem: Typically, process and other design decisions were made with little thought about how they directly address value targets. For example, Synergy's design focus was to drive down labor costs, yet the original business case indicated that the main business value of a few key processes was to reduce their cycle time, not labor expenses.

Solution: Get all the relevant value documented in revalidated business case. Decompose the metrics and attach them to the relevant design areas, such as process x or systems module y. The CIO should educate designers on this approach and then set up this framework once the revalidated business case is complete.

Quick Win #6: Get value on CxO meeting agendas.

The problem: The CEO, his direct reports, the EOG, the SMSC, and the Program Director all had misunderstandings about how program value is created and what they must do to make it happen.

The solution: The CIO will lead the charge to educate, communicate, evangelize, entice, and track value as the ultimate driver of program success. Value actions and results will be a highly visible item on the agendas of leadership meetings.

Jeff planned to present his findings at the special meeting of the EOG, set for the following Wednesday. But first, he wanted to discuss his ideas with a few key committee members. As a first step, he decided to pay a visit to his friend and former business school classmate, Stephanie Duncan, GEI's CFO. She not only understood the personalities of those on the committee, but was a go-getter who could make things happen once she believed.

B. CFO Shift: From NUMBERS OBSESSION to VALUE STORYTELLING

Stephanie responded to Jeff's e-mailed meeting request by suggesting they meet at 3 p.m. in her office. While waiting for him to arrive, she

(continued)

reflected on that fateful EOG meeting a week ago. She recalled watching Bill Smith and others explode about "Jeff's doomed implementation program" in North America. At the time she couldn't suppress her own admittedly defensive outburst. "Bill," she remembered exclaiming, "what were you thinking when we reviewed my financial business case six months ago? You saw all the numbers. My staff spent months developing them, without having to inconvenience you a great deal, I might add. The figures clearly showed an impressive three-year payback from Synergy. You signed off on this." She paused, then quietly said, "Stay patient. The ROI will show up." Stephanie recalled how she had recoiled when Bill responded, "I signed off because I trusted your financial people. I thought you knew what you were doing. Apparently I was wrong."

Jeff walked into Stephanie's office, breaking her train of thought. After getting caught up on the activities of several mutual friends, Jeff laid out his findings about Synergy's value challenges. He then showed her his quick-wins list, and asked for her reaction.

After digesting Jeff's input, she admitted she had not thought about the value challenges of Synergy in quite this way. However, she agreed with his reasoning and recommendations. She told Jeff she would brainstorm some ideas with her finance staff that afternoon and bring them to the EOG meeting. Exhibit 6.4 shows her notes.

EXHIBIT 6.4 Stephanie Duncan's Notes: CFO Quick Wins for Value Success

---

Quick Win #1: **Tell the value story, not the numbers story**.

Problem: N.A. eastern ops VP, Bill Smith, is a sales guy, not a numbers person. Data-heavy business case went right past him. Has no vision of how Synergy will drive a better world for him. He approved the business case only to show he was a team player. Similar challenge exists for other field leaders who do not have a finance background.

Solution: Redo the business case so it tells Synergy's value story with compelling narratives and highly visual graphics. Keep 95 percent of the numbers in the appendix.

Quick Win #2: **Set up quality standards for business case creation**.

Problem: Original business case inconsistent, incomplete. Too focused on cost savings. Not clear how Synergy capabilities will drive certain benefits. Important intangibles buried in appendix.

Solution: Establish checklists for business case content and quality. Promote view that Full Business Value = Tangible (quantified) Value + Intangible (unquantified) Value. Treat both aspects of value with equal rigor. Look for benefits beyond cost savings—revenue uplift and asset improvements can be equally valid. Reject business cases that ignore these quality guidelines.

Quick Win #3: Be clear about rationale for benefits.

Problem: Business case not clear on how Synergy functionality translates to operational improvements. Leap of faith is too great.

Solution: Promote Serge's (CFO mentor from Worldwide Agribusiness) view: "I don't care what the numbers are for a business case. I just need to believe the rationale behind the calculations." Create sample business cases showing clear explanations about what needs to happen for benefits to come true.

Quick Win #4: Embed accountability into program investments.

Problem: Transformation programs getting a "free pass" in terms of management accountability for value success. Unlike GEI's budgeting process, where ownership is established down to the lowest levels of the firm, transformation programs expect value but don't assign it.

Solution: Get CEO buy-in. Work with GEI performance management unit to get program value accountability embedded in manager's annual evaluations and bonus payments.

As she reviewed her own quick-wins list, Stephanie realized she needed to convert her numbers obsession into value storytelling if she was to have any hope of getting field managers to understand both the opportunity and their obligations to help make it happen. It also was clear that some mind-set changes about value needed to be made throughout the executive suite. To do that, she needed the support of Jeff and their mutual boss, CEO Marv Chen. She phoned Marv to request that the three of them meet to discuss "what needs to change in order to get the value we deserve from our big transformation programs." Marv was enthusiastic. "It's a topic that the Board discussed just yesterday at our monthly meeting," he explained. He asked Stephanie and Jeff to come to his office at 6:00 the next morning.

C. CEO Shift: From *SPORADIC ATTENTION* to *VISIBLE LEADERSHIP*

The contentious Board meeting wasn't the only thing on Marv's mind, as he waited for Stephanie and Jeff to arrive. His morning Internet news

(continued)

feed had just popped up a new report on GEI from Hans Deutsch, a widely read Wall Street financial analyst. He minced no words about his reaction to Marv's analyst's conference call the previous week, when record sales and earnings for GEI were reported:

> *GEI is running only on the shaky momentum of large, loyal customers they have had for decades. Few impressive new clients are coming in the door. Once the appalling scarcity of new product announcements is more widely known, combined with the tortoise-like slowness of reacting to even minor, expected market changes (increased regulatory demands on their key customers comes to mind), anxiety among GEI stockholders will heighten. I rate GEI's stock a "Hold." If nothing changes in GEI's strategy in the next 60 days, my rating will probably be dropped to a "Sell."*

Marv wished now that he had mentioned the on-time, on-budget milestone success of the Synergy transformation program to those financial analyst skeptics. Synergy's implementation progress was an example, he would have explained, of GEI moving ahead with determination and focus. His thoughts were interrupted when Stephanie and Jeff entered his office.

After a few words of greeting, Marv asked them to explain what they had in mind. After hearing them out, Marv asked, "Are accelerating new product development and improving GEI's business flexibility two of the major value results we will get from Synergy?" Jeff explained that these two benefit areas had not come up much in earlier business case conversations. Even when they were briefly mentioned, they were deemed too soft to be quantified. Consequently these two intangible payoffs were relegated to a short paragraph in the appendix of the business case. Stephanie was silently puzzled, as she recalled that Marv had signed off on the business case, and thus should have known the answer to his own question.

Marv looked momentarily disgruntled. Then he said "Why aren't we managing to the value of an IT program as intently as we manage to the value of a new manufacturing plant, or of a new warehousing facility? In most cases, those assets are much less expensive, and have less impact on GEI's success, than Synergy."

Jeff reported he had been doing a lot of research on the cause of value leaks and what leading firms had done to overcome them. Foremost among his findings was that transformation programs needed the value-focused time and attention of the CEO if the entire organization was going to take value management seriously.

As hard as this was to hear, Marv had to agree with the findings. He told his two visitors he was going to talk with one of his board members, a CEO with an enviable record of completing a successful transformation program. After that Marv intended to identify several actions he believed that he, as CEO, should take, and would ask for Stephanie's and Jeff's comments.

Four days later, at another early morning meeting, Marv presented his CEO quick wins (Exhibit 6.5) to Jeff and Stephanie, asking for their comments.

EXHIBIT 6.5 Marv Chen's Notes on CEO Quick Wins for Value Success

Quick Win #1: Put the program's value progress on the CEO's personal agenda.

Problem: All direct reports have day jobs independent of the transformation program. This risks value focus being given lip service rather than the needed time and energy commitment. CEO subordinates will take value management discipline only as seriously as their boss does.

Solution: Drop the assumption that "on-value" will be achieved without CEO's personal involvement. Make the key message to the firm "Do as I do." Put the program's value progress on the CEO personal agenda so it gets discussed at every management meeting. Embed value monitoring into the executive dashboard.

Quick Win #2: Get vocal and visible.

Problem: Personal passion for value cannot be believed if it is only seen through words and actions of others.

Solution: Help everyone in the firm "get it" by having the CEO frequently and emphatically evangelize the program's value importance at executive meetings, employee town hall get-togethers, and via internal communications media.

Quick Win #3: Insist upon value ownership down to the first-level supervisor.

Problem: It's not enough if the VP responsible for a million dollars a year in transformation program benefits agrees to own its realization. If the VP has not decomposed that value responsibility down to the first-level supervisor in his or her organization, it risks getting lost in the shuffle. Unassigned value responsibility becomes only a hope and a prayer.

Solution: Make certain that value responsibility is disseminated as broadly and deeply as is budget accountability. Value achievement key performance indicators (KPIs) may or may not be identical to current or planned operational KPIs. Be sure they both exist.

(continued)

After reviewing Marv's list, Stephanie said to him, "This is a great action list. However, it involves a lot of commitment on your part. Given all the other issues on your plate, do you have the time to be this visible and active in the value arena for Synergy?"

Marv leaned forward toward both Stephanie and Jeff and said softly: "My friend told me that his CEO-level involvement was *the* crucial success factor for the value success of his transformation program. Without his personal involvement at this level, he risked authorizing a program that would disappoint hundreds of key stakeholders worldwide."

Marv leaned back, paused, and then looked both his visitors straight in the eye. "Beginning now," he proclaimed, "I am casting aside my habit of giving sporadic attention to Synergy. From now on, my leadership is going to be visible, vocal, and frequent.

"In fact, the first thing I'd like the two of you to do, Stephanie and Jeff, is work with me to get this program repositioned as a business transformation initiative, not as an IT systems program that my managers can just sit back and ignore, with their 'call me when it's over' attitude. I need both of you to get the overlooked value of having a more flexible business platform and accelerating speed to market into that business case. Then help me get the commitments of my entire team to make all of this value happen. Work with our communications director to embed that explanation into all my external and internal talks going forward.

"And one more thing: At our Executive Operations Group meeting this coming Monday, I'm going to be asking those folks to identify the quick wins they need to do to get their focus on making Synergy 'on-value.'"

"See you then."

D. VP-Business Unit Shift from ASSUMED VALUE to MANAGED VALUE

Bill Smith instantly knew something was different. Watching the other regional VPs and the CEO take their seats or connect via conference phone for the weekly EOG meeting, he noticed that the mood seemed more subdued than usual. Typical premeeting chit-chat had vanished. As head of eastern operations, Bill had worked for CEO Marv Chen for over five years. When Marv had something really pressing on his mind, he tended to frown and not say a lot, just like today.

Exactly when the wall clock pointed to 8:00 a.m., Marv called the meeting to order.

"Team," he said, "we've got a serious problem that I didn't even realize existed until a few days ago. It's not just that our North American operations are in some chaos due to Synergy's implementation—that should have been expected and proactively moderated. That will pass. Our real problem is that as Synergy drives the biggest worldwide changes in our history, we, as the senior business leadership of the firm, are pretty much just watching it from the sidelines. True, we are closely tracking timelines and milestones. But we have no clue whether the expected value, which justified this program in the first place, is reflected in the solution's design and occurring on the ground."

He continued, "Let me ask you this: How many of you know the top five monetary benefits your region is committed to realize from Synergy, and by when?" No one made a comment.

"How many of you can personally confirm that the business processes that are now being changed, supposedly for the better, were actually designed to focus on the top five benefits for your region that I just asked you about?" No sound came from the participants.

"How many of you are so committed to value achievement that you have assigned ownership for your region's value achievement across your management hierarchy, down to the first-level supervisor in your plants?" Again, the room was silent.

"How many of you believe that Synergy's value success is essential to your business success?" The participants looked puzzled.

"That's what I feared. If we don't start managing to value, Synergy will be the most visible on-time, on-schedule *value failure* in our history. I see no evidence that we truly understood and agreed upon the full range of business value we need from Synergy. Furthermore, I see no indications that in business operations you are holding your teams and yourselves accountable for achieving that value.

"Tell me—why has value management for Synergy been such a casual focus in your regions?"

That question got the discussion going. In the ensuing heated discourse, the VPs made comments such as:

"Don't look at us, look at IT. They were the ones who designed the program. Why didn't they design to value?" (Eastern Ops)

"I've never seen the original business case. All I know about it is the 10 PowerPoint summary slides that Stephanie showed us six months ago. None of them allocated value to regions." (Central Ops)

"Candidly, I think our ad hoc attitude toward Synergy value management reflected your own, Marv. If it was so important, why didn't you, as the CEO, ask us about it sooner?" (Western Ops)

(continued)

"What the heck does 'manage to value' really mean? If we're supposed to be doing it, explain what I'm to do differently." (North
America VP customer service)

After 20 minutes, Marv signaled that it was time to stop talking.
He said, "I hear all of you loud and clear. And I hope you heard yourselves also. I'd like each of you to do the following within the next six
days, then we'll meet again. First, find out the answers to the questions
I just asked. Second, identify at least four quick wins for yourself—
actions you believe you must take to be sure you accurately understand what Synergy's value is to you, and how you can be assured
you are making progress towards that goal. Please e-mail them to me
at least 24 hours before our next meeting. Meeting adjourned."

Six days later, Marv received e-mails from each VP. He quickly
reviewed Bill's, since he knew that Bill was an opinion leader
among his peers. In the first paragraph of Bill's e-mail, Marv saw the
following:

> *Marv: What I now see, that I didn't five days ago, is that
> getting my region's value out of Synergy is going to take some
> serious focus on my part. That's the bad news. The good news
> is that I'm now convinced it is worth it. Here's my list. [See
> Exhibit 6.6]*

Marv noted with satisfaction Bill's comment at the bottom of this
e-mail:

> *I'm no longer going to assume value happens. I'm going to
> manage value to be sure it becomes real.*

EXHIBIT 6.6 Bill Smith's Notes on Eastern Ops Quick Wins for Value Success

Quick Win #1: Get all my key stakeholders involved and accountable for their
value share.

Problem: Most often programs fail to deliver value because the field
people don't understand them and/or don't believe in them, or are
unwilling to adapt to make this value happen. The frequent root cause
for this is lack of management leadership in enlisting all these people in
the "value cause."

Solution: For every million dollars of annual benefits expected from Eastern operations, it takes at least a dozen stakeholders to make it happen. Every one of them should be brought into the value commitment by (a) providing input to a revalidated business case, (b) studying the justification once it's finalized, and (c) being held accountable for the changes they are responsible for making. I will make sure this happens.

Quick Win #2: Commit best people as program resources.

Problem: Transformation programs are inherently tricky undertakings, due to their complexity, far-reaching impacts and unavoidable business disruption. The sooner the program is finished, and the fewer surprises that arise, the better. Using second-rate people because my "stars" are too valuable becomes a bad choice that can threaten ROI results.

Solution: Identify people who know the most about the processes being impacted to be sure the value will be delivered. Assign the most knowledgeable ones to Synergy. Back-fill their positions with up-and-comers. Using stars is insurance protection from unacceptable value leaks.

Quick Win #3: Don't go to sleep in the middle of the movie.

Problem: Too often operations managers temporarily ignore the design phase of a transformation program, reasoning, "It's all technical and functional details done by specialists." Once the program is launched, managers reappear. This behavior is not smart. During design is where large amounts of value leakage can occur due to designers' lack of knowledge about what's important to the business.

Solution: Insist that requirements prioritization, package customization, launch sequencing, and scope control decisions be primarily value-driven from a business perspective. Assign the right operations people to help identify the most relevant business value criteria to score and rank candidates. For example, if 80 percent of the program's value is coming from customer support, then decision choices should reflect that.

Quick Win #4: Put the program on my top-five priority list.
Problem: Leakage of value that we are depending upon too easily occurs through management inattention. Value losses can occur at hundreds of places, due to actions (or nonaction) by dozens of workers. My employees pay attention to what I pay attention to.

Solution: Elevate program progress as one of my top five personal priorities. Let everyone know. Track value progress weekly. Take prompt and visible action on early warning signs or shortfalls.

(continued)

E. Synergy's Executive Operations Committee Shift: From VALUE CASUALNESS to VALUE RESOLVE

As Marv finished reviewing the quick wins from all four of his regional VPs, he was satisfied that they were now on the right track. As he replayed the events of the past week in his mind, he began to wonder why the SMSC he had specifically set up to oversee the program's success had not picked up on this lack of value focus earlier and taken action. The committee was populated by all his regional executives, as well as the chief operating officer (COO), finance manager, the heads of human resources and the legal department, and Synergy's program director. Surely somebody should have picked up some early warning signs of value inattention. Marv's COO was in charge of this committee.

Marv suspected the committee was focused on everything but value. He decided to do a quick test to confirm his hunch, secretly hoping he would be wrong.

On the train ride home that night he tapped out an e-mail to Praveen Singh, his COO. After explaining the reason for his inquiry, he listed four questions for Praveen:

1. How much time, on average, during the last four SMSC meetings has been spent discussing any aspect of value realization related to Synergy?
2. When the SMSC made decisions three months ago on the sequencing of program rollouts, to what extent did the decision criteria explicitly reflect the impact on business value of options considered?
3. Last month, when the committee spent 45 minutes deciding whether certain additional functionalities should or should not be added to the program, was business value of the proposed new functionality considered?
4. Is ensuring that the Synergy program comes in on-value a part of the committee's formal charter?

Praveen responded to Marv via e-mail within 15 minutes.

You caught me on the train also, so here's a quick response to your questions: zero, none, no, and theoretically, but not explicitly. If you take managing value out of the equation, the SMSC has been doing great work. If you put value oversight back in, I'm afraid we've flopped. Let's get together over lunch tomorrow and talk about what we can do to remedy this major problem. OK?

Marv agreed. Before reaching for the newspaper he e-mailed Praveen that he would forward to him later that night all the value realization improvement quick wins that the CIO, CFO, and regional VPs had completed. He said he hoped these would give Praveen some ideas for quick wins his committee could undertake.

At lunch the next day at Marv's conference table, Praveen handed Marv a copy of the quick wins he proposed discussing with the committee (see Exhibit 6.7). He asked Marv what he thought.

EXHIBIT 6.7 Praveen Singh's Notes on SMSC Quick Wins for Value Success

---

Quick Win #1: Rapidly assess existence of value realization dangers.

Problem: Although committee members have authority to correct value leaks, they often lack awareness this is a problem that needs their attention.

Solution: Ask the program sponsor to provide a list of (a) the top 50 most important Synergy stakeholders, (b) the people who provided input to the business case, (c) people who have reviewed some or all of the final business case, and (d) the stakeholders formally accountable for value results. These lists should match. If they don't, actions need to be taken to get them in sync.

Quick Win #2: Formally track value progress at every SMSC meeting.

Problem: Out of sight is out of mind.

Solution: Embed relevant value progress tracking into the committee's reporting dashboard. Let program stakeholders know the committee not only cares about value success, but is committed to tracking it continuously, and to remedying shortfalls. Invite selected key stakeholders to meetings to discuss their views on value progress.

Quick Win #3: Use a decision framework to maintain scope control.

Problem: Adding new functionality to Synergy at this stage is very costly, and very controversial. However, legitimate requests need to be considered and decided upon.

Solution: Work with CIO Jeff Brown to tailor his quick win #4 (prioritize solution decisions based on value) to the scope control work handled by the SMSC.

(continued)

Marv commented he definitely thought this list was a step in the right direction. Praveen mentioned he intended to have a one-on-one discussion on this topic with Addison Bristow, Synergy's program director, now based in London. Since managing the program was Addison's 24/7 job, Praveen commented, "His perspectives on what is and is not happening regarding value management should be very helpful."

F. Program Director's Shift: From ON-TIME and ON-BUDGET to ON-VALUE

Once he learned that the COO wanted to talk to him about "getting more of our money's worth from Synergy," Addison Bristow was most curious about the likely course of the conversation. Since he was the program director of the entire Synergy project, he already knew about the regional VPs' uproar over North American business disruption. Whatever he said to Praveen should not be inconsistent with what his boss, CIO Jeff Brown, might say. Thus he invited Jeff to join their meeting. Right on time, Jeff and Praveen walked into the room together, laughing about some shared comment, and greeted Addison.

Praveen wasted no time in getting down to business and explained his concern that no one in senior management, including the Synergy Management Steering Committee, was intently watching to be sure that the value expected from the program was driving program design and implementation decisions. "Addison," he said, "to what extent are you personally keeping a close eye on Synergy's value progress?"

Addison was quick to admit that he thought that GEI executives believed value would pretty much automatically occur so long as the program came in on-time and on-budget. "No one," he reminded Praveen and Jeff, "has ever even asked me about value realization progress prior to today."

"Well, Addison, that was then, and this is now," responded Jeff. "Marv Chen is counting on Synergy to not only save us a lot of money in operations, but also to provide us with a more flexible business platform by which to grow and be nimble in responding to the marketplace. How can we be sure Synergy is being designed and implemented to do all this? Needless to say, we can't wait until two years after implementation to find out. We need progress indicators that are early warnings, or hopefully early confirmers, that we are solidly progressing along the on-value track."

Praveen pulled out the list of quick wins that his senior managers, Marv, and Jeff had created. "Look these over, Addison, and let us know when we can get yours."

The program director scanned down the list, quickly grasping the essence of their intentions. "This is really encouraging to see how seriously value achievement is being taken. I'll get back to you by next Monday with my personal quick wins. They will certainly reinforce these," said Addison.

"Great," said Praveen. "See you then," replied Jeff.

After they left, Addison sat back in his chair and began thinking through the difference between being on-time and on-budget and being on-value. As he reflected, he began to make notes.

Two days later, Addison had his list (see Exhibit 6.8).

EXHIBIT 6.8 Addison Bristow's Notes on Program Director Quick Wins for Value Success

---

Quick Win #1: Find out what value is expected, and what decisions the Program Director can influence that help drive that value.

Problem: Hundreds of solution design and rollout decisions impact the program's ultimate benefits, but rarely are such decisions made rigorous based on contribution to business value.

Solution: Identify requirements prioritization, customization, rollout sequencing, scope control, and related decisions that heavily influence value. Set up a mechanism for ensuring that business value is a key input for such decisions. Integrate this decision framework with the ones outlined in the CIO's and COO's quick wins lists.

Quick Win #2: Get my entire program team to be value believers.

Problem: Program directors, managers, and their staff primarily bring technical, process, and functional skills to the program. Rarely do they understand what, if anything, they personally need to do differently to be sure that business case expectations are turned into value reality.

Solution: Create awareness, understanding, desire, and then commitment to perform the needed value roles. Establish workshops and brainstorming sessions to help them understand and believe. Have each manager be a value role model to his or her subordinates.

Quick Win #3: Track value progress on the monthly program status dashboard.

Problem: Value realization status does not exist on the current program dashboard. Value untracked is value unmanaged.

(continued)

Solution: Work with the CFO and business leaders to identify value progress indicators at each stage of Synergy's evolution. Report them on the dashboard. Review monthly. Identify actions to take when progress begins to fall short.

Quick Win #4: Invite CEO Marv Chen to speak at an upcoming weekly program manager's meeting.

Problem: No executive has ever spoken about value focus at Addison's weekly program managers' meetings thus far.

Solution: Invite Marv to speak about his own "quick wins" at our next meeting. Have Jeff and other execs reinforce at subsequent meetings.

Quick Win #5: Clearly and simply communicate Synergy's business value to all stakeholders.

Problem: Synergy has hundreds of important stakeholders worldwide. Each likely has a different, and potentially conflicting, view of Synergy's business value to their area of responsibility and to themselves.

Solution: Map out, visually on a single poster, the value path from Synergy's solution functionality to business improvements to financial payoffs, such as Free Cash Flow. Enable each stakeholder group to see how their value success contributes to the firm's overall value payoff. Help them understand how interdependent everyone is in order to maximize Synergy's overall value to the firm.

As he reviewed his list, Addison acknowledged the fundamental shift taking place in his mind. *From now on,* he told himself, *my programs are going to be on-time, on-budget,* and *on-value.* And based on all the other quick wins lists he saw, it appeared that the entire GEI leadership team was also going to focus on being on-value. Addison hoped that their good plans would endure beyond this initial enthusiasm for curing Synergy's ills.

Executives with mind-sets that focus on value can achieve value. Once mind-set alignment begins to occur, the next most important step in value success is to start making things happen. Part Three, which follows, discusses how.

Plugging Value Leaks: Success Begins Here

To succeed, jump as quickly at opportunities as you do at conclusions.
—Benjamin Franklin, 1706–1790,
American politician, inventor, scientist)

Theme

A simple, structured approach to plugging value leaks accelerates buy-in, and hence results.

Completing the Value Practices Audit in Chapter 4 will typically identify several important areas where management attention and discipline can boost ROI results from IT-enabled programs.

Part Three, containing Chapter 7, provides suggestions for setting the groundwork for quick wins in this area.

Finding the Best Quick Wins

Be quick to learn and wise to know.

—George Burns, 1896–1996,
actor, writer, and comedian

Theme

Actions, not words, create value. Get going with the most important quick wins that best fit your organization.

Dozens of management quick-win actions for discovering and fixing value leaks have been highlighted within this book. But which ones are best for a given enterprise, so stakeholders can see rapid progress and thus become avid supporters? This chapter identifies four quick wins applicable to every situation, and then outlines an approach for selecting other ones that can be tailored to best address an organization's unique needs and culture.

Big Four Quick Wins for Everyone

Everyone likes rapid fixes. Of the more than thirty quick wins discussed in earlier chapters, the four listed below are recommended as essential aspects of any Value Improvement Strategy. Included are cross-references to chapters where the suggested approaches are discussed in more detail.

1. Get Vocal and Visible

Find good reasons to enhance value boosting awareness using messages and examples from this book. Use venues such as business unit meetings, internal bulletins, state-of-the-business gatherings, and so forth to let key stakeholders know that their frustration with continual value shortfalls is going to be addressed head-on. (Reference: Exhibit 6.5, Quick Win #2).

2. Put Value Topics on CxO Meeting Agendas

Steering committees for key initiatives are a natural place to add value topics to meeting agendas. Executive committees responsible for monitoring major strategy and investment outcomes are another. Discussion topics can include:

1. How confident are we that we accurately understand the value expected?
2. Do we have the needed buy-in from stakeholders ranging from senior leaders to first-level field supervisors?
3. Do we have the right measures and proper tracking for knowing if and when value expected is becoming value realized? (Reference: Exhibit 6.3, Quick Win #6.)

3. Do a Speedy Business Case Audit

Because the business case forms the foundation of effective value realization, test to see if existing business cases are up to this heavy responsibility. Pick an important initiative that is underway or about to be launched. Then, assess the trustworthiness of the business case that has set value expectations for this initiative by applying to it the Business Case Quick Audit in Exhibits 8.2 and 8.3 ("Seven C's Content Audit Tool for Business Cases"). If the resulting audit score indicates that the selected business case is less than adequate, give high priority to business case upgrades as part of a Value Improvement Strategy.

4. Dramatize How Hidden Value Can Be Flushed into the Open

One of the most frustrating aspects of dealing with value is the gnawing feeling that some major value for a proposed initiative exists, but no one has yet uncovered it. Consequences can be far-reaching—from inability to justify a highly important initiative, to slowing solution adoption due to lack of belief in the importance of this new way of doing business. Organize and conduct a value discovery workshop, taking inspiration from the true-life vignette shown in Exhibit 7.1.

True-Life Vignette

Quick Win in Action: Uncovering $16 Million in Hidden Savings in Less Than One Day

Situation: Admittedly, it was an embarrassing circumstance for all involved. The board of directors of this $1 billion firm operating coast-to-coast in North America had rejected the chief information officer's and human resources VP's painstakingly developed business case for implementing a vital human resource system. It simply didn't show enough savings to justify the investment. The good news, however, was that these execs were giving the program sponsors one more chance to hit the needed ROI.

Results: In less than a single day of structured brainstorming for selected process teams, the breakthrough came. Twenty attendees were organized into five teams. One of the teams was a group of four training managers who were determined to be the most insightful team in the room. When their turn came to report their value ideas to the group, they stunned the audience by admitting their group was wasting $16 million in developing the wrong training courses, and then delivering them to the wrong audience at the wrong time. With a new HR system able to accurately profile job skills, current roles, career directions, and training completions of each employee, more cost-effective training could be created and provided. Clearly, the employees would benefit, their managers would be happier, and the training group would feel better about their contributions. This unexpected $16 million boost to the solution's benefits total enabled the Board to confidently approve the investment and give the green light to begin system implementation.

Lessons from this workshop approach: Four factors converged to create this happy value ending:

1. Getting all the process owners in the same room for a focused meeting dedicated to finding more value
2. Using a facilitated, structured brainstorming workshop environment to create an exciting yet "safe" atmosphere for teams to be honest about shortfalls and creative about solutions
3. Giving workshop attendees a specific "benefit goal" to strive for
4. Having visible sponsorship by senior executives (one of whom, the chief financial officer, visited the workshop to show his support and encourage insightful thinking)
5. Creating a visual Value Flow Map to show these teams how to link their value findings to goals important to the enterprise (see Exhibit 5.4 for an example)

Tailor Next Steps to Type of Value Challenge

As appealing as the 30-plus quick wins in the earlier chapters of this book may be, everything cannot be done at once. Nor will every quick win necessarily fit every enterprise, or culture, at the same time. For these reasons, Exhibit 7.1 provides guidance on selecting quick wins, best practices and tools discussed in this book based on the "Value Need" of the organization.

EXHIBIT 7.1 Value-Boosting Best Practices by Type of Scenario

ID #	Value Need	Examples of Goal	Examples of Best Practices (Chapter Reference)
1	Improve Stakeholder Engagement	• Motivate stakeholders to be more value-focused • Accelerate and strengthen key stakeholder buy-in	• Leverage committed executive sponsor *(Ch.10, Step 1, Task 3)* • Deeply involve key stakeholder groups *(Value Board, Ch.10, Exhibit 10.5 "Value Board")* • Get visible support from senior management *(Ch. 6, "Management Mind-Set Shifting at GEI")*
2	Build Better Business Cases	• Find hidden value • Convert intangibles to quantified tangibles • Capture financial and nonfinancial value components • Avoid double counting	• Clearly define scope and audience *(Ch. 10, Exhibit 10.5)* • Uncover hidden value *(All of Ch.13)* • Use a framework for Free Cash Flow *(Ch. 5, "Section B: Auditing the Value Flow Map")* • Show HOW value links to firm's strategy *(Ch. 5, "Section B: Auditing the Value Flow Map")* • Make intangibles visible *(All of Ch. 14)*

EXHIBIT 7.1 (Continued)

ID #	Value Need	Examples of Goal	Examples of Best Practices (Chapter Reference)
3	Make Better Decisions Based on Value	• Prioritization—capabilities, requirements, functionality • Prioritization—road maps	• Do value-based prioritization for projects, scope, requirements, customization, etc. *(Ch. 5, Section D: "Program Decision Making")*
4	Improve Accountability, Alignment, and Benefits Tracking	• Ensure value delivery • Assign accountability, track results	• Assign ownership for value results *(Stakeholder Accountability, Ch. 5, "Section C: Stakeholder Accountability")* • Track value results *(All of Ch. 17)* • Embed value practices into PMO *(Ch. 5, "Section G: Value Governance")*
5	General	• Program life cycle value realization support • Expand IT leaders' value-focused discussions with business • Embed a culture and orientation of value	• Address all phases of program's life cycle *(All of Ch. 5)* • Communicate with value stories *(All of Ch. 15)* • Inform and educate senior management on value-based thinking *(Ch. 6, "Shifting the Mind-Sets of Management")*

These Value Needs can be discerned by looking at the results of the Value Practices Audit section of Chapter 4.

For example, if Value Need #3 in Exhibit 7.1 ("Make Better Decisions Based on Value") is a major opportunity for value improvement identified by the Value Practices Audit, then the "Best Practices (Chapter Reference)" column points to the "Program Decision Making" section of Chapter 5. This section discusses decision-making approaches for prioritizing solution requirements and/or implementation road maps.

For additional ideas and insights on addressing these value needs, see the next section, "Using Quick Audits."

EXHIBIT 7.2 Value Realization Quick Audits

ID #	Quick Audit Name	Purpose	Location
1	Process Audit Tool for Value Realization	Rapid quality assessment of how well an organization's processes for maximizing value realization related to business cases are defined, documented, and utilized	Chapter 9, Exhibits 9.4, 9.5
2	Seven C's Content Audit Tool for Business Cases	Rapid quality assessment of how well the calculations, rationale, methods of analysis, and means of communication are embedded into business cases	Chapter 8, Exhibits 8.2, 8.3
3	Seven Tests for Alignment	Rapid quality assessment of how clearly a business case's findings are linked to an enterprise's goals and strategy	Chapter 10, Exhibit 10.11
4	IT -Enabled Project Selection Process Audit	Rapid quality assessment of how well the organization uses a process for IT project selection that is accurate, fair, straightforward, and transparent	Chapter 16, Exhibits 16.2, 16.3
5	IT Benefits Realization Process Audit Tool	Rapid quality assessment of the processes in place to track and report benefits as they emerge.	Chapter 17, Exhibits 17.2, 17.3

Using Quick Audits

In addition to the Value Practices Audit (Chapter 4), five "Quick Audits" are provided to enable you to rapidly gain insight at the next level of detail. Exhibit 7.2 profiles each one.

The Ultimate Goal: 24/7 Value Thinking

Repeated value successes ultimately come when "value thinking" permeates the entire organization. Exhibit 7.3 recaps the scope of what this value thinking includes.

EXHIBIT 7.3 Scope of Value-Based Thinking

---

1. The problem: Value-based thinking is a critical determinant of a program's success. Repeated results across industries, geographies, and economic circumstances demonstrate that programs fail to deliver the desired level of benefits because of a lack of focus on value.

- Value is not clearly understood throughout the program
- Value is not tracked
- Value often overlaps

2. Where and when to apply: Value-based thinking should apply to programs as they are planned, when they are being executed, and in the post-implementation steady state.

The specific way value-based thinking is applied differs slightly depending on the solution's life cycle stage. However, the principles remain the same. The goal is to make the right decisions based on objective measure(s) of value, as opposed to allowing decisions to be based purely on consensus or gut-feel. Here's the focus on value-based thinking across the program life cycle:

- Planning Stage
  - What's the value objective of the transformation program?
  - How should the program's success be measured (metrics and from/to program targets)
  - What is the program worth in free cash flow terms?
  - How will the program be achieved in terms of specific change initiatives?

- Execution Stage
  - Use value maximization as the decision criteria
    - Scope selection (functional and technical requirements prioritization)
    - Technology selection (build versus buy, package A vs. B, technology 1 vs. 2)
    - Implementation road map planning and sequencing
    - Process location selection

- Operation Stage
  - Ensure the organization's continued focus on success metrics
    - Value governance
    - Value ownership and accountability

In the Final Analysis

If, as actor/director Woody Allen suggests, 90 percent of success is just showing up, then getting started on one value-enhancing action can begin an important journey of value maximization.

Getting the Business Case Right

Knowledge consists in understanding the evidence that establishes the fact, not in the belief in the fact itself.
—Charles T. Sprading, 1871–1959,
author

Theme

Maximizing ROI begins and ends with developing and continuously maintaining a reliable, believable business case.

Because business cases are the primary drivers of all value expectations, and directly impact all the measuring, designing, and tracking components discussed in the previous chapters, it is vital to "get the business case right." Since there are so many ways business cases can unintentionally fall short of this goal, Part Four discusses how to be sure they are reliable contributors not only to making insightful funding decisions, but also to ensuring that all promised value of an investment actually comes true. The Part Four chapters are:

The Appendix presents a sample business case that incorporates many of the best practices outlined in this book.

CHAPTER 8

How to Recognize a Trustworthy Business Case

Business more than any other occupation is a continual dealing with the future; it is a continual calculation, an instinctive exercise in foresight.
—Henry Luce, 1898–1967, American publisher
and founder of *Time* and *Fortune*, October 1960

Theme

Trustworthy business cases explain future business value logically and convincingly.

The Business Case as a Trusted Scout

Both real and fictional heroes often have trusted companions that steer them from danger. The Lone Ranger had his loyal scout, Tonto. Red Ryder relied upon Little Beaver. Real-life American explorers Lewis and Clark had Sacajawea, a young female Indian guide to whom they entrusted their lives.

A good business case is the trusted value scout of information technology (IT) investment decision making. It points out promising opportunities, resolves conflicting arguments, flushes out bad reasoning, exposes inappropriate political plays, shores up claims, and simplifies analysis. The result: a management confidence–building path to a dependable investment decision.

However, some scouts are better than others. A bad guide is worse than none, for one is unknowingly led into dire situations, oblivious to the danger.

Thus, the first step toward increasing IT value is knowing how to recognize a good scoutlike business case when one appears.

Using the Seven C's to Assess Content Quality

Like people, some business cases are believable and some are not. Some have slick packaging and deep substance. Some do not.

Fortunately, business cases can be sized up faster and easier than can people. The Seven C's Content Audit Tool for Business Cases described below provides a quick "first-look" way to gauge business case trustworthiness. While not foolproof, this Audit Tool contains a list of known characteristics of good business cases, garnered from the authors' review of hundreds of business cases from around the globe. The closer the match of these audit factors to a given business case, the more likely that business case can be trusted. Once a business case passes this "first-look test," it can be examined in more detail using techniques described in the remaining chapters of this book.

Trustworthy business cases are all about *quality*. Quality is the degree of fit between a selected object and a standard of value for that object. With business cases, the higher the quality, the more dependable their contents.

The Seven C's of Content Quality

The Seven C's Content Audit Tool for Business Cases measures the following seven aspects of quality:

- **Correct** fit to the decision being made
- **Concerns** of decision participants fully identified and reflected in the decision criteria
- **Complete** analysis of all value areas, both tangible and intangible
- **Connections** from IT features to business goals
- **Credibility** of analysis
- **Conciseness** of expression
- **Compelling** story usage

Examples of applying these content quality components in real life include:

Correct fit: Is the audience and scope of this business case clearly defined and in proportion to the investment decision's impact?
Not this: "This business case examines the value of customer relationship management (CRM)."

But this: "This business case examines the business value of a proposed $500,000 project to implement a CRM solution in the consumer division of ABC Corporation's Asia-Pacific operations (except for Singapore) during the next five fiscal years. Budget for this business case analysis was 3 percent ($15,000) of the proposed CRM cost."

Concerns: Are true concerns of the business case audience fully addressed in the decision criteria?

Not this: (No explicit mention of the audience for the business case, nor of their individual concerns that the CRM system addresses.)

But this: "This business case is written for the CRM investment decision participants shown in Exhibit A. The decision criteria, which were derived based on the highest concerns of each decision participant, are shown in Exhibit B."

Complete: Are all relevant tangible and intangible value areas assessed?

Not this: "Only two areas of monetary benefits were identified. Intangible benefits are excluded from this business case."

But this: "Five key benefit areas have been quantified, including lower customer service cost per phone inquiry, fewer inquiries per customer, more inquiries via the Web, lessened IT costs, and fewer customer defections. The last benefit, while often considered intangible by many people, has significant tangible value to us, as detailed in Exhibit C.

"Two key intangible benefits, which have important strategic implications for our enterprise's vision, values, and goals, are discussed in Exhibit D."

Connections: Does a clear link exist from investment features to business goals?

Not this: "An integrated database will improve data integrity."

But this: "Easier access to more accurate product maintenance data enables customer services reps to complete customer inquiries faster, thus enhancing customer satisfaction, a key element in our firm's drive for increased market share during the next fiscal year."

Credibility: Is the analysis convincingly supported?

Not this: "Labor savings are easily $500,000 over 5 years."

But this: "Labor savings of $500,000 over 5 years derive from a 10 percent decrease in errors. This 10 percent decrease is half of what similar firms in our industry report (see details in the Appendix). Our vice president of customer service, Sally Lawrence, states 'This 10 percent assumption has my support. It is very conservative in view of our current operations.'"

Conciseness: Is the entire analysis clear, yet succinct?

Not this: "In summary, the data warehouse–based richness and integrity of this Internet-enabled CRM system will provide a technical architecture platform of unlimited expandability into the future."

But this: "In summary, this CRM system offers a 120 percent return on investment with a 14-month payback. Risks are minimal, while upsides are substantial."

Compelling: Are stories of interest and conviction used to illustrate key themes?

Not this: "The key message of this business case is that a good return is available from the proposed CRM investment."

But this: "Jim Smith, chief executive officer of XYZ, our largest customer, said this after reviewing our CRM investment plans: 'Our firm's success is intertwined with yours. Just last week we decided to forgo a multimillion-dollar sales opportunity, which was heavily dependent on the quality and responsiveness of your customer support operation. At that time we felt your ability to support us was insufficient for us to be successful with our own customer. If you had your proposed CRM system already implemented, we believe we could have bid and won that business. That, in turn, would have provided you with $1 million a year in contracts from us. Invest in your proposed CRM system now. We both need it!'"

Each of these seven quality factors is explained in more detail in Exhibit 8.1 and is expressed as a scoring category on the Seven C's Content Audit Tool for Business Cases in Exhibits 8.2 and 8.3.

The Seven C's Content Audit Tool for Business Cases

Exhibits 8.2 and 8.3 provide the instructions and a scoring tool, respectively, for rapidly determining how closely a given business case incorporates the seven C's of content quality discussed above.

Having a reliable business case document is a crucial, but not sufficient, approach to ensuring that IT investment value is maximized. How the business case is used after it has been developed will ultimately determine project success or failure. The following chapter explains three key processes for successfully applying a good business case to real-life IT investment opportunities. These processes are the:

- Project proposal process
- Project selection process
- Project tracking process

EXHIBIT 8.1 Explanation of Content Quality Factors of Business Cases

	CORRECT Fit (Nature and boundaries of this analysis are clear.)
Explanation	The scope and level of effort of the business case reflects investment size and impact.
Importance	An ill-defined business case boundary or level of effort undermines the reliability of the business case.
Guideline	Invest up to 3 percent of a project's potential investment in a business case analysis.
More information	See Chapter 10
	CONCERNS ("Who cares about what" is clearly documented.)
Explanation	All decision participants and their true concerns are accurately identified.
Importance	Overlooking people involved in the decision reduces business case credibility.
Guideline	IT investment decisions typically impact four or more organization groups: for example, operations, staff, IT, division management, executive management, customers, partners.
More information	See Chapter 10
	COMPLETE (Every important cost and benefit area is assessed.)
Explanation	Has no major gaps in costs or benefits; includes both tangible and intangible factors; assumptions and rationale are carefully explained. Enterprise issues related to this investment are appropriately included.
Importance	Information gaps of significance weaken validity of the entire business case.
Guideline	Fully explain at least five quantified and two nonquantified (intangible) benefits areas.
More information	See Chapters 10, 15
	CONNECTIONS (Key features are linked to business goals.)
Explanation	Major features of each investment option are clearly linked to business goals.

(continued)

EXHIBIT 8.1 (Continued)

Importance	Only consider investments unambiguously supporting major goals of the business.
Guideline	Show at least one cause-and-effect link between investment option features and each organizational group involved in the decision. For example, "Improved data sharing cuts rework due to errors in invoicing, as well as cost of salespeople's time to soothe clients."
More information	See Chapters 10, 11

CREDIBILITY (Analysis is convincingly supported.)

Explanation	Evidence/support for assumptions, assertions, and calculations is relevant and believable.
Importance	Analysis is useless without rational support for assumptions and logic.
Guideline	Show visible support from subject-matter experts and politically influential people.
More information	See Chapter 11

CONCISENESS (Message is succinct.)

Explanation	Document does not exceed maximum length specified by decision makers.
Importance	Lengthy documents discourage readership and comprehension.
Guideline	Main body of business case is 5 to 15 pages, not including appendices.
More information	See Chapter 12

COMPELLING (Stories illustrate key themes.)

Explanation	Key themes, rationale, and messages are reinforced with convincing stories.
Importance	Loss of interest means loss of comprehension, thus reducing business case impact.
Guideline	Use at least one story to illustrate each major message of the business case.
More information	See Chapters 12, 15

EXHIBIT 8.2 Instructions: Seven C's Content Audit Tool for Business Cases

---

INSTRUCTIONS

This Seven C's Content Audit Tool provides a quick assessment of how well the calculations, method of analysis, and means of communication of a business case match the characteristics of business cases known to be highly effective.

Note: This quality audit tool assumes that the individuals doing the scoring are familiar with the characteristics of a high-quality business case outlined in this book and illustrated in the Appendix, "Sample Business Case."

Instructions below refer to the Scoresheet in Exhibit 8.3.

1. Complete heading information (name of business case, date, person(s) doing assessment).
2. Score each Quality Factor as either a 0 (little or none), 1 (some), or 2 (much), according to how well it accurately describes the business case being assessed.
3. If desired, add explanatory comments at the bottom of the Scoresheet.
4. Upon completion of all the scoring, total the score points as shown at the bottom of the Scoresheet in Exhibit 8.3.
5. Use the Scoring Table below to assess the content quality of the business case.

SCORING TABLE
(maximum possible score = 30)

Over 25: VERY GOOD (Contains most factors found in trustworthy business cases.)

15 to 25: ADEQUATE (Use with caution.)

Under 15: WEAK (Important to remedy weak points before using.)

TERMINOLOGY

Decision participants: Individuals (or groups) who will influence, recommend, or make the buying decision.

Decision criteria: Factors used by decision participants to determine the attractiveness of investment alternatives.

Decision-participant concerns: Business issues decision participants care about. Equivalent to "decision criteria."

Tangible benefit: A benefit whose value is quantified in monetary terms.

Intangible benefit: A benefit whose value is *NOT* quantified in monetary terms.

EXHIBIT 8.3 Scoresheet: Seven C's Content Audit Tool for Business Cases

(See Instructions and Terminology in Exhibits 8.1 and 8.2)

Name of business case assessed: _____

Date of assessment: _____

Person(s) doing assessment: _____

	Circle Score			
	A	**B**	**C**	
	Little	Some	Much	
Extent of Match >>>	or			*More*
Quality Factors	None			*Information*
CORRECT Fit (Nature and boundaries of this analysis)				
1. Audience and scope of business case proportional to decision's impact?	0	1	2	Chapter 10
CONCERNS (Who cares about what)				
2. Decision participants are identified from all relevant organizational areas?	0	1	2	Chapter 10
3. Decision criteria reflect true concerns of *each* decision participant?	0	1	2	Chapter 10
COMPLETE (Addressing every important value area)				
4. Tangible benefits have considered the full spectrum of value opportunities?	0	1	2	Chapters 10, 15
5. Benefits of systems' impact on groups *outside* of main users also assessed?	0	1	2	Chapter 10
6. Total cost of ownership of investment is assessed?	0	1	2	Chapter 11
7. Key nonquantifiable (intangible) benefits are identified?	0	1	2	Chapter 14
8. Risks when implementing investment options are identified?	0	1	2	Chapter 10
CONNECTIONS (Alignment to business goals)				
9. Clearly shows how system features directly link enterprise goals?	0	1	2	Chapter 10, 11
CREDIBILITY (Analysis convincingly supported)				
10. Metrics used are convincingly justified?	0	1	2	Chapter 11
11. Rationale supporting benefit calculations is logically constructed?	0	1	2	Chapter 11
12. Credible sources have validated the calculations and assertions?	0	1	2	Chapter 11
13. Politically influential people support key claims?	0	1	2	Chapter 11
CONCISENESS (Message succinct)				
14. Business case contained in 15 pages or less (not including appendices)?	0	1	2	Chapter 12
COMPELLING (Stories illustrate key themes)				
15. Key messages conveyed via convincing, interesting stories?	0	1	2	Chapters 12, 15

Add the score for each column >>>   ☐ + ☐ + ☐

Total audit score (Columns A+B +C) >>>   ☐

Comments:

CHAPTER 9

The Importance of Good Processes for Value Realization

If you get all the facts, your judgment can be right; if you don't get all the facts, it can't be right.
— Bernard Baruch, 1879–1965, presidential adviser and investment broker, *St. Louis Post-Dispatch*, June 21, 1965

Theme

To be fully effective, business cases must be melded to simple, but powerful, value realization proposing, selecting, and tracking processes.

Why Value Realization Processes Really Matter

Business Case–Grounded Processes Drive Business Results

Having the best business cases on the block does not automatically mean saying good-bye to value disappointments. Carefully designed processes are needed to ensure their correct usage.

In an enterprise, well-designed processes (or methods, as they sometimes are called) drive success. Banks succeed by being the best at processing a resource called "money" from owner to borrower. Supermarkets become industry leaders by most effectively processing a resource called "groceries" from source to consumer. Airlines gain market share via superior processing of a resource called "people" from City A to City B. Schools cement a quality reputation by excellent processing of resources called "student minds" from entry to graduation.

In one sense, it seems almost laughable to imagine management not paying close attention to all key processes in their organization. Certainly executives would never launch a great new product if no method existed for delivering it to customers. Similarly, senior decision makers would never advertise a new miracle drug if methods for its manufacture were ad hoc and opportunistic.

However, unfortunately in many organizations, business cases are allowed to float in a process-muddled sea. To be fully successful, business cases need to be the key input of three simple but powerful processes: proposing, selecting, and tracking.

- The proposing process (to provide standards and methods for building and submitting useful business cases)
- The selecting process (to define who decides which projects get funded, how, and why)
- The tracking process (to report the progress of information technology (IT) investment value by comparing actual value with that forecasted by the business case)

Substandard Business Case Processes Abound

Throw a dart at a list on the wall of the *Fortune* 1,000 global enterprises. Chances are at least 90 percent that it will hit an enterprise that gives more thought to the processes for approving $50 expense reports than to the business case processes for ensuring IT value realization. The situation at smaller firms is even bleaker.

This situation is especially ironic given that we now live in a business process reengineered (BPR) world. In the past decade, BPR teams have focused reengineering on practically every process known to humankind, except one—the decision-making process for managing IT investments. This is a serious problem. IT investments impact the success of almost every business process in the firm. For example, try reengineering a supply chain process using inappropriate software chosen by a flawed IT investment decision-making method. Not a pretty sight.

Costs of Tolerating Process Problems Are High

The penalties are high for ignoring the presence of substandard value realization processes. Consider these examples:

- When the proposing process is flawed:
    - A high-payoff IT investment option is overlooked because no process exists to encourage an accurate business case analysis.

- A low-payoff IT investment option is accepted, thus, during times of scarce capital, preventing higher-value investment options from seeing the light of day.
- When the selecting process is flawed:
  - A brilliant business case is developed, but it is ignored when politically powerful decision makers ram through an alternative investment. Discouraged users resist the chosen system, which then fails.
  - The best investments for the firm are overlooked. No consistent decision criteria are employed to enable an apples-to-apples comparison with competing funding proposals.
- When the tracking process is flawed:
  - A high-potential system is selected, and yet it flounders during implementation. Management realizes, too late, that the scope of the failed system was modified during rollout. This new scope negated value assumptions outlined in the original business case.
  - In spite of early awareness at the plant level that workers' productivity on a new system was poor, management never got the message in time to revise flawed training methods. The implementation flopped.

Given that sound value realization processes are essential to IT value achievement, it pays to stay alert for indicators that processes may, in fact, be standing in the way of success.

Symptoms of Process Problems

Numerous early warning signs, such as those shown in Exhibits 9.1, 9.2, and 9.3, can indicate significant process problems.

EXHIBIT 9.1 Common Symptoms of PROPOSING Process Problems

The **proposing** process explains standards and methods for building useful business cases.

The proposing process may need fixing when:

- Business cases are not used for important projects.
- Business cases are weak, misleading, and/or overly complex.
- No standards exist for constructing effective business cases.
- Business case creation standards are inconsistently applied.
- Score is under 15 on Seven C's Content Audit Tool for Business Cases (see Chapter 8).

EXHIBIT 9.2 Common Symptoms of SELECTING Process Problems

The **selecting** process defines who decides which projects get funding, how, and why.

The selecting process may need fixing when:

- Complaints are frequently made about an unfair funding process.
- The selecting methodology is not documented.
- Existing selection methods are inconsistently applied.
- Business cases are inconsistent in use of decision criteria.
- Business cases do not address standardized project selection criteria.
- There is no feedback to projects submitters on why funding was withheld.
- Score is under 17 on IT-Enabled Project Selection Process Quality Audit Tool (see Chapter 16).

EXHIBIT 9.3 Common Symptoms of TRACKING Process Problems

The **tracking** process reports IT investment value progress by comparing actual value with that forecasted by the business case.

The tracking process may need fixing when:

- The business case is not used for monitoring value realization.
- The tracking process is inconsistently applied.
- Out-of-date business cases are used in the tracking process.
- No feedback is given on why projects had value shortfalls.

Types of Value Realization Process Problems

The first step in resolving process problems is to identify them as quickly as possible.

The symptoms described in Exhibits 9.1 to 9.3 can be signs of serious business case process problems, such as:

- *Design weakness,* which risks the creation of flawed business cases and/ or erroneous selection and tracking methods, thus directly degrading IT value maximization.
- *Complexity of procedures and forms,* which increases training costs and decreases users' desire to embrace the process.

- *Missing or confusing documentation,* which lengthens the learning curve and contributes to user frustration.
- *Lack of acceptance of the process,* thus accelerating its demise.
- *Lack of maintenance of the process,* leading to out-of-date business case creation and usage, thus directly subverting the goals of IT value maximization.

Detecting Value Realization Process Problems

The fastest way to determine if existing value realization processes are flawed is to look back at the past 24 months and ask these questions:

- Was the true value that was actually realized from all IT investment implementations analyzed?
- Were payoff results reported to management for review and action?
- Was action taken from payoff reporting?
- Is there certainty that no strong IT investment opportunity was overlooked due to process shortcomings?

If the answer to any of these questions is no, the value realization processes deserve more scrutiny.

The process audit described next provides a quick way to determine the soundness of the processes of proposing, selecting, and tracking. The closer the match of these factors to a given process, the more likely that process is helping to maximize IT value.

The Process Audit Tool for Value Realization measures the following aspects of process quality:

- Strength
- Simplicity
- Documentation
- Acceptance
- Maintenance

Strength: Does the process design reflect industry best practices, adapted to the organization's goals and culture?

Not this: The design of this process was the result of a brainstorming exercise from a recent indoctrination class of new hires to the firm.

But this: The design of this process reflects our research of worldwide best practices, consultations with internal and external process experts, and interviews with senior managers and staff within the firm.

Simplicity: Are the methods and forms simple and easy to learn and use?

Not this: The 25 steps, 15 exhibits, and 20 forms are detailed in the 185-page user guide attached.

But this: The seven steps and four forms can be understood with less than 30 minutes of effort.

Documentation: Is the process described in ways that easily communicate its content and requirements?

Not this: The 185-page user guide explains in textual detail all aspects of every step necessary to operate this process.

But this: The 12-page user guide includes visual input-output charts that summarize the scope and requirements of each step.

Acceptance: Is the process actively and enthusiastically used as intended?

Not this: Although not used in many key situations, this process is available should managers wish to employ it.

But this: A recent review showed that this process was used in 98 percent of all eligible situations. Management's active endorsement is clear and visible.

Maintenance: Is the process updated annually to reflect changes in the organization's strategy or structure?

Not this: Process development and maintenance dates are unclear.

But this: This process was developed on [date] and last reviewed and updated on [date] by [name(s) of responsible persons].

The Process Audit Tool for Value Realization

Exhibits 9.4 and 9.5 provide the instructions and scoring tool, respectively, for rapidly determining how closely a given value realization process incorporates the quality factors discussed above.

Once process problems have been identified, it is time to get into fix mode. To help with this endeavor, many best practices for process design are presented in Chapters 10–12, 16, and 17 for proposing, selecting, and tracking processes.

EXHIBIT 9.4 Instructions: Process Audit Tool for Value Realization

INSTRUCTIONS

The process audit tool for value realization provides a quick assessment of how well each of three business case processes (proposing, selecting, and tracking) within an organization incorporates quality factors shown in Exhibit 9.5.

Note: This quality audit tool assumes that the individuals doing the scoring are familiar with the characteristics of high-quality processes outlined in Chapters 10–12, 16, and 17 of this book.

Instructions below refer to the Scoresheet in Exhibit 9.5.

1. Complete the heading information [process audited, date, person(s) doing audit]
2. Score each of the 16 Quality Factors as a 0 (little or none), 1 (some), or 2 (much), according to how well it accurately describes the business case processes being assessed.
3. If desired, add explanatory comments at the bottom of the Scoresheet.
4. Upon completion of all scoring, total the score points as shown at the bottom of the Scoresheet in Exhibit 9.5.
5. Use the Scoring Table below to assess the process's overall quality.

SCORING TABLE: PROCESS AUDIT TOOL FOR VALUE REALIZATION
(maximum possible score = 32)

Over 24: VERY GOOD (Has most factors found in a reliable business case process.)

16 to 24: ADEQUATE (Use with caution.)

Under 16: WEAK (Important to remedy weak points before using.)

EXHIBIT 9.5 Scoresheet: Process Audit Tool for Value Realization

Business Case Process Audited _____
Date of Audit _____
Person(s) Doing Audit _____

Quality Factors	A	B	C	More Information
STRENGTH				
1. Process contains at least 90% of relevant best practices in this book.	0	1	2	All Chapters
2. Process design has been reviewed by subject-matter experts.	0	1	2	All Chapters
SIMPLICITY				
3. Simple templates are provided to guide data collection.	0	1	2	Chapter 11
4. Process has no more than seven major steps.	0	1	2	Chapters 10, 11, 12
5. Process uses no more than four templates.	0	1	2	Chapters 10, 11, 12
6. Automation is well used to reduce manual input analysis and output.	0	1	2	
7. Process can be understood in 30 minutes or less of effort.	0	1	2	Chapter 9
DOCUMENTATION				
8. Methods and forms are well described in writing.	0	1	2	Chapters 10, 11, 12, 16, 17
9. Inputs, outputs, and internal processes are clearly explained for each step.	0	1	2	Chapters 10, 11,12
10. Documentation includes a process flow.	0	1	2	Chapters 10, 11, 12
11. Sample inputs and outputs are included in training media.	0	1	2	Chapters 10, 11, 12, 16, 17
12. Keys to success guidelines and tips are identified.	0	1	2	Chapters 10, 11, 12, 16, 17
ACCEPTANCE				
13. Process is visibly endorsed by senior management.	0	1	2	Chapter 9
14. Process is used for at least 90% of eligible IT investment opportunities.	0	1	2	Chapters 8, 9
15. Process is rated "satisfactory or better" by at least 75% of users.	0	1	2	Chapters 10, 11, 12, 16, 17
MAINTENANCE				
16. Process is reviewed, and needed changes are made at least annually.	0	1	2	Chapter 9

Add the score for each column >>>
Total audit score (Columns A + B + C) >>>

☐ + ☐ + ☐

☐

Comments:
_____
_____
_____
_____
_____

CHAPTER 10

Defining: Steps 1, 2, and 3 to Building Better Business Cases

What one sees depends upon where one sits.

—James R. Schlesinger,
American politician and
presidential cabinet member

Theme

Effective business cases require a clear purpose, supported by carefully considered decision criteria.

Seven Hats for Seven Steps

A business case is a unique document:

- Its goal is to analyze, and yet it is not a truly financial document.
- Its goal is to sell, and yet it is not a sales tool.
- Its goal is to explain, and yet it is not an instruction manual.
- Its goal is to convince, and yet it is not a marketing guide.

The main goal of a business case is to help management decide, in a rational way, the true business value of a potential investment. But this seemingly benign role masks a challenge worthy of a Solomon. The reality is that investment choices, especially information technology (IT)-enabled investment choices, are a hotbed of misunderstandings, confusion, politics, and emotion.

Compounding the situation is that even if "building a business case" is identified as a good way to help overcome these challenges, another problem sets in. How can a business case be built that both its creators and its management audience can trust?

Fortunately, it is not hard to build a good business case. But it can be tricky. For an analogy, recall people's first attempts at riding a bicycle. Although the learning period was short, it required serious focus while it lasted. However, once mastered, bicycling became second nature.

Why is it so tricky to compose a reliable business case? Primarily because it involves a small, but carefully orchestrated, set of skills that rarely reside in just one person. The realities of technology investment decision making require that business case creators wear, at various times in the creation process, seven different hats. These chapeaus of distinction are:

- The *project manager* hat (to astutely organize and wisely administer the entire business case development process)
- The *politician* hat (to discern who matters, how, and why)
- The *salesperson* hat (to accurately unearth needs of the decision influencers)
- The *detective* hat (to cleverly uncover information)
- The *investigative reporter* hat (to clearly interview and convincingly write)
- The *analyst* hat (to accurately calculate and insightfully assess)
- The *attorney* hat (to convincingly construct evidence and rationale, and compellingly present it)

With so many challenges at stake, and so many ways to go astray, putting a little bit of structure into business case development can do wonders for producing a quality document.

The process of building a business case can be outlined in three phases, comprising seven steps. Each of these seven steps has associated tasks, shown in Exhibit 10.1.

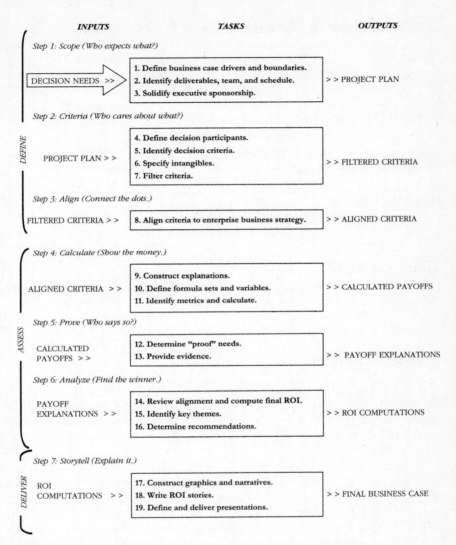

EXHIBIT 10.1 Seven Steps Road Map to Creating Successful Business Cases

Step 1: SCOPE (Who Expects What?)

Watchword: *"Front-end precision reduces back-end confusion."*

SCOPE in a Nutshell (Main Hat to Wear: Project Manager)

Purpose	Define the business case contents and project plan.
Input	Decision needs.
Output	Project plan.
Why Do This Step	• Identify needed resources. • Avoid time-wasting detours. • Accurately set management expectations.
Templates, Tools	Business Case Scope, Summary Table of Contents (draft), Project Plan.
Key Principles	• Clarify final output of the project. • Confirm the business case creation project cost is proportional to decision importance.

SCOPE Explained

A business case is too important analytically and too visible politically to contain avoidable mistakes. A surprising number of these needless errors originate at the scope stage.

Scope involves three key tasks, as shown in Exhibit 10.2

Description of Tasks

TASK 1: DEFINE BUSINESS CASE DRIVERS AND BOUNDARIES   The need for an IT investment decision does not spontaneously burst from the ether. Hidden somewhere in the cosmos of the enterprise are major business factors that propel the need to make this decision now, rather than six months ago or six months from now.

Flushing out and documenting these key "drivers" is extremely important. The correct drivers establish the direction of the business case and set the stage for the "theme" of the business case analysis (discussed in more detail in Task 15). A good business case will clearly link the functionality of the solution being considered to these high-level management concerns.

The correct primary business drivers always address issues of direct concern to senior management. If the proposed drivers do not meet this test, then more research is needed until such drivers are found.

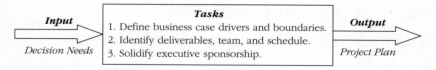

EXHIBIT 10.2 Process Flow for Scope

Take extra pains to be sure the business drivers are correct. Best bet: Talk to one or more of the most influential decision participants. Ask "What are the strategic business conditions that are causing the need to make this IT investment decision right now, rather than six months earlier or six months later?" Express the business drivers in the language of the most senior decision participants.

Boundaries identify exactly what is and is not included in this business case relative to:

- Investment options to be assessed
- Span of the systems to be justified
- Organizational units involved in the value assessment
- Level of detail of the business case analysis and report
- People and resources to be consulted

TASK 2: IDENTIFY DELIVERABLES, TEAM, AND SCHEDULE Enlist and document all members of the business case evaluation team. These are the people who formally are responsible for the development and delivery of the business case. For this task, deliverables (e.g., final report) and project timeliness should be specified in detail.

TASK 3: SOLIDIFY EXECUTIVE SPONSORSHIP Any business-case document that will influence senior management in making IT investment decisions requires an executive sponsor. This sponsor has overall responsibility to senior management for the quality and timeliness of the business case. To be effective, an executive sponsor should:

- Have access to and the confidence of the decision participants who will use the business case
- Know the organizational workings and realities related to the system being justified
- Understand clearly the IT investment decision process (both the formal and informal components)
- Have enthusiasm for the potential value of the investment under consideration
- Encourage subject-matter experts to cooperate with the business case team
- Actively support, guide, and encourage the business case team

Step 2: CRITERIA (Who Cares About What?)

Watchword: *"People embrace what they understand, care about, and believe in."*

CRITERIA in a Nutshell (Main Hats to Wear: Reporter, Politician, Salesperson)

Purpose	Accurately determine the audience for the business case and the factors they will use (criteria) to make the investment decision.
Input	Project plan.
Output	Filtered criteria.
Why Do This Step	• Avoid missing key decision criteria. This could lead to undermining the validity of the business case and its creators. • Focus team resources on those payoff areas of most importance to the final decision.
Templates, Tools	ValueBoard, Scoresheet.
Key Principles	• The business case audience is always the decision participants. • Be sure the highest-level decision maker is accurately identified. • Have at least one criteria for each decision participant. • Express criteria in language undestood by each level of decision participant. • Include some intangibles. • Address risks. • Weight all criteria to indicate their relative importance to the decision. • Be clear how investment opportunity aligns to high-level business goals.

CRITERIA Explained

Imagine trying to win a friendly poker game and being ignorant of the rules. Are the aces high or low? Are jacks wild or not? Are there any betting limits? How long will the game last? Under such conditions, it would be easy to be a superior player, play hard, and yet still lose the game.

A similar situation exists when trying to compose a business case. The "game" being played is called "IT-enabled investment selection and value maximization." The players are the decision participants (who have rules by which they decide if the business case wins or loses) and the developers of the business case (who must prove superior value). The business case developers "win" if their proposed investment is selected and actively used throughout the investment's lifetime.

The "main rules" of the IT investment selection game are the decision criteria.

This criteria step is designed to provide strategies and methods for avoiding these serious problems. The criteria step involves four key tasks, shown in Exhibit 10.3.

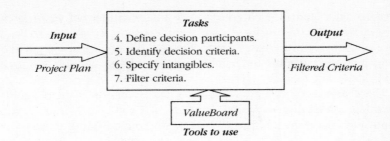

EXHIBIT 10.3 Process Flow for Criteria

Description of Tasks

TASK 4: DEFINE DECISION PARTICIPANTS   Decision participants are people who either directly influence or actually make the decision to invest in the system evaluated by the business case at hand. The audience for the business case is always these decision participants. They in essence, are the only ones who count. It is these people whose vision, values, and goals must be clearly understood if the business case is to succeed.

To be confident that this audience is accurately understood, document all decision-participant groups by name, enterprise responsibility and/or title, and decision process role.

TASK 5: IDENTIFY DECISION CRITERIA   Decision criteria are factors (both tangible and intangible) used by decision participants to determine the attractiveness of investment alternatives. They are expressed as benefits, costs, and/or risks.

This task focuses on flushing out decision criteria that decision participants will use to assess the value of the investment. Task 5 recommends that 30 to 40 decision criteria candidates be identified at this point. Task 7 calls for these candidates to be filtered down to the top 6 to 12. Common pitfalls in Task 5 are:

- Asking the right people, who give wrong answers (either inadvertently or on purpose)
- Getting the right answers from the right people, but then having the business case team inadvertently misinterpret such remarks
- Being unable to contact the right people (not available, don't know who they are, etc.)
- Overlooking valuable secondary sources, such as publications, articles, blogs, and so on

The impact of these criteria-gathering curveballs is major. Having erroneous or missing criteria can mislead management into making the wrong investment decision. If such criteria defects are caught before or after the decision is made, the business case team loses significant credibility with senior executives. If the flaws go undetected, the enterprise may make the wrong investments, thus ultimately penalizing all stakeholders, including the business case team.

There are a couple of simple tools and methods to help avoid this misguided criteria discovery: the ValueBoard (Exhibit 10.5) and the Project Prioritization Scoresheet (Chapter 16). Driving the design of these tools are three principles of good decision criteria gathering:

- *Business results focus:* Defining value in terms of business results, not system features or functions
- *"Who cares about what":* Linking value to personal concerns of individual decision participants
- *Alignment:* Explicitly linking investment features to enterprise business needs (Task 8)

Hitting the "Dartboard of Value"

To help ensure that the right decision criteria have been fully identified, think of darts trying to hit the target on a dartboard. The goal of a "business case darts" game is to pick up the dart and then—with proper skill and timing—hurl it to the highest payoff area of the dartboard. This, in essence, is the goal of Task 5—to identify criteria. The objective is to find the right criteria and then place those criteria in the business case exactly where they have the highest value.

To envision this dartboard-of-value approach, consider a dartboard that is shaped like an organizational pyramid, such as in Exhibit 10.4. Only a few decision criteria should appear in the shaded "Systems/Data" zone at the bottom of the pyramid.

The areas on this target to aim for are the areas above the Systems/ Data area: One is the area directly above—objectives/tactics for directors and VP-level managers. The area especially important is at the top—strategic business results for C-level executives, including the board of directors. These two groups think, plan, and operate in the realm of business results. It is a common failure of many business cases that decision criteria under-address their interests. Thus, the goal is to find and throw decision criteria darts so as many as possible land above the systems/data area.

Decision criteria must not only target the enterprise area where business results live, but also align with the interests of decision participants. In addition, the criteria must clearly link, in a cause-and-effect manner, to the features of the investment option. These methods can be effectively addressed using a tool called a ValueBoard, discussed next.

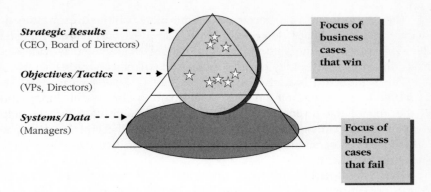

EXHIBIT 10.4 Effective Business Cases Target Business Results, Not System Features

Using the ValueBoard

A quick and easy way to help ensure that the value darts (decision criteria) are hitting the right business results is to use a visual mapping tool called a ValueBoard. Exhibit 10.5 shows a ValueBoard example.[1]

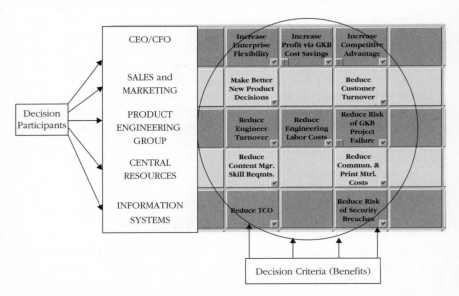

EXHIBIT 10.5 ValueBoard: (by Decision Participant Levels): Final Criteria for an Intranet Global KnowledgeBase Evaluation for ABC Corporation

---

1. For clarity of explanation at this point in this chapter, Exhibit 10.5 shows only 12 payoff areas, although Task 5 calls for identifying 30 to 40 candidates before filtering them down to 6 to 12 (Task 7).

The ValueBoard is a rectangular equivalent of the organizational-shaped value dartboard described above. The idea is to place proposed decision criteria on the ValueBoard. The patterns that evolve provide signals concerning the validity of distribution and balance of criteria.

The ValueBoard is useful on the front end of business case analysis as a criteria brainstorming aid. The ValueBoard is also useful during and at the end of the business case effort as a communication tool to help decision participants quickly visualize the nature of the criteria used. The ValueBoard can be simulated manually by using flip chart paper and some sticky notes.

The ValueBoard shows two types of crucial relationships between payoff opportunities and investment functionality that will make the payoff possible. These relationship types are:

- *Who cares about what?* This links potential payoff areas to the interests of different decision participants. (On the ValueBoard, these relationships are shown horizontally, as can be seen in Exhibit 10.5.) A CEO concerned with enterprise strategy and operations is more likely interested in different benefits than an accounting communications manager responsible for reducing the costs of phone services.
- *What causes what?* This is the cause-and-effect link between payoffs of interest to different types of stakeholders. For example, the billing manager may be excited about reducing invoice errors, but the CEO is not. However, if fewer invoice errors could provide a major improvement in customer satisfaction, thereby increasing sales and thus enterprise profits, then the CEO might be extremely interested. Applying this principle to the example in Exhibit 10.5, the central resources group is enthusiastic about reducing communications and printed material costs, but the CEO is not. However, if such costs are significant enough to make a noticeable improvement in profits, then the CEO will take notice.

Using a Balanced Scorecard–Oriented ValueBoard

A powerful and popular technique for aligning business objectives with business strategy, and with one another, is the Balanced Scorecard.[2] The ValueBoard can be recast as a Balanced Scorecard by renaming the levels and then assigning the payoff areas to match those levels. In addition,

---

2. The Balanced Scorecard method, created by Dr. Robert Kaplan and Dr. David Norton, has become a major strategy-performance measurement technique for enterprises worldwide. See Bibliography.

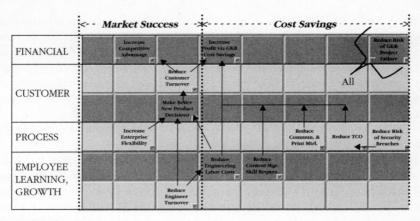

EXHIBIT 10.6 ValueBoard (by Balanced Scorecard Levels): Final Criteria for an Intranet Global KnowledgeBase Evaluation for ABC Corporation

further insights are available by making the left section of the ValueBoard a revenue-oriented "Market Success" category and the right section "Cost Savings." Exhibit 10.6 remolds Exhibit 10.5 into the Balanced Scorecard view of the world. This approach is discussed in more detail in Task 8 (align criteria to enterprise business strategy), Task 14 (review alignment and compute final ROI) and Task 15 (identify key themes).

Establishing Key Themes

A business case should ultimately have one primary message of value, supported by no more than two or three related messages. In other words, a dozen or two pages of analysis should be able to be summarized into a couple of succinct messages.

While the final decisions on key messages can be postponed from Task 5 (identify decision criteria) until Task 15 (identify key themes), now is the right time to begin looking for such opportunities.

The "Summary of Value Results" for the ABC Corporation business case in the Appendix also illustrates this principle of having a succinct, key theme:

Improving engineering productivity and loyalty are the main, core advantages of the intranet Global KnowledgeBase (GKB) solution. These benefits translate into improving the quality and quantity of new products, a key for enhancing ABC's competitive advantage, and thus its revenue and profits.

TASK 6: SPECIFY INTANGIBLES   No business case concept is more misunderstood than the "tangibility" of decision criteria. Tangibility is an attribute
indicating the extent to which decision participants believe a payoff can
be quantified in monetary terms. A criterion called "Reduce the average
price of raw materials" could be classified as tangible if decision participants believed it could save "$100,000 per year by cutting $5 from the unit
price of every 20,000 widgets we buy."

However, if they felt such savings could not legitimately be quantified,
then the criterion would be classified as "intangible."

The reality is that any criterion in the world can be classified as either
intangible or tangible. The answer depends upon the answers to five "tangibility" questions discussed in Chapter 14 ("Handling Intangibles: The
Emotional Enigma of Value Realization"). (See Exhibit 14.1.) These answers
place a given criterion along a scale of "extent of tangibility." In the final
analysis of business case work, tangibility is an opinion adopted by a
group, not an absolute.

When making the tangibility decision, remember the only answer that
counts is that which the decision participants will use during investment
decision time. See Exhibit 10.7 for guidelines for determining "tangibility"
of a specific decision criterion.

Misgauging the relative importance of tangible and intangible factors
is easy to prevent. Best bet: Have the business case team do an educated
guess on a first-cut basis. Then soon thereafter review their classifications
with the executive sponsor and decision participants.

Guideline: Assign at least 20 percent of the criteria as intangible. This
reflects the realities of how IT investment decisions are made.

Guard against feeling that classifying a criterion as intangible somehow places it in a lower state of usefulness than if it were considered
tangible. Chapter 14 discusses the crucial value of intangibles in today's
economy. Typically, 50 percent or more of executive IT investment decisions are based on intangible factors, even if decision makers do not admit
it in public.

TASK 7: FILTER CRITERIA   It is now "survival of the fittest" time.

In Task 5 (identify decision criteria) above, 30 to 40 criteria were to be
identified during the brainstorming sessions. These candidates were then
assigned to the most appropriate levels on the ValueBoard. In Task 7, this
ValueBoard of impressive but actually unmanageable criteria is to be con-
densed to an easier-to-handle 6 to 12.

Why such a small number of criteria? Experience has shown that much
work is required to determine and prove value for each criterion selected.
Having more than a dozen criteria to analyze will risk overwhelming the
business case team. More importantly, having more than 12 criteria in

EXHIBIT 10.7 Guidelines for Determining the "Tangibility" of Decision Criteria

GUIDELINES: Some factors for deciding tangibility at this stage in the business case development cycle:

Consider classifying the criteria as TANGIBLE if ALL of the situations below apply:
- The formulas for calculating hard-money value are relatively noncontroversial.
- The assumptions upon which the formulas depend are believable.
- The metrics used for the quantification are readily available and believable.
- Important political allies will support such calculations and their related assumptions.

Consider classifying the criteria as INTANGIBLE if any ONE of the situations below apply:
- Formulas required for quantification seem to be a stretch in terms of complexity and/or assumptions required.
- No one of influence with decision participants will support the calculations, regardless of their mathematical correctness.
- Metrics are not considered believable.
- Decision participants insist criteria is intangible despite the fact the criteria can be quantified, and the criteria are popularly believed to be inherently intangible.

Important note: It is not a good reason per se to classify a criterion as intangible just because a similar criterion in the past has been classified that way. Chapter 14 gives dozens of examples where criteria can be quantified even though they are popularly believed to be inherently intangible.

---

the business case risks overwhelming some members of the decision team with excessive detail. When this happens, the main value message of the business case is often lost.

Of all the value calculations in a typical business case, experience shows that it is typically three or four (out of the 12) that ultimately drive the decision to invest or not. However, a dozen are needed so the decision team can pick and choose which ones they have the most confidence in.

If the business case team is convinced that more than four are required for one ValueBoard level (refer again to Exhibits 10.5 and 10.6), then perhaps the definition of that level is too broad. The level may need to be split into two or more decision-participant groups (i.e., levels). Or it is possible that there are too few criteria on levels above and below the overpopulated one. A common mistake when justifying process improvements is to overpopulate criteria for the level that actually uses the system being valued. When this happens, it typically means that the higher business results areas (e.g., senior management) are missing important criteria.

Here are some tips on how to filter 30+ criteria candidates down to no more than a pithy dozen:

- Do not use more than four criteria per decision-participant group (i.e., per level on the ValueBoard).
- Look for decision candidates that cover the same criteria but use different words. For example, a criterion called "Improve engineering productivity" may be similar to "Reduce engineering labor costs." Consider combining them into one.
- Ask if the tangible value of a given criterion is likely to be large enough to keep. For example, a value of $10,000 over five years is probably not worth including if every other criterion provides at least $500,000 in value.

Step 3: ALIGN (Connect the Dots)

Watchword: *"Everyone must pull together."*

ALIGN in a Nutshell (Main Hats to Wear: Analyst, Detective)

Purpose	Confirm all decision criteria and link to key business goals.
Input	Filtered criteria.
Output	Aligned criteria.
Why Do This Step	Best business value occurs if solution directly supports enterprise needs.
Templates, Tools	ValueBoard.
Key Principles	• Lower-level criteria link to higher-level criteria.

ALIGN Explained

Alignment is an often misunderstood, but profoundly important, management skill. Alignment is the process of keeping all activities and resources headed in the same direction in a mutually reinforcing manner.

An enterprise consistently succeeds only when all of its parts are in a strong cause-and-effect relationship (alignment) with one another. Starbucks thrives because its entire worldwide organization is aligned to ultimately focus on one thing—produce a uniquely satisfying refreshment experience that encourages repeating. To succeed, Starbucks must align

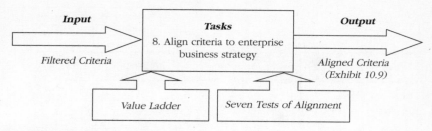

EXHIBIT 10.8 Process Flow for Align

activities in a carefully orchestrated cause-and-effect manner. From the fastidiously selected coffee beans, to the precision roasting, to the exact brewing, to the comfortable surroundings, to the experience-related merchandise for sale, every element of Starbucks's enterprise links to that goal. Using brand extension strategies, Starbucks also "re-creates" this experience virtually by selling Starbucks-branded items to the consumer via other channels. As Starbucks evolves, so will its alignment.

Alignment is foremost on the minds of executive decision makers when faced with choices on IT-enabled investments. How strong, they want to know, is the cause and effect between investing in Project X and realizing key business objectives? It is the job of the business case team to discover and communicate the strongest possible, truest value alignment related to the investment being analyzed. This align step provides an approach (Exhibit 10.8).

TASK 8: ALIGN CRITERIA TO ENTERPRISE BUSINESS STRATEGY   "Align criteria" is the process of first checking, then adjusting, for a compelling cause-and-effect relationship among successively higher-level decision criteria, so that all criteria ultimately support the enterprise's business strategy.

Using the Value Ladder to Display Alignment

The Value Ladder (Exhibit 10.9) is a tool to help in this regard. It consists of concise, cause-and-effect, graphical depictions of how an investment option's features and/or functions impact the objectives and ultimately the business results of an enterprise. Exhibit 10.9 shows the alignment process as applied to ABC's evaluation in the Appendix.

To check on the strength of any individual component, Exhibit 10.10 shows how to examine one Value Ladder (i.e., cause-and-effect display) dealing with reducing customer turnover. This Value Ladder is saying that the payoff area of an intranet GKB called "Reduce customer turnover" is driven by (i.e., made possible via) another payoff area called "Make better new product decisions."

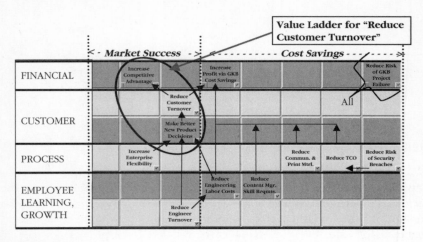

EXHIBIT 10.9 ValueBoard (by Balanced Scorecard Levels): Showing a VALUE LADDER Example for an Intranet Global KnowledgeBase Evaluation for ABC Corporation

This ValueBoard shows a Value Ladder named "Reduce Customer Turnover."* This ValueLadder begins with the payoff named "Make Better New Product Decisions," and indicates that it helps drive a higher-level payoff called "Reduce Customer Turnover," which in turn helps drive an even higher-level payoff entitled "Increase Competitive Advantage." Taken together, this Value Ladder visually shows the rationale of how making better new product decisions ultimately helps increase competitive advantage. Value Ladders provide insight into potential major cost-benefit themes that can evolve as key messages from the business case (see Task 15—Identify Key Themes in Chapter 11).

*See Appendix to see how this ValueBoard is integrated in a business case.

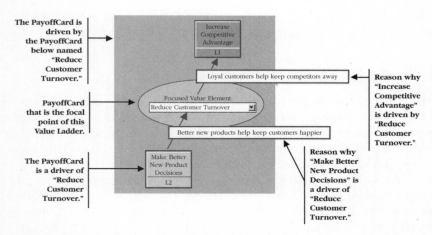

EXHIBIT 10.10 A Value Ladder for "Reduce Customer Turnover"

This entire Value Ladder can now be read as two connected sentences that drive home the point to decision participants:

Making better new product decisions helps make customers happier, thereby reducing customer turnover. Less turnover means having more loyal customers, which help keep competitors away, thus increasing our competitive advantage.

Value Ladders are especially useful for helping the decision team distinguish the forest from the trees. By grouping sets of payoff areas together in a logical cause-and-effect message, the decision team can quickly see the extent (or absence) of mutually reinforcing payoff areas. This "connect the dots" result can be seen in Exhibit 10.10.

Using the Seven Tests of Alignment

The seven tests of alignment (Exhibit 10.11) are helpful to quickly confirm that a business case's alignment of payoff areas is as strong as possible. Simply apply the following tests to the decision criteria defined at the completion of Task 7 (filter criteria).

EXHIBIT 10.11 Seven Tests of Alignment

- Test 1: Does every payoff area have a logical cause-and-effect (alignment) relationship with one or more other payoff areas? (Yes. Every payoff area either drives or is driven by at least one other payoff area.)

- Test 2: Are these relationships as strong and convincing as they can be? (Maybe. See Test 6 below.)

- Test 3: Are payoff areas relatively evenly distributed among the four Balanced Scorecard levels—financial, customer, process, and employee learning and growth? (Yes. We want a business case that addresses different levels relatively evenly.)

- Test 4: Does this collection of payoff areas emphasize one or the other of the two primary strategies of executives: market success or cost savings? (While Exhibit 10.9 shows more payoff areas under the "Cost Savings" side of the ValueBoard, later analysis (see Appendix) will show that the quantified value of the payoff areas favors the "Market Success" side.)

- Test 5: Do the messages of individual Value Ladders communicate the message that resonates with the decision team? ("Reduce engineering labor costs" may not support the team's goal of "More frequent and successful new products.")

(continued)

EXHIBIT 10.11 (Continued)

- Test 6: Is the language chosen to define each payoff area the most appropriate for the value message desired? (Most seem to be. However, what about "Reduce engineering labor costs"? If the primary message management wants to hear is "market success," then lowering engineering costs may not be the way to go. This is a clue that "increase engineering productivity" in terms of producing more new products faster may be more important. Thus, this Value Ladder analysis leads us to change the title of this payoff area from "Reduce engineering labor costs" to "Increase engineering productivity", which helps engineers create new products faster.)

- Test 7: Do the monetary savings (from the main messages that we are trying to discover from the Value Ladder payoff areas) constitute a majority of the total savings of the entire analysis? (Yes. See the "Tangibles Worksheet" in Exhibit 11.12.)

With the completion of Tasks 1 through 8, the business case project is now well under way. Boundaries and scope have been clarified. People involved with the decision are identified. Decision criteria have been created and filtered down to a dozen or less. Chapter 11 will explain time-efficient ways to calculate, prove, and analyze business case information so that the true business value is identified.

Assessing: Steps 4, 5, and 6 to Building Better Business Cases

All business proceeds on beliefs, or judgments of probabilities, and not on certainties.

—Charles William Eliot, 1834–1926, President, Harvard University, *The New Dictionary of Thoughts,* 1957

Theme

Effective business cases require believable assertions and well-reasoned recommendations.

Introduction

Successfully completing the **define** phase (described in Chapter 10) means that the scope of the business case, its audience, and key decision criteria are all well understood and documented. Now it is time to enter the assess phase, outlined in Exhibit 11.1.

In the assess phase, the focus is on doing computations, gaining insights, and establishing credibility for conclusions reached.

DEFINE

Step 1: Scope

Task 1. Define business case drivers and boundaries.
Task 2. Identify deliverables, team, and schedule.
Task 3. Solidify executive sponsorship.

Step 2: Criteria

Task 4. Define decision participants.
Task 5. Identify decision criteria.
Task 6. Specify intangibles.
Task 7. Filter criteria.

Step 3: Align

Task 8. Align criteria to enterprise strategy.

ASSESS

[This Chapter] →

Step 4: Calculate

Task 9. Construct explanations.
Task 10. Define formula sets and variables.
Task 11. Identify metrics and calculate.

Step 5: Prove

Task 12. Determine "proof" needs.
Task 13. Provide evidence.

Step 6: Analyze

Task 14. Review alignment and compute final ROI.
Task 15. Identify key themes.
Task 16. Determine recommendations.

DELIVER

Step 7: Storytell

Task 17. Construct graphics and narratives.
Task 18. Write ROI stories.
Task 19. Define and deliver presentations.

EXHIBIT 11.1 Steps/Tasks List: Building a Better Business Case

Step 4: CALCULATE (Show the Money)

Watchword: *"When it's about money, get it right."*

CALCULATE in a Nutshell (Main Hats to Wear: Analyst, Detective)

Purpose	Compute realistic hard-money costs and benefits of investment options.
Input	Aligned criteria.
Output	Calculated payoffs.
Why Do This Step	Money impacts have a major influence on investment decisions.
Templates, Tools	PayoffCards, Tangible Worksheet.
Key Principles	• Establish credibility with clear, believable calculations. • Explain every computation. • Cite convincing evidence for every assumption, reason, and conclusion. • Use agreed-upon estimates if no concrete data are available.

CALCULATE Explained

The two most frequent reactions that kill business cases are "I don't understand it" and "I don't believe it."

Common reasons decision teams reject calculations within business cases include:

- *Computation errors:* Arithmetic errors, regardless of how few, convey a devastating image of carelessness on the part of the business case team. (*Example:* 200 times 20 is shown as 400, instead of the correct 4,000.)
- *Formulas' assumptions invalid:* Formulas make assumptions the audience will not accept. (*Example:* "Market share" multiplied by "profit per market share point" equals "value of market share." The audience may not agree that "profit per market share point" is an appropriate way to calculate market share value.)
- *Metric disbelief:* Regardless of what the business case team believes, the decision team considers stated metrics as inappropriate for the investment decision being faced. (*Example:* Business case states that "employee turnover is currently 15 percent." The decision team believes that the "15 percent" metric is invalid.)

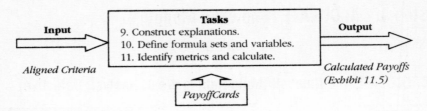

EXHIBIT 11.2 Process Flow for Step 4: Calculate

- *Convoluted formulas:* These include computations involving a dozen or more variables and/or multiple subformulas.
- *Terminology confusion:* Words have different meanings for different cultures. (*Example:* Workers in one firm might be called "associates" if they are full-time employees and "staffers" if they are from temporary placement agencies. In another firm, the very same workers might be called "staffers" if they are full-time employees and "associates" if they are from temporary placement agencies.)
- *Explanation omission:* No definitions are supplied for potentially misunderstood terms. (*Example:* What exactly is meant by the word "clients"? At what point in time? Includes existing clients who have bought new products? Includes clients who no longer buy from the firm but once did?)
- *Calculation obscurity:* The exact mathematical computations are nowhere in sight.

Calculation involves three key tasks, which are shown in Exhibit 11.2.

Using the PayoffCard

A core tool for this calculation step is a template called a PayoffCard. A PayoffCard is typically a one-page, structured document designed to collect and communicate succinctly the essence of what senior decision makers need to know regarding the value-based implications of a single decision criterion. Its components are shown in Exhibit 11.3.

A PayoffCard typically has three uses: (1) to **review** the eligibility of its information for use in a business case being developed, (2) to **document** specific factors unique to the ROI analysis being created, and (3) to **communicate** these factors to decision participants and others who need to know.

A PayoffCard provides advantages such as:

- *Clarifies data* needed, thus helping to ensure crucial information is not inadvertently omitted

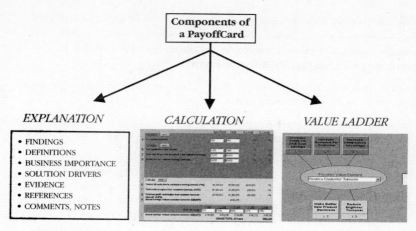

EXPLANATION

- FINDINGS
- DEFINITIONS
- BUSINESS IMPORTANCE
- SOLUTION DRIVERS
- EVIDENCE
- REFERENCES
- COMMENTS, NOTES

CALCULATION

VALUE LADDER

The **explanation** component describes in text what this payoff area is, why it is important as a decision criterion, how the solution being evaluated supports this payoff area topic, and what evidence and rationale exist to support key value assertions and calculations.

The **calculation** component displays all computations used to compute the tangible value of the PayoffCard topic area.

The **Value Ladder** component graphically shows how this PayoffCard topic is aligned to other PayoffCard topics.

EXHIBIT 11.3 Components of Each PayoffCard

- Encourages *succinct explanations*, thereby forcing sharpness of thinking and thus enhancing business case appeal and comprehension by busy decision makers
- *Provides flexibility*, thus accelerating revisions, changes, and reuses
- *Speeds comprehension*, thus increasing understanding

Description of Tasks

TASK 9: CONSTRUCT EXPLANATIONS

Explanation Section: The explanation section of the PayoffCard (an example is shown in Exhibit 11.4) contains all text information concerning descriptions, evidence, references, and notes. The explanation section text fields are:

- *Findings:* A summary statement of the business result conclusions reached from the value assessment information contained in the PayoffCard. The statement should be 20 words or less.

EXHIBIT 11.4 Explanation Section of "Reduce Customer Turnover" PayoffCard

---

Findings: Faster, better new products cut customer turnover by 1 percentage point, saving $855,000 annually.

Definition: Customer turnover: ratio of those who leave during a given period of time to total customers at the beginning.

Business Importance: Losing customers not only is expensive from a cost and profit margin point of view, but also risks negatively impacting employees' morale and ABC's market image.

Solution Driver: GKB enables product design engineers to respond faster to proposal requests. The proposals can be sent faster to existing customers with demanding time frames, who then experience "great service" which assists retention. Better new products with high appeal to existing customers can also be developed quickly.

Evidence, References: ABC's annual survey of defecting customers indicates that lack of new products is main reason they leave.

Comments, Notes: "Cost to replace each customer leaving" includes sales and other expenses to find a replacement customer, as well as the annual profit contribution lost from sales the departed customer did not generate.

USEFULNESS: Nets out the main message. Essentially this section is an "executive summary" of value of this particular payoff area (decision criterion).

- *Definition:* An explanation of the meaning of the title of the PayoffCard. USEFULNESS: Helps to avoid confusion and misinterpretation by readers. For example, a PayoffCard title might be "Increase Customer Satisfaction." The definition section would clarify if this PayoffCard addresses only those customers based in northern Europe using products sold by the European division versus all customers worldwide.
- *Business importance:* Explains the primary impact of the management issue covered by the topic of this PayoffCard. USEFULNESS: Helps remind decision participants of the importance of this PayoffCard topic, educates non–senior management business case developers about the value of a specific PayoffCard.
- *Solution Drivers:* Highlight specific features of the investment being analyzed that help make possible the payoff described in the calculation section. (See the example solution driver for a Global KnowledgeBase in Exhibit 11.4.) USEFULNESS: Enables decision participants to quickly understand which components of the solution are the main drivers of the payoff areas of most interest to them.

- *Evidence, References:* See Task 13 (Provide Evidence).
- *Comments, Notes:* Any additional information relevant to decision participants when viewing the specific PayoffCard. Length should not exceed 100 words.

TASK 10: DEFINE FORMULA SETS AND VARIABLES Misconceptions abound concerning how to develop and communicate a convincing set of formulas for calculating hard-money savings. Consider this business case example:

> *Productivity savings has been calculated to equal $855,000.41. This comes about from 10 lost customers that could be saved, at a cost of $18,000.04, to replace a customer.*

What's wrong with this example?

- *Mathematical accuracy is unverifiable:* The exact formulas for calculating the savings, while implied, are mathematically invisible.
- *The time period is unclear:* Is the savings for one year? Five years? Some other period?
- *The magnitude of change required is ambiguous:* Is saving 10 customers from leaving a huge change, a minor one, or somewhere in between? Showing what percentage 10 customers is of all customers would give a quick clue.
- *The primary driver of change in unspecified:* What variable in this formula set is the primary, management-controllable change that this business case is addressing? Is the purpose to reduce the cost per customer lost, the number of customers lost, or some other factor?
- *The input data required may be misinterpreted:* What constitutes "cost to replace a customer"? Does it include the lost profit from goods or the lost profit from services the lost customer would have purchased, or both?
- *The level of accuracy is not believable:* The savings is calculated to the penny, even though the input data realistically could be accurate only to the nearest thousands.

Being successful when calculating payoffs involves mastery of three best-practice factors:

- *Relevance:* A single business case payoff area can often be quantified dozens of ways, even to get the same answer. The formula set selected must be appropriate to the situation and acceptable to the decision team. If senior managers do not want to address profits lost from missed sales to defecting customers, then regardless of the affront to economic theory, that information should not be included. Mention can be made in the Notes section, however, if desired.

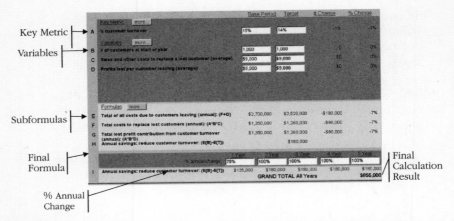

Key Metric
Variables
Subformulas
Final
Formula
% Annual
Change
Final
Calculation
Result

EXHIBIT 11.5 Sample PayoffCard: Calculation Section of "Reduce Customer Turnover"

- *Availability:* Rely on data input that is readily located, accurate, and easily tracked during systems implementation (see Chapter 17, "Tracking").
- *Easily understood:* Most decision team members are typically nonfinancial people. It is vital that they can rapidly comprehend the rationale and implications of the calculations. This puts a premium on clarity and simplicity.

Calculation Section: An example of a Calculation section of a PayoffCard is shown in Exhibit 11.5.

Calculations, no matter how clever or thorough, do not work if no one believes them. The evidence and references section explains why the calculations should be believed. Tasks 11 and 12 below explain this principle in more detail.

TASK 11: IDENTIFY METRICS AND CALCULATE   Metrics are the variables specified in the formula set of each PayoffCard. The term "variable value" refers to the quantities assigned to a variable (or metric). Generally, a good business case will have from 20 to 60 individual metrics as input items. If more inputs are required, there is a danger the business case is too detailed. If fewer are required, there is a risk that the business case might fall apart if some of the areas of payoff are rejected by the decision team.

In the case of the "Reduce customer turnover" PayoffCard (Exhibit 11.5), the metrics used for the base and target[1] periods relate to the variables:

- Percentage of customer turnover
- Sales and other costs to replace a lost customer (average)
- Profits lost per customer leaving (average)

The most common mistakes related to metric usage include:

- Missing available metrics due to lack of knowledge of where and how to look
- Reluctance to use a metric that is only an "estimate"
- Use of a metric that is misleading due to a failure to carefully define its meaning
- Use of a metric with an unclear source

A number of principles exist for avoiding or overcoming the problems mentioned above:

- Know exactly **what** you are looking for. If the metric required is "employee compensation," clarify if this means all employees or just certain types. Does compensation include wages as well as benefits? Is it annual compensation? An average for the group? If yes, is it based on the most recent year?
- Look in all the **right places**. The right metrics can be as close as a few clicks on your Internet browser's search engine or as far away as a trip to the other side of the world. Chapter 13, "Finding Hidden Value That Others Miss," provides multiple suggestions for where to search for metrics that are often overlooked.
- **Document the source** of the metric selected. The notes in the appendix of a business case should specify the source of every metric used.
- **Estimate** when appropriate. Estimating numbers such as metrics is not inherently an evil act. Educated guesses form the backbone of the world's economy. Millions guess each day on stock prices for the future. Weather forecasters guess for a living. So do industry analysts. It is okay to guess if the result is identified as a guess and the rationale and assumptions of the guess are clear.

---

1. The base period is often considered the status quo in many business cases. The target period is the value of a variable once the proposed solution is installed and its benefits are being realized to their fullest extent.

It is as important to get the costs right as it is the benefits. Nevertheless, a business case team should spend no more than one-fourth of its cost and benefit research and analysis time on cost issues. The other three-fourths (or more) should go to benefits discovery. This is because costs, while extremely important, are inevitably an order of magnitude easier to locate and verify than most benefit findings.

Once the formulas are set and the metrics gathered, the calculations for each PayoffCard can begin. The goal at this stage of business case development is to get a feel for the magnitude of benefits from each pay-off area (i.e., each PayoffCard). As important is the identification of why these calculations should be believed. Step 5 explains how to do this.

Step 5: PROVE (Who Says So?)

Watchword: *"Make 'em believe."*

PROVE in a Nutshell (Main Hats to Wear: Attorney, Detective)

Purpose	Use compelling evidence to make calculations and claims believable.
Input	Calculated payoff.
Output	Payoff explanations.
Why Do This Step	To be accepted, business case claims must be credible.
Templates, Tools	PayoffCard text fields: Evidence, References, Business Importance.
Key Principles	• It is reasons, not arithmetic, that ultimately make a business case a winner. • Keep explanations logical and rational. • Follow the "rules of evidence."

PROVE Explained

Calculations can be exquisite. Criteria may be inspired. Descriptions may be found to be crystal clear. But so what, if no one believes them?

Proof is defined as evidence sufficient to convince someone that something is true or believable. Evidence is especially important in business cases because skepticism is high among people charged with approving IT-enabled investment requests. They know all too well that IT investments are fraught with risks of overruns, missed deadlines, and even failed implementations.

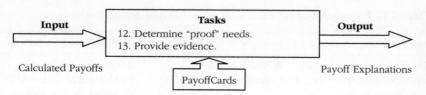

EXHIBIT 11.6 Process Flow for Step 5: Prove

Common stumbling blocks when establishing proof in business cases are:

- Misunderstanding the different types of proof needed
- Using reasoning that is ambiguous, illogical, or untrue
- Not knowing where to find proof that already exists
- Using weak proof—proof that is unable to withstand management pushback
- Assuming some point is self-evident when it is not
- Failing to provide evidence behind crucial arguments
- Relying on external sources that, on closer examination, are fallacious
- Making mistaken assumptions
- Rejecting any evidence that is not hard data

The prove step suggests how to avoid such difficulties (Exhibit 11.6).

Description of Tasks

TASK 12: DETERMINE "PROOF" NEEDS   Deciding on what types of proof are needed is vital. Otherwise, finding evidence can be a frustrating and time-consuming activity. To determine proof needs, be aware of the different types of evidence available and the places in the business case it is most needed. Exhibit 11.7 provides some examples.

Tip

Be good at bulletproof reasoning. Experienced attorneys are not the only ones highly skilled at detecting weak or erroneous reasoning. It is likely a key skill of the executives to whom the business case is addressed.

EXHIBIT 11.7 Examples of Business Case Areas Needing Strong Evidence

Business Case Challenge	Example of Challenge	Type of Evidence Source
Justification for including a potentially **controversial payoff area** in the business case.	"Reduce customer turnover."	1. Opinion-based survey from internal research. 2. Internally conducted survey.
Key metric value.	"Customer turnover can be 1 percentage point with the GKB implementation."	Internally conducted survey of influential people.
Value of an **input variable** with high sensitivity to payoff calculations.	"Average compensation of engineers at ABC."	Financial reports known to be accurate.
Validation of a key **cause-and-effect** statement.	"Poorly performing engineering design systems risk increasing engineering turnover."	Data-based survey.
Demonstration of the importance of a **key management principle** underlying a PayoffCard analysis.	"Decision making is arguably one of the most important jobs of the senior executive and one of the easiest to get wrong."	Expert opinion from well-respected publication.

TASK 13: PROVIDE EVIDENCE Once it is clear (from Task 12) what type of proof is needed, the evidence discovery process can begin. The first three columns of Exhibit 11.8 are similar to those of Exhibit 11.7. However, Exhibit 11.8 has a fourth column that provides examples of evidence that can be added to the business case in support of assumptions made in the "Example of Challenge" column.

Exhibit 11.9 shows an example of how evidence and references are recorded on a PayoffCard. Fields include:

- *Evidence:* Provides quotes from key publications, industry analyst firms, and individuals—these add credibility to the importance of the PayoffCard. Also can include endorsements—names of internal, external, and/or third-party people who support the explanations of the PayoffCard.
- *References:* Names, dates, and so on, of key publications, industry analyst firms, and individuals for each piece of evidence cited.

EXHIBIT 11.8 Examples of Evidence Statements for Business Case Areas Needing Strong Evidence

Business Case Area	Example of Challenge	Type of Evidence Source	Example of Evidence Statement
Justification for including a potentially controversial payoff area in the business case.	"Reduce customer turnover."	1. Opinion-based survey from internal research. 2. Internally conducted survey.	1. "An increase in customer retention rates of 5 percent increases profits by 25 percent to 95 percent." (*Source: Loyalty Rules*, F. F. Reichheld (Harvard Business School Press, 2001, p. 10) 2. "ABC's annual customer survey of defecting customers indicates that our customer turnover is now twice the industry average." (P. Perowski, VP Sales for ABC).
Key metric value.	"Customer turnover can be cut by 1 percentage point with the GKB."	Internally conducted survey.	"ABC's annual customer survey of defecting customers indicates that lack of timely, compelling new products is the number one reason our customers are leaving us." (P. Perowski)
Value of an **input variable** with high sensitivity to payoff calculations.	"Average compensation of engineers at ABC."	Financial reports known to be accurate.	"This compensation average validated by G. S. Ridgeway, general manager of Human Resources Payroll Department."
Validation of a key **cause-and-effect** statement.	"Poorly performing engineering design systems risk increasing engineering turnover."	Data-based survey.	"A recent survey (2010) by Associated Engineers of the World indicated that engineering turnover increased 22% when core IT system projects failed."
Demonstration of importance of a **key management principle** underlying a PayoffCard analysis.	"Decision making is arguably one of the most important jobs of the senior executive and one of the easiest to get wrong."	Expert opinion from well-respected publication.	"What You Don't Know about Making Decisions," D. Gavin and and M. Roberto, Harvard Business Review, September 2001, p. 108.

EXHIBIT 11.9 Evidence and References Section: "Reduce Customer Turnover" PayoffCard

---

EVIDENCE AND REFERENCES

Evidence:

- "An increase in customer retention rates of 5 percent increases profits by 25% to 95%." Ref. 1.
- "X: Decreasing customer turnover is one of the effective ways for us to increase profits." Ref. 2.
- ". . . research . . . by James Heskett at the Harvard Business School . . . holds that the endgame of business is growth and profit, which are tied to the ability . . . to create customer loyalty & retention." Ref. 3.

References:

- Ref. 1: *Loyalty Rules, How Today's Leaders Build Lasting Relationships,* F. F. Reichheld, 2001, p. 10.
- Ref. 2: M. Powers, CEO, ABC Corp., at annual companywide meeting, October 2002.
- Ref. 3: *The Power of Alignment,* George Labovitz & Victor Rosansky, 1997, p. 15.

When looking for and documenting evidence:

- **Be very clear what proof is needed**: Completing a matrix similar to Exhibit 11.8 often helps sort out what type of evidence is needed for what part of the business case.
- **Prioritize evidence needs**: Rank what is needed in order of importance to the credibility of the overall message of the business case. If the key message is freeing up more time for scarce product design engineers to create winning new products, then focus the evidence discovery strategy primarily on this area.
- **Be open to all types of evidence**: While hard data from reputable and relevant sources get top billing, if such data cannot be found, other types can be highly useful. For example, be open to opinions from respected experts, especially if published in trusted media. Anecdotes about field experiences can be useful.
- **Ask people on the front lines**: Send an e-mail to headquarters and field managers and employees who can be positively impacted by the IT solution being justified by the business case. Ask them for data, experiences, stories, and concerns that relate to your evidence needs. One *Fortune* 500 firm business case team uncovered a treasure of field-inspired evidence from just one broadcast e-mail request to a few dozen employees.

- **Enlist skilled information resource specialists**: While nothing is to prevent business case team members from firing up their own browsers for some quality Internet time on their favorite search engine, getting professional information searchers can often be even more productive. Business research librarians, as well as market research professionals, are a good place to start.
- **Put vendors to work**: Vendors who can benefit from a successful business case have a large incentive to provide resources to assist your search. Let them know what is needed. Be clear that any feedback they provide must be specific, highly credible, and nonbiased.
- **Apply due diligence**: Once evidence candidates are found, ask tough questions about their relevance and authenticity.
- **Document well**: Record evidence accurately in the business case, with clear notations concerning where it was found and when.
- **Start early and stay late**: Finding useful evidence requires time. Leads need to be identified and then explored. Checks and double-checks must be applied. Begin looking as early as possible in the business case development process and continue looking until the last minute.

Step 6: ANALYZE (Find the Winner)

Watchword: *"The envelope, please."*

ANALYZE in a Nutshell (Main Hats to Wear: Analyst, Project Manager)

Purpose	Identify the investment to be recommended and why.
Input	Payoff explanations.
Output	ROI computations.
Why Do This Step	Vital output of the entire business case process.
Templates, Tools	ValueBoard, Tangibles Worksheet.
Key Principles	• Match to a Balanced Scorecard matrix, if being used. • Align values computed to key management drivers of business success. • The recommendation needs to be logical, believable, and clear. • Base recommendations on both tangible and intangible factors.

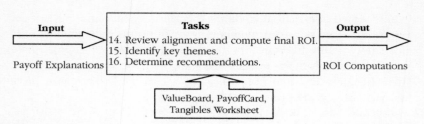

EXHIBIT 11.10 Process Flow for Step 6: Analyze

ANALYZE Explained

So how valuable is this IT-enabled investment? Thus far in the business case creation we have been collecting data. Criteria, calculations, evidence, and rationale have been gushing into "business case central" in varying degrees of volume, speed, and relevance.

Analyze is the step where we discover what type of information has been created from all the data gathered and what recommendation should be made and why.

The analyze step involves three tasks for ensuring a correct and defensible recommendation (see Exhibit 11.10).

Description of Tasks

TASK 14: REVIEW ALIGNMENT AND COMPUTE FINAL ROI This task deals with three activities:

- *Realign:* Recheck for a compelling cause-and-effect relationship between payoffs benefiting different levels of the organization.
- *Compute:* Calculate the overall financial results, using internal rate of return (IRR), net present value (NPV), return on investment (ROI), and payback period, or whatever computations are requested by the decision team.
- *Compare:* Match the financial results to the minimum acceptable standards (hurdle rates) for the enterprise.

Review Alignment: It is now time to do a final check on the decision criteria alignment that we defined in Task 8 (align criteria to enterprise business strategy). We want to be sure that each payoff area most effectively and logically supports the others. At this point, return to Chapter 10 and review the ValueBoard in Exhibits 10.6 and 10.9, which show the alignment displayed at the completion of Task 8.

When reapplying the Seven Tests of Alignment (from Chapter 10), the business case team noticed an inconsistency. The payoff area "Reduce

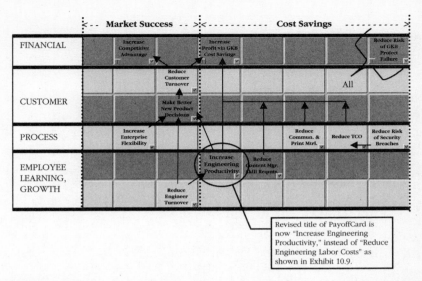

EXHIBIT 11.11 Revised PayoffCard Title—ValueBoard Alignment (by Balanced Score-card Levels): Intranet Global KnowledgeBase Evaluation for ABC Corporation

engineering labor costs" has an arrow pointing to "Make better new product decisions." This implies that somehow a decrease in labor costs helps drive better new-product decisions. After discussing this issue with numerous subject-matter experts, the business case team concluded that this link did not make sense. However, when examining the calculation section of the PayoffCard for "Reduce engineering labor costs," the calculations are all about engineering efficiency (see example in Exhibit A-3.2, in the Appendix). The team concluded that a key benefit of improving the efficiency of engineering was to make better new-product decisions. Since the calculations made sense in this regard, the team decided to change the name of the PayoffCard from "Reduce engineering labor costs" to "Improve engineering productivity." By doing this, a logical Value Ladder could be constructed, as seen in the revised ValueBoard in Exhibit 11.11. With alignment now solid, the next task is to compute the full value of each payoff.

Compute Final ROI: To determine the economic attractiveness of the investment being analyzed, one must compute the financial results from all costs and payoffs accumulated thus far. The goal at this point is to determine if the minimally acceptable ROI results (hurdle rates), provided by the decision team, are being reached or exceeded.

| Payback Period (Mo.) | 12.5 | ROI: | 125% |
| NPV | $3,019,582 | IRR: | 109% |

Costs	Year 0	Year 1	Year 2	Year 3	Year 4	Year 5	Grand Total
Software License Fees	200,000						
Installation Costs	600,000						
Hardware Costs	100,000						
Annual Maintenance Fees		60,000	60,000	60,000	60,000	60,000	300,000
Other Ongoing Expenses		150,000	150,000	150,000	150,000	150,000	750,000
Total All Costs Per Year	900,000	210,000	210,000	210,000	210,000	210,000	1,950,000

Payoffs

Level	Value Element	Year 1	Year 2	Year 3	Year 4	Year 5	Grand Total
CUSTOMER	Reduce Customer Turnover	135,000	180,000	180,000	180,000	180,000	855,000
CUSTOMER	Make Better New Product	150,000	200,000	200,000	200,000	200,000	950,000
PROCESS	Reduce Commun. & Print M	52,500	70,500	70,000	70,000	70,000	332,000
PROCESS	Reduce Risk of Security Br	75,000	100,000	100,000	100,000	100,000	475,000
PROCESS	Increase Enterprise Flexib	101,250	135,250	135,000	135,000	135,000	641,250
PROCESS	Reduce TCO	158,100	210,800	210,800	210,800	210,800	1,001,300
EMP. LEARNING & GRO'	Reduce Content Mgr. Skill	42,188	56,250	56,250	56,250	56,250	267,188
EMP. LEARNING & GRO'	Increase Engineering Prod	180,000	240,000	240,000	240,000	240,000	1,140,000
EMP. LEARNING & GRO'	Reduce Engineer Turnove	162,000	216,000	216,000	216,000	216,000	1,026,000
Total Payoff Per Year		1,056,037	1,408,050	1,408,050	1,408,050	1,408,050	6,688,237
Total Net Payoff Per Year		846,037	1,198,050	1,198,050	1,198,050	1,198,050	5,638,237
Net Cash Flow Per Year	-900,000	846,037	1,198,050	1,198,050	1,198,050	1,198,050	4,738,237

EXHIBIT 11.12 Tangibles Worksheet* for ABC Corporation Intranet Global KnowledgeBase Evaluation

*NPV based on a discount rate of 10%.

Decision team members are typically most comfortable with a spreadsheetlike report recapping this calculation. Exhibit 11.12 shows an example of a Tangibles Worksheet for the ABC Corporation evaluation.

Once the financial calculations are made, the next activity is to check the results with the known hurdle rates. (Those rates should have already been gathered, typically from the chief financial officer [CFO]. They highlight the minimum financial results that the company will accept for any proposal for a similar investment.) Exhibit 11.13 shows those results for the GKB business case in the Appendix. A table similar to Exhibit 11.13 should be used in the business case itself, so that the decision team can quickly understand the business case's relative strength versus hurdle rates.

A *caveat:* Usually IT-enabled investment decision teams compare the attractiveness of a business case relative to other investment opportunities facing them at the time. In this mode, the difference between the hurdle rates and the business case results is less important than the difference between one business case and another. See Chapter 16 ("Selecting: Prioritizing Programs with Confidence and Ease") for a more detailed

EXHIBIT 11.13 Financial Results Comparison: Global KnowledgeBase Business Case

Formula	Hurdle Rate	Business Case Result	Results versus Hurdle Rates
IRR	30%	109%	GKB is over three times greater
NPV	$1,000,000	$3,019,582	GKB is three times the minimum NPV
Payback Period	18 months	12.5 months	GKB is one-third faster
ROI	25%	125%	GKB is five times greater

discussion of techniques for making these business case–to–business case comparisons.

TASK 15: IDENTIFY KEY THEMES   A business case runs an inherent risk of ending up as a hodgepodge of information, mostly devoid of meaning. This is not surprising: The very nature of a business case requires dealing head-on with myriad confusion factors, such as subject-matter complexities, political realities, and power bias, not to mention decision-making subtleties.

It is important to remember that the reason a business case is initially requested is that the decision team recognizes that these challenges exist, and it wants the business case team to help make sense of the IT-enabled investment opportunity. This is why it is so important to identify and communicate business case themes.

A "theme" is a dominant idea within a larger work. Themes are vital because they aid the audience in not only understanding but also accepting the messages in the subject matter. It is especially important to use themes in business cases when dealing with inherently risky IT-enabled investment options. Decision teams will never accept what they do not understand.

The responsibility of the business case team is to discover key themes and communicate them to the decision team. These themes can be postulated in advance, but they can only be honestly confirmed during the analysis. For example, the team may want to find a theme of "Reducing labor costs" (perhaps because of political pressure), but if their research keeps suggesting a more relevant payoff of "Improve new-product successes," then the latter should be a focus.

Now that the key themes have been identified, verified, and documented, the team is ready to determine recommendations (Task 16), the final activity in the **assessing** phase.

EXHIBIT 11.14 Recommendation of ABC Corporation Business Case

---

Immediately install Intranet GKB. It has an IRR of 109 percent, NPV over $3 million, ROI of 125 percent, and a payback period of 12.5 months—all much better than ABC's hurdle rates. Intangible advantages include enhancing ABC's competitive advantage via more, better new products, thus increasing revenues and profits.

TASK 16: DETERMINE RECOMMENDATIONS   The recommendation portion of the business case states in succinct terms which option the business case team suggests the decision team select. Specifically, the recommendation is the outcome of the interpretation of:

- Financial results from ROI calculations
- Intangible factors
- Risk analysis
- Sensitivity analysis

All of the factors, which enter into the recommendation by the team, should be clearly spelled out, in an objective manner, in the main body of the business case itself. Exhibit 11.14 shows an example of a recommendation from the ABC Corporation business case. Notice what the recommendation *does*. It:

- Unequivocally specifies a recommendation.
- Includes a time frame for the decision, that is, "immediately" (if that has emerged as an important issue in maximizing the value of the proposed investment).
- Summarizes major financially based tangible results known to be of high interest to the decision team.
- Summarizes major intangible factors that reinforce the key value themes established for the business case.
- Reflects the logical outcome of the analysis discussed in the business case.
- Says it all in 50 words or less. (So the decision team can cut to the chase.)

Notice also what the recommendation does *not* do. It:

- Does not discuss in detail why the recommendation is made (that discussion goes elsewhere in the business case).

- Does not explicitly use judgmental adjectives. (For example, the recommendation in Exhibit 11.14 does not take a stand on whether the IRR, which is three times the hurdle rate, is good, bad, or indifferent. That judgment is left up to the decision team.)
- Does not judge how well the recommended choice fares in relation to other investments to be considered by the decision team, but not included in the scope of this business case. However, astute business case developers will ferret out the relative attractiveness of these other investments and keep such factors in mind during their analysis.

Positioning the recommendation section in the business case is important. Since it is an important clue concerning the theme of the business case, it should be the first piece of information the decision team sees in the executive summary.

This completes the discussion of the activities related to the assessing process. The next chapter, "Delivering: Step 7 to Building Better Business Cases," describes how to package the business case analysis and effectively deliver the results so that the decision team "gets it" quickly.

CHAPTER 12

Delivering: Step 7 to Building Better Business Cases

Self-expression must pass into communication for its fulfillment.
—Pearl S. Buck, 1902–1973,
Pulitzer Prize–winning author and Nobel laureate
in literature, in Hull, *The Writer's Book*

Theme

Well-done graphics, narratives, and stories make or break the ability of the business case to succinctly communicate to those who need to know.

Introduction

Now that the assess phase of building a business case has been completed, it is time to wrap it up by packaging the material in a manner that accurately conveys the intended message of the business case—and to do it in a way that is succinct and compelling. This is the purpose of the **deliver** phase, which is outlined in Exhibit 12.1.

Step 7: STORYTELL (Explain It)

Watchword: *"Tell it well and they will listen."*

EXHIBIT 12.1 Steps/Tasks List: Building a Business Case

DEFINE

> *Step 1:* Scope
>
>> Task 1. Define business case drivers and boundaries.
>> Task 2. Identify deliverables, team, and schedule.
>> Task 3. Solidify executive sponsorship.
>
> *Step 2:* Criteria
>
>> Task 4. Define decision participants.
>> Task 5. Identify decision criteria.
>> Task 6. Specify intangibles.
>> Task 7. Filter criteria.
>
> *Step 3:* Align
>
>> Task 8. Align criteria to enterprise business strategy.

ASSESS

> *Step 4:* Calculate
>
>> Task 9.   Construct explanations.
>> Task 10. Define formula sets and variables.
>> Task 11. Identify metrics and calculate.
>
> *Step 5:* Prove
>
>> Task 12. Determine "proof" needs.
>> Task 13. Provide evidence.
>
> *Step 6:* Analyze
>
>> Task 14. Review alignment and compute final ROI.
>> Task 15. Identify key themes.
>> Task 16. Determine recommendations.

DELIVER

> *Step 7:* Storytell
>
>> Task 17. Construct graphics and narratives.
>> Task 18. Write ROI stories.
>> Task 19. Define and deliver presentations.

STORYTELL in a Nutshell (Main Hats to Wear: Salesperson, Attorney, and Reporter)

Purpose	Craft easily understood and compelling business case narratives.
Input	ROI computations.
Output	Final business case.
Why Do This Step	• Improve rapid understanding of the business case findings and rationale. • Enhance the likelihood of acceptance of the business case recommendation. • Improve the audience's ability to articulate the message to others.
Templates, Tools	Tips and guidelines below and in Chapter 15, "Using ROI Storytelling to Drive Home the Message."
Key Principles	• Convert key themes and data to visual media as much as possible. • Build a logical sequence of topics. • Speak the audience's language. • Uncover and tell stories that illustrate key points. • Encourage presentations and then prepare well with highly visual content.

STORYTELL Explained

This storytell step exists because in my experience, incorrect communication of the business case findings and rationale accounts for close to 20 percent of all the reasons why business cases fail. Here are a few examples of communication-related problems:

■ Fifty pages of business case data and no pages of "so what does this mean to us"
■ Abundant use of technical terminology to which the audience cannot relate
■ Details about systems features, but little explanation of how they help the enterprise
■ Unclear reasoning behind the conclusions offered
■ A writing style that does not communicate well to an executive audience

Communications-related problems are particularly troublesome because they can mask the quality and relevance of the research and analysis

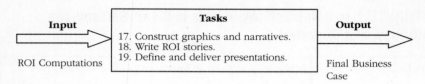

EXHIBIT 12.2 Process Flow for Step 7: Storytell

completed by the business case team. Fortunately, many of the solutions to these problems, as described in the tasks below, are relatively easy to implement.

Storytell involves the key tasks shown in Exhibit 12.2.

Description of Tasks

TASK 17: CONSTRUCT GRAPHICS AND NARRATIVES   At its core, the worth of a business case is not in its mass of numbers. A business case's worthiness always springs from the quality of the guided *conversation* it stimulates about the shape of the future. Conversations move people to action. Data are merely the backdrop, although admittedly an essential one.

For these reasons, the words, diagrams, and drawings presented in the business case report must engender conversations that reflect an accurate understanding of the findings and rationale. Here are some tips and suggestions for how to do this. (See examples in the Appendix, "Sample Business Case.")

- Confirm who the **audience** is (Task 4). Know the members of the audience by name, rank, and serial number. The report should be written to known individuals, not to "To whom it may concern" types. Ask if any additions or deletions to the audience have occurred since the last time the team had asked.
- Confirm understanding of the **key themes** the business case is to present (Task 15). The goal is to communicate a small number of messages very clearly and very compellingly.
- Speak the **audience's language**. For business cases, this means speaking the language of business, as practiced by decision participants identified as your audience. This usually means avoiding detailed discussion of financial concepts and issues. It also means steering very clear of technical jargon.
- Help the **data to talk**.
  - Summarize data numerically.

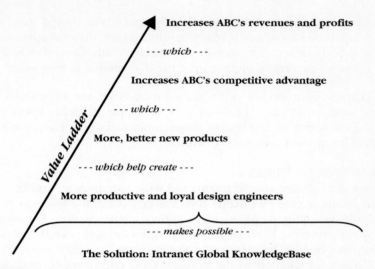

EXHIBIT 12.3 Concept Visual Example: Summary of Intranet GKB Business Value to ABC Corporation

- Use charts as much as possible to show proportions, trends, and so on. A good guideline: Use at least one chart for each table of data presented.
- Use text to draw attention to important findings within the data and charts.
- Use **concept visuals** whenever possible. Concept visuals are drawings that illustrate key points. A text-based Value Ladder such as that shown in Exhibit 12.3 is an example of a concept visual taken from the business case example in the Appendix. Note that the entire theme of the business case is summarized in this one diagram. Arrows and hierarchies drive home the point of the cause and effect of the key theme of the business case.
- Write **succinct, vivid text** that delivers messages in a few words. (See Executive Summary section of the Appendix.) Business case readers are typically very busy, short-attention-span people. They, frankly, would most likely rather be doing something else other than reading this business case.
- Make the **rationale clear**. The business case is a logical, rational, objective analysis of the likely consequences of investing in a specific solution. The explanations, logic, and reasoning behind conclusions should be visible and clear.

- Use an **executive summary**. Every business case should have a summary. If the document is more than five pages, the executive summary should be a separate section. An executive summary should average about 10 percent of the length of the document it is recapping.

Sharpen your written communication skills via use of resources such as the ones in Exhibits 12.4 and 12.5. A couple of hours spent reviewing the messages of any one of these publications will bring rewards far beyond improved business case writing.

TASK 18: WRITE ROI STORIES

It is not enough to construct graphs and write narratives around key themes of the business case. No matter how cleverly done, the business case will still undercommunicate unless the narratives are sharpened via storytelling.

ROI storytelling is about relating people-oriented tales that illustrate a key theme, finding, or message of the business case. ROI storytelling can be a powerful addition to the business case effectiveness, provided it is used carefully and sparingly. The best times to apply it are:

- When a key, somewhat complex, point needs to be clearly understood
- When a key point needs to be believed
- When a key point needs to be easily remembered

EXHIBIT 12.4 Excellent Resources for Visual Communication Techniques*

Publication/Author	Comments
Visual Language: Global Communications for the 21st Century by Robert E. Horn, 1998	The cleverest and most pragmatic of authors who publish techniques regarding visual and text communication in the business realm. His masterpieces of explanation of how to use visual techniques (themselves cleverly told visually) are must reading for business case writers who seek the best of ideas. Contains some material, not all, in his earlier book *Mapping Hypertext* . . . listed below.
Mapping Hypertext: Analysis, Linkages and Displays of Knowledge for Next Generation of On-Line Text and Graphics by Robert E. Horn, 1989	This book is a precursor to Robert Horn's *Visual Language* . . . cited above. Although in computer evolution years, this is an antique, his visual examples are timeless in concept. Many examples are very entertaining.

All references listed in Exhibit 12.4 are detailed in the Bibliography.

EXHIBIT 12.5 Excellent Resources for Written Communication Techniques*

Publication/Author	Comments
Story by Robert McKee	Eloquent, succinct, riveting exposition on the glories of screenwriting. Many principles apply to ROI storytelling as well. Just reading McKee's prose cannot help but make the reader a better writer.
Bird by Bird: Some Instructions on Writing and Life by Anne Lamott, 1994	Pithy advice, written in a compelling, storytelling style that makes you want to read her prose, independent of the depth of your interest in the topic!
Writing Down the Bones by Natalie Goldberg, 1986	Another master teacher who writes as well as she dispenses golden nuggets of advice to those seeking to write better.

All references listed in Exhibit 12.5 are detailed in the Bibliography.

ROI storytelling generally should *not* be used when descriptions of technically oriented features or functions are needed.

The best type of ROI story is that which resonates with the business case audience. Usually this kind of story deals with the enterprise and the people who compose it, as well as its customers, suppliers, and investors.

Learn to keep an eye and ear open for stories, even before their exact use is identified. Generally, intriguing or compelling stories dealing with customers, suppliers, or employees and the value they get, or do not get, from the enterprise are worth remembering. A vignette from a top customer of ABC Corporation is used in the executive summary of the business case in the Appendix to drive home the point about the urgency of getting more new products to market.

For more information on effective ROI storytelling, see Chapter 15 ("Using ROI Storytelling to Drive Home the Message").

TASK 19: DEFINE AND DELIVER PRESENTATIONS   Often business case teams are asked to deliver oral presentations in addition to creating a written report. Here are some tips:

- Use all the procedures and suggestions from Task 17 ("Construct graphics and narratives") and Task 18 ("Write ROI stories") when preparing and delivering a presentation.
- Be clear on the **purpose** and **duration** of the presentation(s).
- Understand who the **audience** is and how the presentation audience(s) differs from the report audience(s), if at all.

- **Clarify visual aids** usage. Even if told none are needed, try to do some anyway.
- Use **charts and diagrams liberally** if visual aids are encouraged.
- Make **liberal use of stories**. Try to build at least 20 percent of your presentation time around them.
- **Focus on explaining** the business case findings, emphasizing their objectivity and thoroughness.
- Allow plenty of time for **questions**, as much as 20 percent of your allotted time if possible.
- Be ready for **challenges** from the audience.
- **Anticipate animosity** from one or more audience members. If the business case did not have some type of controversy attached to it, it would not have been commissioned in the first place. Treat potentially antagonistic questions or comments with professionalism and respect.
- Get **feedback** after the presentation is done.

Making business case presentations is a great opportunity that should be encouraged. Preparation is the key to success.

This chapter concludes the discussion of the seven steps to building a successful business case. The next three chapters discuss more detailed techniques for enriching the content and the communication of the business case.

CHAPTER 13

Finding Hidden Value
That Others Miss

There are more things in heaven and earth, Horatio, than are dreamt of in your philosophy.

—William Shakespeare, 1564–1616, *Hamlet*

Theme

Rich value opportunities missed by others can be revealed by looking in the right places and asking the right questions.

Who Has the Value?

Some have the "right stuff" to find their quarry, and some do not. Sherlock Holmes, the world-famous fictional detective, had it. So did the fictional lawyer Perry Mason, who exhibited that talent in numerous books and in the popular TV series of the 1970s. Likewise, Indiana Jones had it in movies like *Raiders of the Lost Ark*.

Uncovering benefits for an information technology (IT)-enabled investment's business case has a lot of similarities to a detective story— especially in relation to the quarry. Just as in Sherlock Holmes tales, our quarry is clear (i.e., locate legitimate benefits)—we know the benefits are out there somewhere. The search has stymied lesser souls, but not us.

This chapter is about how to be a value discovery hero. It requires surprisingly little skill and practice. Mostly, it is all about having focus, being persistent, and learning where to begin.

Consider these true stories:

A Canadian government organization had failed to uncover enough savings, after investing months of concerted effort, to justify a badly needed human resources system. Yet under the guidance of a value discovery facilitator, the organization uncovered $16 million in a single day of brainstorming! That was enough to seal the board of director's approval for the system. The key to success: the synergy created when the right people were brought together with the right motivation, a deadline, and a common goal—find the money!

A university administration group had spent weeks of effort to trying to justify a financial system and then found a $1 million savings area during a lunch hour. Their secret of success: a team contributor who knew where to look.

These examples illustrate a key reality of value discovery—more value opportunities are residing in your enterprise than you would dream possible. All that is needed is a good *process* for finding the savings.

Finding Commonly Overlooked Value Areas

Successful value discovery searchers have two skills in common:

- Knowing *where* to look
- Knowing *what* to look for

By enhancing these capabilities, time can be saved, business cases can be rescued, and project selections can be accurately made.

Knowing Where to Look

When time is tight, the last thing a business case team wants to do is to waste efforts going down unproductive pathways. The six strategies listed below provide some suggestions for quickly finding tangible savings.

Setting Up the Search

Strategy 1: Ask the execs what they care about (do executive interviewing). See Exhibit 13.1.

Strategy 2: Examine public pronouncements (find revelations from records). See Exhibit 13.2.

EXHIBIT 13.1 Ask the Execs What They Care About (Executive Interviewing)

Goal	Uncover the primary business concerns of key decision makers.
Why	Executive decision makers want the business case to highlight the best business decision for the organization. The most spectacular payoff is worthless, and will therefore rarely be supported, if decision team executives do not care about the issue it addresses.
How	Ask for a short interview (20 minutes). Primarily query executive decision makers about what business issues (not data issues) are of key importance to them. Link these answers to tangible savings from the proposed investment.
Example	Use interview questions like these: "What are your main business objectives and challenges for the next six months? The next one to three years?" "What are the critical success factors associated with these objectives?" Continue with questions such as: "What type of information do you need to do your job better?" "What reports are most useful to you?"

EXHIBIT 13.2 Examine Public Pronouncements (Find Revelations from Records)

Goal	Quickly locate executives' "hot buttons."
Why	Executives invest in technology that solves major business problems of importance to them. Executive hot buttons and concerns provide insights for targeting benefits of the proposed investment.
How	Publications related to enterprise activities can be a treasure trove for discovering executives' concerns. Examine easy-to-find documents, such as annual reports, trade press articles, and stock market and industry analyst reports. Ask your firm's public relations department for locations and/or copies of relevant public documents. Search your organization's web site. Use Internet search engines to do a search on your firm's name and/or industry.
Example	To uncover the most important issues driving Jewel Weston, the chairperson of ABC Corporation, search the Internet using keywords such as "ABC Corporation" + goals + chairperson.

EXHIBIT 13.3 Ask the Neighbors (Talk to Organizational Neighbors)

Goal	Look outside the system's primary owner/user for other organizational groups that could benefit from the proposed investment too.
Why	In today's interconnected world, no department or group is an island. Each impacts as well as depends on others in both dramatic and subtle ways.
How	Identify payoffs within "neighboring" departments by asking: "Who else inside or outside the organization, besides the key system owners, will benefit from data produced by the proposed system? In what ways could they benefit?"
Example	• Field operations is a neighboring department to finance. Workers can be scheduled more effectively if field operations receives better, faster sales and profit data from the finance department.
	• Customer service is a neighboring department to engineering. Engineering can design more successful new products if it receives more helpful, accurate, and timely customer complaint data from the customer service department.

Narrowing the Search

Strategy 3: Ask the neighbors (talk to organizational neighbors). See Exhibit 13.3.

Strategy 4: Follow the money chain (locate cause and effect). See Exhibit 13.4.

Strategy 5: Do the right thing (be effective *and* efficient). See Exhibit 13.5.

Strategy 6: Go where the action is (interview stakeholders at their workplace). See Exhibit 13.6.

Knowing What to Look For

Many overlooked tangible payoff areas keep reappearing in one organization after another. Examples include these tangible savings:

Savings 1: Eliminate wasted time locating data. See Exhibit 13.7.

Savings 2: Empower the end users. See Exhibit 13.8.

EXHIBIT 13.4 Follow the Money Chain (Locate Cause and Effect)

Goal	Locate savings that are relevant to decision participants at different levels within the organization. Show how they are linked.
Why	Executives may not understand how changes to processes at lower levels within the enterprise can directly impact high-end results; for example, making people more productive at lower levels can improve the bottom line.
How	Document the concerns and goals of people at all levels of the enterprise who are impacted by the proposed systems investment. Then look for cause-and-effect relationships between the goals of lower-level personnel and those of middle and executive levels. Use those links to build a rationale that explains why an improved "Operation A" helps realize the achievement of "Strategy B," which in turn creates a desired "Business Result C."
Example	Providing better, more accurate customer data to a help desk service rep can create happier customers via better, faster response to phone inquiries. More satisfied customers are typically more loyal, which means the enterprise cost to sell them additional products and services is less than that for a new customer. This can result in decreased costs of selling, which in turn can improve profits, which is often high on the list of executive interests.

EXHIBIT 13.5 Do the Right Thing (Be Effective *and* Efficient)

Goal	Do not overlook "effectiveness," which is often confused with "efficiency." Effectiveness is defined as "doing the right thing" in the first place (i.e., producing the right product for the market, rather than reducing the manufacturing cost of a product that is wrong for the market). Efficiency is defined as "doing a thing right" (i.e., using less time and effort to build a product).
Why	Effectiveness payoffs are often missed because they frequently are less obvious than efficiency payoffs. Effectiveness payoffs are often much larger than efficiency payoffs.
How	For processes, ask the question "Is the object or output of this process needed by the enterprise?" Look for effectiveness payoffs from doing higher-value-added activities with the additional time made available through efficiency improvements.

(continued)

EXHIBIT 13.5 (Continued)

Example	• Purchase order processing:
	– Efficiency payoff—Reduce labor cost of processing a purchase order via easier access to purchasing data.
	– Effectiveness payoff—Eliminate the entire cost of some purchase orders by freeing up staff time to determine if the item being purchased is even needed by the enterprise.
	• A classic article on this "elimination" concept is Michael Hammer's "Don't Automate, Obliterate!", (published in *Harvard Business Review*, July/August 1990). This insightful write-up described Ford Motor's discovery that eliminating invoices was even more productive than processing them in the first place.

EXHIBIT 13.6 Go Where the Action Is (Interview Stakeholders at Their Workplace)

Goal	Finding overlooked benefits from those who will be using the system/data.
Why	Often, users know best where the savings are.
How	Find out the names and roles of key "hands-on" users of a proposed investment. Schedule a time to visit them at their site. Ask them what system features and functions will assist them in having a more productive and satisfying job.
Example	An enlightening but terrifying interview of a logging crane operator five stories above the ground showed a determined business case developer how better data (from the proposed system) could significantly increase the operator's productivity. The operator was extremely candid in the interview since he was impressed that the interviewer thought enough of him to make the perilous trip to the operator's 50-foot-high "workplace in the sky."

EXHIBIT 13.7 Eliminate Wasted Time Locating Data (Savings 1)

Issue	Most often, "information searching" is a highly *in*effective use of employee time.
Why	As an enterprise's success becomes more data dependent, requests increase for information. Time spent on searching for data offen takes employees away from their core business functions.

EXHIBIT 13.7 (Continued)

How	Identify how many people must access the data, the amount of time they spend doing it, and the percent reduction in this effort that is possible with a new system.
Example	A $1.1 million per year savings unexpectedly surfaced from an HR staffer's off-handed complaint. When she mentioned to coworkers about her "lost lunch hours due to chasing data requests," it triggered an analysis revealing thousands of wasted person-hours by many employees throughout the work year. Calculations revealed the million-dollar savings opportunity.

EXHIBIT 13.8 Empower the End Users (Savings 2)

Issue	Finding ways to give end users direct access to needed data.
Why	Providing end users with personal access to needed information not only saves time and effort of information providers (often expensive IS or departmental resources), but also can improve users' job satisfaction since they *get* data they *want* when they want it.
How	Review end users' jobs to identify how much time they (and others) spend locating data. Examine the proposed systems investment to identify instances where data could exist in a format more easily accessed by the data users. Also consider payoffs available if the employee had more free time to devote to other, higher-value activities.
Example	Instead of waiting hours, if not days, for human resource (HR) staffers to respond to requests for 401K status data, employees can directly access the information from a browser on their personal computers or mobile devices in seconds. Say, for instance, 100 non-HR employees reduce by only 5 percent their average time spent per year on questions to the HR department. The labor savings easily could total $1 million over a 5-year period.

Savings 3: Find the hidden asset. See Exhibit 13.9.
Savings 4: Eliminate duplicate systems. See Exhibit 13.10.
Savings 5: Ensure better scheduling of discretionary employees. See Exhibit 13.11.
Savings 6: Reduce turnover of key employees. See Exhibit 13.12.

Additional tangible savings are shown in Exhibit 13.13.

EXHIBIT 13.9 Find the Hidden Asset (Savings 3)

Issue	Locate resources (e.g., equipment) that exist but are hidden from those who could use them.
Why	Lack of awareness of enterprise-owned assets often triggers unnecessary costs in terms of storage, maintenance, rentals, and so on.
How	Inventory key assets and match them against rental records and other asset expense records.
Example	A mid-sized Canadian municipality discovered that an inaccurate fixed-asset accounting system was costing over $1 million a year in unnecessary equipment rentals. Project teams, under time pressure, would incorrectly assume that certain critical machines were not available internally and would thus rent similar machines from outside suppliers. The problem was that the current fixed-asset system was not correctly accounting for certain equipment, thus effectively "hiding" it from those who sought to use it.

EXHIBIT 13.10 Eliminate Duplicate Systems (Savings 4)

Issue	Uncover duplicate, unnecessary systems that are not used for backup purposes and thus are candidates for elimination. These "extra" systems are unofficial, user-maintained processes that duplicate and/or extend the functionality of an "authorized" system. (Such systems are also called "redundant" or "shadow" systems.)
Why	These systems usually exist because the users do not have confidence in the reliability of the official system, and/or the official system does not provide the information they need in a timely and cost-effective manner.
How	Confirm that the proposed system investment will reliably and effectively provide results that are equal to or even better than the existing shadow system. Uncover shadow systems by asking end users for examples of unofficial systems that use data that are the same as or similar to the data used in the primary system.
Example	Elimination of shadow systems can often save from 5 to 20 percent of the proposed systems investment. A new HR system in a mid-sized firm was substantially justified by discontinuing shadow systems. Over $1.5 million was saved annually in labor (elimination of duplicate data entry), equipment and maintenance services, and upgrade costs.

EXHIBIT 13.11 Ensure Better Scheduling of Discretionary Employees (Savings 5)

Issue	Examine the efficiency and effectiveness of the scheduling of temporary, part-time, overtime, and other discretionary labor costs.
Why	Lack of timely data for matching labor supply to demand can result in costly overstaffing of discretionary labor, especially in field operations relying heavily on such resources.
How	Determine the number and cost of person-hours that are discretionary but are not well utilized due to missing, inaccurate, and/or late data that could be rectified by the new system.
Example	A $2 billion retailer was paying over $1 million annually for store-level scheduling of discretionary labor. More rapid reporting of weekly sales enabled field managers to better understand new sales trends and thus better match labor availability to customer needs. Overstaffing could be drastically reduced.

EXHIBIT 13.12 Reduce Turnover of Key Employees (Savings 6)

Issue	Look for opportunities to reduce the departures of hard-to-replace workers.
Why	Certain types of employees can be 10 times (or more) costly to replace than others, because of the scarcity of their skills and/or experience. These people are often knowledge workers.
How	Identify opportunities where improved systems could help reduce departures by alerting management to early warning signs of employee dissatisfaction.
Example	The departure of experts in a new technology could be slowed by introducing new human resource software that encourages more targeted training, performance measurement, and competitive compensation. Slowing turnover by 5 percentage points at an enterprise could save over $2 million annually. Typically the cost to replace a knowledge worker is at least one-half of the worker's annual salary. Such costs can be multiple times higher for key workers whose skills are especially critical, such as new-product development designers dealing with demanding rollout schedules.

EXHIBIT 13.13 Eleven Additional Tangible Savings (Savings 7 to 17)

7: *Save management time via faster, easier approvals.* Reducing time that managers spend on routine approvals frees them to be more effective at their primary jobs. *Example:* Via automated workflow (e.g., e-mail approvals), the average 5 percent of management time spent approving expense reports can be decreased to 1 percent.

8: *Speed up time-sensitive processes.* Time is money. *Example:* Filling job vacancies of workers who directly impact revenue generation can be a measurable benefit. A salesperson hired two weeks sooner could generate two weeks of sales otherwise lost in the first year of employment.

9: *Eliminate ad hoc reconciliations and reporting.* Typically, the amount of effort and time required for financial ad hoc reconciliations and reporting is underestimated. In addition to labor savings, consider the value of improved accuracy and timeliness of such reconciliations. *Example:* For an enterprise with finance and administration (F&A) annual labor costs of $1 million, over $100,000 per year in F&A staff labor is saved by eliminating the 10 percent of time spent per closing period on identifying and resolving reconciliations. Another 5 percent is saved due to fewer errors.

10: *Reduce audit costs.* The cost of auditing is often directly related to the complexity of the audited process and the volume of errors that must be examined. *Example:* Streamlining time sheet processing by 50 percent (which saves $500,000 per year) also eliminates 90 percent of the need to conduct manual audits. Thus an additional audit cost savings of $180,000 is realized ($200,000 audit costs $\times$ 90 percent = $180,000).

11: *Reduce leakage.* Prenegotiated discounts that are not used by employees can be very costly. This activity is sometimes called "maverick spending." *Example:* Traveling salespersons bypass headquarters-approved hotels (which have prenegotiated hotel room discounts) for ones more convenient to their travel plans.

12: *Improve labor relations via better grievance management.* Use better data to resolve minor labor grievances before they become major, more costly conflicts. *Example:* Instead of dealing with 100 minor grievances (at an average resolution cost of $500 each) and 10 major grievances per year (at an average resolution cost of $10,000 each), an improved grievance management system, one that focuses on detecting early warning signs of problems, can reduce the number of grievances to 60 minor grievances and 5 major grievances annually, for a savings of $350,000 over five years.

13: *Improve collaboration of teams.* When complex activities are involved, the interdependence of workers can significantly impact the project's outcome. *Example:* A study of data warehouse teams revealed that improved training and management could reduce the cost of that team by 20 to 30 percent.* This is because the complex nature of data warehouse tasks makes each team member's productivity highly dependent on the effectiveness and efficiency of others on that team. Thus, data warehouse developers are highly dependent on the clear and timely communication from coworkers such as data warehouse designers.

14: *Reduce time helping colleagues.* Time spent by more experienced employees in answering job-related questions from newer workers can be unnecessarily expensive, especially in situations where job knowledge is complex and critical to productivity. Improving processes such as employee training can help reduce such occurrences. *Example:* By saving 20 minutes a day of 50 managers with a combined annual payroll of $2.5 million, a five-year savings of $525,000 can be realized.

15: *Make small changes.* Small changes can have big effects. For example, if 5 seconds can be saved from each of the 1,500 daily help-desk calls that generally run one minute each, 100 additional calls can be handled with no increase in staff.

16: *Avoid errors:* A transaction may cost $1, but correcting errors in that same transaction can add up to an additional $10. Avoiding errors leads to happier customers (which encourages the purchase of additional products) and lowers employee frustration (which leads to less turnover).

17: *Eliminate ineffective training:* Savings can be accrued when an enterprise focuses on giving the *right* training course to the *right* employees. Savings can come from eliminating wasted course development costs and training costs and lost productivity of employees.

De Long, David and Keen, Jack, Hidden Costs That Threaten Data Warehouse Payback, *May 1999. White paper.*

Value lives in many, many places. "Looking" strategies and a little practice can reveal surprising opportunities.

The value discovery examples above suggested examples of tangible, hard-money savings. However, Chapter 14 explains how to recognize and handle payoffs that many people consider to be intangible.

Handling Intangibles: The Emotional Enigma of Value Realization

Whenever decisions are made strictly on the basis of bottom-line arithmetic, human beings get crunched along with the numbers.

—Thomas R. Horton, CEO,
American Management Association,
Management Review, January 1987

Theme

Intangible benefits are central to business case validity, both as the basis for conversion to tangibles and "as is."

The "Intangibles" Factor: Controversial Yet Crucial

Want to inject some life into a subdued meeting of folks involved with information technology (IT) project selection? Then take an emphatic stand on whether or not intangibles should be a fundamental element of decision making.

Intangibles are an emotional enigma of IT-enabled investment decision making. Opinions differ widely on what should be done about nonquantified benefits put forth in defense of making an IT investment. Examples include:

"They should be an integral part of credible IT project selection."
"They should be used as a tiebreaker only."
"Ban them entirely—they reflect wishful thinking."
"They are the only true decision factors and thus should drive everything."

Not surprisingly, because of these differences, many decision teams, evaluation committees, and business case members are confused and frustrated concerning what approach to take with these "soft benefits."

This chapter discusses the nature and origin of this controversy, explains why it is a crucial issue worth spending time to resolve, and then suggests some policies, tools, and tips for helping to bring closure on the issue.

The issue of handling intangibles sometimes strikes without warning:

Bob Stone, the chief financial officer (CFO) of the $500 million retailer Foley Foods, had just officially convened the meeting of his financial system software evaluation teams. Ten people on the committee, recruited from every major department impacted by the software proposal, took their seats. Glancing around the room to be sure everyone was present, he began:

"We've spent over six months and untold thousands of person-hours trying to get a handle on what our corporation needs, what's available, and what it's worth to our firm. Today, our software evaluation project comes down to this: How can we find at least $1 million in believable benefits which will ensure that the software proposal will be accepted by the executive committee? Today is do or die. Our window of opportunity for project acceptance may pass."

Walking up to the whiteboard, he wrote down four areas where such benefits might come from. Turning to Jan McConnell on his left, he said:

"As you know, your job is to lead us through this benefits brainstorming session today." Then turning to the committee members, he continued:

"Remember that we need hard-money benefits. Things we can quantify that the decision team can relate to. Let's keep those flimsy intangible factors off the table for today."

Jan stood up, looked around, and then, turning to the CFO, said,

"Based on our conversations last week, Bob, you indicated that 'closing financial books faster' was a prime benefit your department is seeking. Why isn't it on the list of benefits to brainstorm today?"

"I've thought about it a lot, Jan. Unfortunately, it's an intangible payoff. Whatever people time we save, we still have to pay their salaries. Our cash flow isn't going to change one cent. However much our field managers will appreciate getting their business unit financial statements sooner, I don't know any way of quantifying 'thanks.'"

"I understand, Bob," replied Jan. "However, how about exploring this issue just a little to see if there are any angles that would allow us to quantify the value of closing books faster. Who on the committee could tell us what the ultimate users of the financial data might actually do if they had financial data faster?"

After 15 minutes of discussion, little was revealed except "it would be nice to have more data faster." Then, just as the momentum of the conversation was winding down, Mary Ann Ramsey, vice president of retail operations, raised her hand. As soon as Jan called on her, she replied:

"I've been thinking about your question ever since you asked it. I just now recalled a conversation I had with one of my store managers last week. She was complaining about the high cost of her discretionary labor these past few months, since sales have become more volatile. By discretionary labor, Jan, I mean nonemployees whom we use only as needed. For example, temporary part-timers would fall into that category. Overtime would also. The store manager told me she had spent $10,000 more last month on discretionary labor than she really had to. Because of the lag in getting historical store sales and profit data from headquarters, each week she had to guess at the level of sales. She had to 'gut-feel' extrapolate future sales—and thus store staff she would need to have on hand. Thinking a recent sales surge was still continuing, she went heavy on discretionary labor. Once the financial results came in, however, she discovered her 'guesstimate' on past sales was way out of line. As a result, most of the store staff were just hanging around for the subsequent week. She told me that had she had more frequent store financial data, she could have easily saved half of the $10,000. You know, Jan, if we extrapolated that out to all our stores, the savings could be significant!"

Meanwhile, unbeknown to the committee, another conversation was going on between the chief executive officer (CEO) and the chief information officer (CIO) in the former's office.

"Andy," said Amy Crawford, Foley Food's CEO, to the CIO, "I am getting concerned about the way we are doing cost-benefit analysis on our IT project proposals. Every time I turn around, someone is claiming we can save labor costs, and that becomes the whole justification. I suspect that if I added up all the labor cost savings claimed

(continued)

by business cases I've seen for the past year, it would exceed our total payroll by two times. From now on, let's treat labor cost savings as an intangible. That way, we'll make the cost-benefit folks work harder trying to find some real savings that will justify an IT expenditure."

"I understand your concern. I'll run it by Bob Stone when I have lunch with him tomorrow. My guess is that he would have no problem with a policy of treating labor savings as an intangible."

Foley Foods managers are dealing with a common dilemma. What's the "right" way to handle benefits that may or may not be tangible? Fortunately, there are some straightforward explanations and techniques to solve the puzzle. To begin, we need to understand what really is the nature of a tangible or intangible benefit.

What Is "Intangibility," and Why Is It Controversial?

"Intangibility" is a concept with multiple meanings, depending on the context of its usage (the intention and viewpoint of the speaker).

To a financial analyst, an intangible is an asset for which there are no generally acceptable standards of accounting to allow it to be quantified.

"The premium we paid over the book value of our most recent acquisition is carried as an intangible on our financial statements."

In this case something is intangible by regulatory decree. Government and/or industry regulatory bodies have said so.

To a football fan, an intangible is that mysterious, unexplainable factor that enables one team to beat another.

"Our team has always beaten its opponent whenever we played on the home field. This gives us a real intangible advantage."

In sports, intangible is a personal opinion, which may or may not be challenged.

To an IT project selection participant, an intangible is a benefit of a proposed investment that is not expressed in monetary terms.

"Implementing this IT project brings a key intangible benefit, namely a vastly improved image of our firm with its customers, partners, investors, and future employees."

For IT investments, intangibility is an especially hot, disputed, and widely misunderstood issue. Reasons include:

- The definition of "intangibility" is widely misunderstood and thus misused.
- No central "authority" exists to decree a standard definition; thus opinions, whether informed or not, flow freely.
- Management thought leaders have conflicting positions on it, although upon closer examination such differences are often semantic.
- IT project selection based on a business case analysis often could go one way or another, depending on how intangibles are handled.

The reality is that the use of intangibles "as is" is a valid component of effective IT project selection and benefits realization. All decisions in life have an intangible component to them, whether we realize it or not. Jung said it best in 1923:

[Decisions] have as a rule far more to do with the instincts and other mysterious unconscious factors than with . . . well-meaning reasonableness.[1]

A good deal of business success hinges on management decisions driven by a gut feel of experience and intuition.

Alfred Sloan invented the concept of the successful decentralized corporation when he was leading General Motors in the early part of the twentieth century. No data, analysis, or precedents could conjure for him in advance something that had never existed before. It was all intangible, and he had the insight and guts to push ahead.

Sam Walton had little "tangible analysis" that told him that his Wal-Mart strategy of discounting would eventually overturn the giants of the day, Sears and K-Mart.

IT project selection decisions need intangible input to clarify important differences among alternative courses of action.

Is it important to know that Project A will use a vendor with 100 happy customers, whereas Project B relies on a supplier that simply

1. Carl Jung, *The Psychological Types*, (1921), reprinted in Bollinger Series XX, Volume 6, Princeton University Press, 1971, 1976.

acquired a smaller company, dismissed most of its employees, and incorporated the products into its product line. Which is a better investment? It is an intangible call all the way.

The issue thus becomes not *if* intangibles should be included as an integral part of IT project selections, but *how*. The how is addressed next.

Managing Intangibles with Skill and Style

Five Ways to Handle Intangibles

Intangibles are typically handled by organizations in one or more of five ways:

1. Ban intangibles from use in any business case.
2. Allow intangibles on a case-by-case basis only.
3. Use individual intangibles as scorable items.
4. Group multiple intangibles together and quantify them as a set.
5. Convert as many intangibles to tangibles as possible.

We will discuss each approach below.

BAN INTANGIBLES   When using this approach, senior management decrees that no intangibles are allowed in business cases.

ALLOW INTANGIBLES ON A CASE-BY-CASE BASIS   This option is one of the more frequently used. Intangibles are allowed into the business cases, but primarily on an exception basis. They are mostly treated as second-class citizens.

USE INDIVIDUAL INTANGIBLES AS SCORABLE ITEMS   This is the approach taken by ABC Corporation in the examples in Exhibit 14.6 and 14.7. Intangibles are encouraged, and in most cases are expected.

GROUP INTANGIBLES TOGETHER   This approach is used successfully at some firms. Sets of similar intangibles are grouped together, and then a calculation is assigned to the group. For example, the following three benefits could be grouped under the heading "Labor savings available from more automated expense report processing":

- Decrease in time required by employee to complete each expense report
- Reduction in time spent by auditor reviewing each expense report
- Reduction in wasted management time for approvals

If the business case team is prevented, for whatever reason, from making each of these a tangible benefit, the three could be combined and assigned a dollar benefit. An example of the combined dollar benefit could be $100,000 per year. In this case, the hard-money amount was computed by assuming that the combined total of hours saved from the three areas above was two hours per expense report. Assuming an average hour costs the firm $40, and that 5,000 expense reports are processed annually, then the labor savings is $400,000 per year ($40 per hour times 5,000 reports times 2 hours per report). This total "savings" was then cut by 75 percent to reflect the uncertainty of exactly how many hours might be saved and what would be done with those hours if they were saved.

The advantages of this approach include ease of explanation and a good deal of latitude for the decision team to exercise in determining how much of the logic and calculations it is comfortable with. A disadvantage of this "group" technique is reliance on numbers that are heavy with assumptions.

CONVERT AS MANY INTANGIBLES TO TANGIBLES AS POSSIBLE All things being equal, most IT investment decision makers prefer tangible ("hard money") benefits to intangible ("soft money") payoffs. Unfortunately, people over-estimate the difficulty of "flipping" what seems to be an intangible over to a powerful tangible benefit. The next section provides guidance on some straightforward ways to make those flips into hard money values.

Converting Intangibles to Tangibles

Reasons an intangible *could* be converted to a tangible include:

- An analogy was discovered that the decision team was comfortable with.
- Politically respected stakeholders endorsed the assumptions and calculations.
- An approach to quantification not considered by the decision team was presented (this was the case with Mary Ann Ramsey's assessment in the Foley Foods scenario mentioned above).
- A formula was identified for making the calculation, which was considered believable and relevant.

Converting intangibles to tangibles is made much easier by understanding what exactly differentiates the two. This is called the DNA of tangibility.

THE DNA OF TANGIBILITY What at the core makes a benefit tangible or intangible? If a biologist were asked a similar question: "What is it that makes a dog a dog or a cat a cat?" the answer would be DNA—the genetic code of life that directs living cells to evolve into one form or another.

Tangibility also has "DNA." If we understand it, it helps us decide what benefits should be tangible or intangible. It also helps make us more successful in converting intangibles to their more socially accepted cousins—tangibles.

As shown in Exhibit 14.1, the primary elements (DNA) that distinguish a tangible are:

- A **premise** (fundamentally held belief)
- An expression of a logical **cause and effect** that implies that given X, then Y can occur (i.e., a Value Ladder)
- Mathematical **formulas** to calculate such a benefit
- **Metrics** (values assigned to variables) that enable the formulas to be calculated into a monetary value
- **Proof** citations backing up the claims of the previous components

---

The extent of "tangibility" of a benefit depends on the strength (in the opinion of the decision team) of each of the five components (premise, mathematics, cause-and-effect ladder, metrics, and proof) shown below. Benefits with only one component are much more likely to be considered intangible than those with four or five.

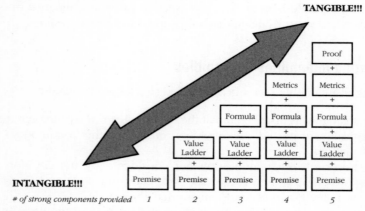

EXAMPLE: A benefit called "Close Books Faster" is proposed as a tangible. However, at the point in time when it is proposed, it has only one strong component, a premise. That premise says that "Closing books faster is a highly valuable goal." At this point in this benefit's "tangibility evolution," it is more likely to be treated as an intangible. There is just not enough rationale or data for it to be convincing as a tangible. However, if more research and analysis is done, and the result is that this same benefit has strong data related to all five components (premise, Value Ladder, formula, metrics, and proof), it is more likely to be accepted as a tangible. If only three out of the five components had strength, it typically would be a close call whether a decision team would consider this as a tangible or an intangible. See Exhibit 14.2 for an example of what this information and reasoning might look like to have this benefit qualify as a tangible.

EXHIBIT 14.1 The DNA of Tangibility

Drawing a picture of the DNA of tangibility, Jan asked the group to apply it to their "close books faster" discussion. Exhibit 14.2 shows the results of their efforts.

EXHIBIT 14.2 Example of Converting "Close Books Faster" from an "Intangible" to a "Tangible"

Tangibility DNA Component	Explanation	Comment
Premise/ assumption	Closing books faster is a desirable goal. Employees like to know financial results as soon as possible.	Nonfinancial people typically need examples of "books," such as a profit and loss statement, balance sheet, general ledger accounts, sales trends, etc.
Cause and effect (Value Ladder)	Closing books faster will enable field retail store managers to adjust their resources more quickly in response to changing market conditions.	An "aha" occurs here when a former field manager on the committee remarks that retail directors waste a lot of money by overcommitting to discretionary labor, due to uncertainty concerning near-term demand. If they had their sales figures 5 days after the period close, instead of 15 days, they could be more accurate in lining up such labor. Conversely, if they **underestimated staffing** and a sales surge occured, significant revenues, as well as customer goodwill, might be lost.
Formula	The average cost of discretionary labor per year multiplied by the percentage; this could be reduced if discretionary hiring decisions were made with more accuracy.	The formula measures the expected reduction in the difference between discretionary labor actually used versus that which should have been used.
Metrics	Percentage improvement possible with more timely store sales and profit reporting.	Percentage improvement is usually expressed as a change from the base period (status quo).

(continued)

EXHIBIT 14.2 (Continued)

Proof (evidence and references)	Who, with credibility, can be cited as believing this analysis to be accurate and credible?	"Mary Ann Ramsey, VP Retail Store Operations, confirms that the logic and metrics of this analysis are realistic. In fact, she believes the percentage improvement might even be conservative." All stores, in her opinion, would benefit, as accurately forecasting labor needs is a universal problem.

Next, Jan drew on the whiteboard an organizationlike chart showing how the cause and effect jumped across organization groups before it was quantified (Exhibit 14.3). After a couple of minutes of questions and answers, she calculated a figure of $1.5 million savings over five years in discretionary labor. Added to that would be another $800,000 in savings from decreases in finance and administration (F&A) staff labor costs and distribution costs (e.g., mailing and printing) to close books. This grand total would be $2.3 million savings from closing books faster. "Does that seem plausible, Mary Ann?" she asked. "Absolutely," Mary Ann replied.

The CFO, Bob, followed the entire 45-minute discussion and analysis with great interest. When Jan asked how he felt about quantifying "Close books faster" using the analysis on the whiteboard, he replied, "My skepticism is dissipating. I agree with the rationale. I have great regard for Mary Ann's opinion. The math seems to make sense. Let's document and submit it!"

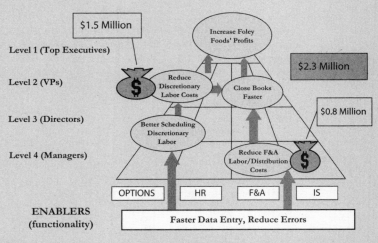

EXHIBIT 14.3 Cause-and-Effect Value Chart for "Close Books Faster"

Their document is shown in Exhibit 14.4. A more detailed explanation of this PayoffCard Format is found in Chapter 11 "Assessing" Step 4 (Calculate). Intangible conversion strategies learned from this example include:

- Look for value beyond the department that is to be the *primary* beneficiary of the project (in this case, the finance department).
- Have access to people who know the world of the data users intimately.
- Get influential people to endorse the analysis.
- Be bold.

Findings:
By reducing the closing cycle from 15 to 5 days, we can save $2.3 million, 65% of which is via reduced discretionary labor costs.

Definition:
Closing books faster reduces the cycle time for generating and distributing the financial statements of the company.

Business Importance:
Getting critical financial data out to the organization faster enables managers to make more informed decisions.

Solution Driver:
New financial application software can aid closing books faster by (1) faster data entry (no rekeying), (2) reduced error correction reconciliation time, and (3) automated business processes.

Calculations:

		Base Period	Target	# Change	% Change
	Key Metric more...				
A	# of days to close books	15	5	-10	-67%
	Variables more...				
B	F&A labor costs (avg. hourly) of staff closing books	$35	$35	$0	0%
C	# of F&A staff to close books per cycle (base period)	2	2	0	0%
D	# of closing cycles (annual)	12	12	0	0%
E	Printing and mailing costs of financial statements (annual)	$150,000	$50,000	-$100,000	-67%
F	% decrease in field store discretionary labor costs	0%	15%	15%	0%
G	Discretionary labor costs, all field stores (annual, base per.)	$2,000,000	$2,000,000	$0	0%
	Formulas more...				
H	Total F&A labor and distribution costs to close books (annual): (A*B*C*D*B[B])+E	$250,800	$83,600	-$167,200	-67%
I	Total discretionary labor costs in field stores (annual): (100%*[1]-F)*G	$2,000,000	$1,700,000	-$300,000	-15%
J	Total closing and discretionary labor costs (annual): (H+I)	$2,250,800	$1,783,600	-$467,200	-21%
K	Annual savings: close books faster: (H(B)-H(B))+(I(B)-I(B))+(J(B)-J(T))		$467,200		

		1 Year	2 Year	3 Year	4 Year	5 Year
	% annual change	100%	100%	100%	100%	100%
L	Annual savings: close books faster: (H(B)-H(B))+(I(B)-I(B))+(J(B)-J(T))	$467,200	$467,200	$467,200	$467,200	$467,200
			GRAND TOTAL All Years			**$2,336,000**

EXHIBIT 14.4 "Close Books Faster" PayoffCard

(continued)

EXHIBIT 14.4 (Continued)

Evidence:

Mary Ann Ramsey, VP of Retail Operations, stated that one of her store managers told her that she had overspent $10,000 in a past month, due to the lag in getting historical sales and profit data from headquarters. The store manager went on to state that she believed that with better data she could have saved at least half of that $10,000. Mary Ann believes this issue resides in all our stores.

Put all these elements together into a cohesive and believable story, and a benefit becomes tangible, because *its intended audience believes it to be*. In the final analysis, tangibility is an opinion, influenced by all the things that opinions are shaped by.

Postscript: The committee added the $2.3 million savings to the business case. The decision team agreed with the analysis. The "Close books faster" savings item pushed the ROI past other investment options that the decision team was considering. The software was implemented as planned. The CFO gained a new view of opportunity for systems justifications.

EXAMPLES OF HOW INTANGIBLES CAN BE CONVERTED TO TANGIBLES The thinking behind the conversion of intangibles to tangibles can be further illustrated by reviewing the tangibles version of benefit areas many consider to be intangible. Seven such examples are shown Exhibit 14.5.

EXAMPLES OF OTHER INTANGIBLE CONCEPTS CONVERTED TO TANGIBLE

- Increase strategic alliance success.
- Increase the value of intellectual capital.
- Maximize corporate portal value.
- Reduce litigation exposure.
- Improve the quality of a process.
- Demonstrate customer commitment.
- Value being a "continuous learning company."
- Make users more self-sufficient.

EXHIBIT 14.5 Tangibles Versions of Intangible Benefits

Intangible View	Tangibility Theme
Increase Shareholder Value Shareholder value is impacted by too many factors to be quantifiable.	Savings increase profits. Share prices generally reflect profit trends, which is why the price/earnings ratio is a popular, albeit not perfect, metric. *Calculation approach*: System benefits boost profits, which, when multiplied by the price/earnings ratio, boost share prices and thus shareholder value.
Increase Competitive Advantage Competitive advantage is too elusive a concept for calculating a value.	An improvement in competitive advantage can translate into increases in the firm's operating margin contribution from various value chain activities, such as sales, marketing, customer service, product, procurement, and/or logistics. *Calculation approach*: Determine a defensible percentage improvement in all value chain areas relevant to the impact of the system investment and multiply that times the current margins.
Improve Marketplace Image Image cannot be directly measured; thus it cannot be translated to hard-money value.	Positive marketplace image, such as perceived consumer value of products, goodwill, quality, and so on, can make it easier for the firm to attract, with less effort and expense, not only customers but also employees and even investors. *Calculation approach*: Determine a reasonable percentage improvement in these acquisition expenses.
Enhance Intranet Effectiveness Because a single intranet typically performs multiple functions, getting a handle on its economic value is tough.	Intranet investments are often significant and contain a high percentage of fixed costs. Once an intranet is in place, the additional expense of adding new applications is typically small. *Calculation approach*: Spread the benefits of each new application across the intranet user population, on a "per-user" basis. Multiply that by the number of intranet users in order to calculate the "value of an intranet application." Add all the intranet applications together to get a "total intranet value."

(continued)

EXHIBIT 14.5 (Continued)

Increase Customer Satisfaction

"Satisfaction" is a very subjective action—hard to capture and hard to measure.

Reducing customer turnover saves replacement costs, as well as avoids lost sales. It also encourages larger and more frequent purchases.

Increase Employee Morale

Having employees who are happier or more satisfied is nice, but too fuzzy to quantify.

Poor morale ultimately translates into higher turnover costs. Turnover costs of knowledge workers can average 50 percent of their annual compensation.

Improve Project Success via Better ROI Tools

Hard to quantify the *value* of using ROI-based project selection and management methods.

Monetary project payoffs are increased because ROI tools help management avoid missteps. *Calculation approach:* Multiply the increase in the percent likelihood of project success by the number of projects by the net payoff from each project.

Using the Scoresheet to Manage Intangibles

If, for whatever reason, intangibles will not, or cannot, be converted to tangibles, the Scoresheet is a useful and popular way to integrate intangibles into the IT selection process. Usage of this Scoresheet is described in more detail in Chapter 16 ("Selecting"). However, a portion of it is shown here as Exhibits 14.6 and 14.7.

The Scoresheet is used to grade how closely various investment options match each criterion. Once this grading is complete, the total scores of each investment are compared, as an indication of the relative value of each to the enterprise.

Note the following about the Scoresheet excerpt in Exhibit 14.6:

- The first column lists all decision criteria (both tangible and intangible) that are relevant to this business case.
- The second column shows the weights assigned to each criterion. These weights reflect the importance of each criterion to the entire group. In Exhibit 14.6, all the weights total 100.
- The weights should reflect the relative importance of each criterion in the eyes of the decision team (and no one else).

Several important principles of tangibles and intangibles are represented in this Scoresheet excerpt:

- A **balance** is shown between tangible and intangible decision criteria (benefits). In the case of Exhibit 14.6 that balance is 50–50. The split

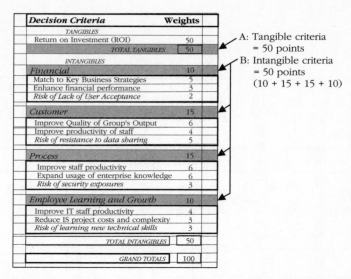

Decision Criteria	Weights
TANGIBLES	
Return on Investment (ROI)	50
TOTAL TANGIBLES	50
INTANGIBLES	
Financial	10
Match to Key Business Strategies	5
Enhance financial performance	3
Risk of Lack of User Acceptance	2
Customer	15
Improve Quality of Group's Output	6
Improve productivity of staff	4
Risk of resistance to data sharing	5
Process	15
Improve staff productivity	6
Expand usage of enterprise knowledge	6
Risk of security exposures	3
Employee Learning and Growth	10
Improve IT staff productivity	4
Reduce IS project costs and complexity	3
Risk of learning new technical skills	3
TOTAL INTANGIBLES	50
GRAND TOTALS	100

A: Tangible criteria
= 50 points

B: Intangible criteria
= 50 points
(10 + 15 + 15 + 10)

EXHIBIT 14.6 Decision Criteria for Business Case Submission to the IT Steering Committee

of weighting factors between tangibles and intangibles represents the decision team's judgment concerning the relative contribution of each to-the team's final decision. The split could have been 90 percent tangibles to 10 percent intangibles, or 80 percent to 20 percent, 100 percent to 0 percent, or anywhere in between. As a side note, the process by which these splits are set is a very enlightening exercise for the decision team members. It forces them to think out and then reach consensus on how a variety of important factors are to influence their final decision.

- Intangibles are subdivided into **categories**. In Exhibit 14.6 they are the typical Balanced Scorecard categories of "Financial," "Customer," "Process," and "Employee Learning and Growth."[2] Once again, this categorization enables the decision team to reach agreement concerning how much various factors, all of which have proponents and opponents, will impact the decision.
- **Risks** are actively incorporated into the criteria. Four risk criteria are also shown in Exhibit 14.6.

2. For more information on how and why the Balanced Scorecard categories are chosen and used, refer to Robert Kaplan and David Norton's seminal books on this subject. Also refer to Paul Niven's excellent book describing detailed processes for Balanced Scorecard implementation. See Bibliography.

Decision Criteria	Wts.	Global KBase Grade	Global KBase Score	Inventory Grade	Inventory Score	Budget System Grade	Budget System Score
TANGIBLES							
Return on Investment (ROI)	50	3	150	4	200	5	250
TOTAL TANGIBLES	50		150		200		250
INTANGIBLES							
Financial	10		32		16	1	17
Match to Key Business Strategies	5	5	25	2	10	2	10
Enhance Financial Performance	3	3	9	4	12	5	15
Risk of Lack of User Acceptance	2	-1	-2	-3	-6	-4	-8
Customer	15		41	1	9	1	-10
Improve Quality of Group's Output	6	5	30	2	12	1	6
Improve Productivity of Staff	4	4	16	3	12	1	4
Risk of Resistance to Data Sharing	5	-1	-5	-3	-15	-4	-20
Process	15		48	1	18	1	0
Improve Staff Productivity	6	4	24	1	6	1	6
Expand Usage of Enterprise Knowledge	6	5	30	3	18	1	6
Risk of Security Exposures	3	-2	-6	-2	-6	-4	-12
Employee Learning and Growth	10		32		4	2	-5
Improve IT Staff Productivity	4	5	20	1	4	1	4
Reduce IS Project Costs and Complexity	3	5	15	3	9	1	3
Risk of Learning New Technical Skills	3	-1	-3	-3	-9	-4	-12
TOTAL INTANGIBLES	50		153		47		2
GRAND TOTALS	100		303		247		252

EXHIBIT 14.7 ABC's Project Prioritization Scoresheet (Balanced Scorecard Categories)

Once the criteria are established by the decision team, then project candidates can be compared by scoring each against the criteria. Exhibit 14.7 shows how the IT Evaluation Committee (ITEC) did this for ABC Corporation's (see the Appendix, "Sample Business Case") project candidate.

In the case shown in Exhibit 14.7, intangibles played a decision role in making the intranet Global KnowledgeBase (GKB) the highest-scoring option. Its intangibles score of 153 was so much greater than the other two alternatives, that it more than made up for GKB's lower score of 150 from the tangible portion of the calculations.

An Intangibility Policy Memo

Because of the importance as well as the inherent confusion regarding the use of intangibles in IT project selection, it can be very helpful if the decision team sends out to all business units a policy memo clarifying the approach the firm will take in handling intangible benefits. Exhibit 14.8 suggests key topics for that memo. Much of the content can come from other sections in this chapter.

Tips on Management of Intangibles

Here are a few more suggestions to assist in "intangibles management." Details of many of these tips, as well as additional suggestions, are contained in Chapter 13 ("Finding Hidden Value That Others Miss").

- *Upgrade research skills*, such as interviewing and publication searching. Very frequently tangibility acceptance hinges on the availability of metrics. If comparative metrics, such as for similar firms in similar industries, can be uncovered, the deal is often sealed for an acceptable hard-money calculation.

EXHIBIT 14.8 Contents of Policy Memo on Using Intangibles as Benefits for Justifying IT Projects

Topics to Cover in Memo
Need for policy
Definition of intangible
Pros and cons of using intangibles
Policy for usage
Types of intangibles allowed
How they will be handled in the business cases
Examples
Person to contact for additional information

- *Be good at focused interviewing*. What hinders workers in getting a quality job done? What inefficiencies exist in costly processes? Who is impacted if a certain event does not happen? Pick your interviewees and find out what they would like to see happen to make them more effective and more satisfied.
- *Beat the clock*. Searching for analogies, metrics, formulas, and related items takes time. Allow enough elapsed time not only to refine your search, but to permit needed interviewees to be available to you.
- *Keep your eyes and ears open*. Like Sherlock Holmes, cast a practiced eye on out-of-the-ordinary behaviors ("the dog that did not bark") that might give clues to tangibility possibilities.
- *Be prepared for pushback*. Certain types of objections to converting intangibles to tangibles are heard very frequently. Be prepared with answers.
  - **Labor savings**
    Objection: Labor savings do not count. We still have to pay their salaries every month.
    Answer: Ask for a medium- and long-term view to be considered. For example, cost avoidance is a real savings if the enterprise's operations seem reasonably predictable during the time frame of the business case analyses.
  - **Missing metrics**
    Objection: Cannot get any metrics to support the logic.
    Answer: Give very conservative guesstimates, backed up with explanations of assumptions and rationale. This at least gets decision makers thinking about the possibility.
- *Monitor the evolution in business thinking*. Attitudes about handling intangibles are continuously assessed by leading academics as well as by high-profile business leaders. Follow the business press to learn their latest ideas and applications. Often their papers and pronouncements can be used to help gain buy-in to a more open acceptance of intangibles.

In the final analysis, whether a benefit is tangible or intangible is an opinion. In most cases that opinion can be influenced by sound research, a clear understanding of the nature of tangibility, and tools that make such pronouncements easy to comprehend.

No matter how seemingly compelling a benefit calculation, or logical an intangible analysis, the acceptance of it by the decision team is by no means a slam-dunk. Someone needs to explain it in a way that maximizes the likelihood that decision makers will listen, understand, and agree. The next chapter, "Using ROI Storytelling to Drive Home the Message," provides a technique that supports this goal.

CHAPTER 15

Using ROI Storytelling to Drive Home the Message

Executives will have to invest more and more on issues such as culture, values, ethos and intangibles. Instead of managers, they need to be cultivators and storytellers.

—Leif Edvinsson, 1946– , executive,
pioneer in knowledge capital management

Theme

Good ROI storytelling is the secret ingredient of highly compelling and effective business cases.

Why ROI Storytelling Drives Home the Message

Great business cases and bestselling books have one thing in common. They succeed by telling great stories in simple, convincing ways.

The chief financial officer (CFO) of a $100 million service organization urgently convened an elite team. Their goal: Develop an airtight business case justifying a new $200,000 human resources system. Dozens of trusted staff people were mobilized. Scores of field people were

(continued)

interviewed. In the end, the return-on-investment (ROI) numbers looked great. But the CFO knew it would take more. The most important vote was that of the founder and chairman, who was legendary for his penny-pinching ways. Although the cost savings looked great, the CFO knew a secret that was even more important. The soon-to-retire leader wanted badly to leave a legacy of greatness, to overcome recent years of business disappointment. So the CFO downplayed the cost savings and focused instead on dramatic stories describing how this information technology (IT) investment offered the best hope to restore the firm to its former greatness. The chairman was inspired, and the investment was approved.

A common mistake in writing business cases is spending too much time on numbers and too little time explaining their significance. Many business cases fail because their all important message misses its mark.

Storytelling, like the air we breathe, sustains us without our conscious awareness. No other narrative process can gain attention, stimulate retention, and encourage retelling better than storytelling. In business, storytelling is especially effective in moving people to action:

Master storytelling is a core skill of many revered chief executives. One of the best storytelling execs is the mega-successful former chairman of Southwest Airlines, Herb Kelleher. For example, rather than spend big money on lawyers to fight a high-profile business dispute, Kelleher masterminded a mock pro-wrestling match between the defendant and himself to determine the outcome. The story about the whys and hows of this live "drama" became the most talked about event in Southwest's 31-year history. For details about this incredible clever storytelling triumph, view the excerpt "Malice in Dallas" at http://search.barnesand noble.com/Nuts/Jackie-Freiberg/e/9780767901840, or see it on video at www.youtube.com/watch?v=51a5xuxxxZQ.

Great storytelling is the essence of good news reporting. On any given day major business media, such as the *Financial Times* or the *Wall Street Journal*, use over a dozen stories to gain attention and accelerate understanding of top business events. It is not by accident that many journalists refer to anything they write, be it breaking news or a reflective essay, as a "story."

Storytelling can be the hidden underpinning of organizational success. It worked to effect major changes at the World Bank. This story and others were brilliantly chronicled at the Smithsonian Institution–sponsored "Storytelling: Passport to the 21st Century" conference in 2001 (www.creatingthe21stcentury.org).

Why do stories work? Because they get attention by connecting to deep-felt issues of the listener. Such an impact can endure for years. An example:

An ROI storyteller helped win funding for the biggest IT investment a $20 million consulting firm had ever made, by telling reluctant executive decision makers a story with an ego-appealing vision. This vision was that the success of this investment had such power for the firm that it would put the executives on the cover of *Fortune* magazine. With that statement, he whipped out a *Fortune* front cover mock-up showing the smiling faces of every decision maker. The headline exclaimed "Visionary Execs Hit Global Home Run." While everyone laughed at such an obvious appeal to pride, the funding was approved. Years later the *Fortune* cover story was still remembered, long after the details of the ROI had faded away.

Principles of Good ROI Storytelling

Good ROI storytelling is an easily learned skill if the right principles are followed. Here are some key ones.

Pick the Right Story for the Right Audience

Effective stories carefully **match** the narrative and audience. Use answers to the following questions to facilitate such an alignment.

- What is the primary **goal** of the story? Is it to gain attention, clarify difficult or controversial points, get buy-in from influential decision participants, or something else? Use one goal per story.
- Who is the **audience?** The story's audience is always one or more of the decision participants for whom the business case is written. For example, if a CFO is known to be skeptical of the data contained in the business case, then a key ROI story might describe an interview with a respected finance department employee concerning the extra steps taken to ensure the credibility of the cost savings identified.
- **How many** stories are needed? Use one story (the business case theme story) for the main message of the business case. In addition, use "microstories" (typically a few sentences long) for all supporting messages needing storytelling help.

- What story **delivery format** should be used? Business cases are most often delivered in report and/or presentation formats. Even when a business case is delivered in hard copy, it is desirable to have conversational versions of the key stories available to reinforce the business case message at opportune times. Encountering a key decision participant alone in an elevator is an example of a powerful 20-second storytelling occasion.

Build Stories That Touch Human Hearts

Stories work because they reach inside people's souls and speak in images and language they want to hear. Here are some principles to make this happen.

- Address **universally compelling** themes, such as:
  - Achieving great rewards (via existing resources or from future ones)
  - Avoiding great loss (now or in the future)
  - Winning widespread respect (for results, leadership, innovation, and so on)
  - Strengthening security (reduction of risk)
- Use **familiar** situations:

  Executives within a forest products firm want forest-related examples. One successful ROI storyteller told about journeying to the southeast United States and then climbing 50 feet to the top of a logging crane operator's tiny control hut. Inside this dangling skybox, the operator bared his soul about problems keeping him from doing his job better. Back at headquarters, the crane-climbing storyteller dramatically linked these needs to the IT investment being requested.

  This memorable story helped win IT funding because it was attention getting, compelling, vivid, and believable. It also enhanced the business case writer's credibility by dramatizing the thoroughness of his research.

- Keep it **truthful**: ROI stories are of two kinds: factual and visionary. For the former, guard against natural tendencies to embellish. It is both dangerous and foolish to be less than truthful. These types of stories are typically easy to confirm. For visionary stories, be clear that they are about future opportunities.

Use Vivid Language

Vibrant language spawns attention-getting mental images. Competition for reading awareness is tough. On the average, professional managers read

EXHIBIT 15.1 Terms to Gain the Attention of Business Case Readers

High Importance	To Win
Compelling	Conquer
Gripping	Crush
Vital	Triumph
Potent	Overcome
Sense of Urgency	**Avoid Problems**
Time Sensitive	Avoid a loss
Immediate	Steer clear
Instant	Skirt a hazard
Vital	Shun
Distinctiveness	**Warning**
Elite	Caveat
Exclusive	Admonition
Unique	Troublesome
Special	Caution

hundreds of thousands of words a year related to work issues. To get and keep mind share during the short time the business case is being reviewed, use expressions that pulsate with relevance. Search out adjectives describing sensation, color, and action. To see the difference in impact, examine the two sentences below.

Sentence 1: The return on this IT investment is 105 percent annually.

Sentence 2: The annual return on this IT investment is an unusually high 105 percent. This return is double what senior management demands for system investments to help stomp competition in the hotly contested European market.

While Sentence 1 is succinct, Sentence 2 is better for the business case. The latter vividly tells not only what, but even more importantly, why.

Exhibit 15.1 lists some vivid terms to help make business cases come alive. Take care to ensure that such emotion- and image-producing text is relevant within the primary message of the business case.

Be Succinct

Like business cases themselves, ROI stories must be brief. Busy executive decision makers demand brevity. Lengthy stories risk becoming unread stories. A rule of thumb: The "main message" business case story should be one page or less. Microstories should be no more than a couple of sentences each.

The goal is succinctness in the context of attention-getting and compelling narratives. A tip: Study stories in the business press. They are typically short, punchy, and relevant. A further tip: Be a good self-editor. Get the thoughts on paper without worrying about conciseness. Then double back on that draft and aggressively chop words and condense thoughts.

Stay Alert for Story Ideas

Compelling candidates for business case stories abound in every enterprise. Tune ears to listen. Hang out where such stories live. Physical and virtual water coolers are a good place to start, such as coffee/break rooms, storyteller-populated lunch tables, e-mail chat rooms, and threaded discussion groups. Publications can be goldmines. Study employee newsletters, media articles interviewing key stakeholders, and industry analyst reviews.

Additional examples of ROI stories are found in the sample business case in the Appendix.

In summary, good ROI storytelling is one of the most potent, yet frequently neglected, aspects of effective business cases. Being a good ROI storyteller begins with a commitment to the principles, and grows with heightened sensitivity to story opportunities, ideas, and role models.

Thus far in this book, the strategic framework for creating and using business cases has been described. Chapter 16, which follows next, outlines how to confidently select the best-value IT projects when there is not enough funding to invest in all eligible projects.

CHAPTER 16

Selecting: Prioritizing Programs with Confidence and Ease

Take time to deliberate, but when the time for action has arrived, stop thinking and go in.

—Napoleon Bonaparte, 1769–1821,
Emperor of France, *Maxims*

Theme

Successful IT project selection methods are simple, accurate, fair, timely, and open.

IT Project Selection: Replacing Anxiety with Confidence

Earlier chapters described how to bring order out of the chaos of unstructured business case building. Once the business case is built and presented before the decision committee, a related activity comes into play: project selection. How does the decision committee choose which projects to fund when there is not enough money for all? This, too, is a process replete with confusion, anxiety, and misinformation among those who decide, as well as among those who wait anxiously for the "vote" on their cherished proposals.

197

*If someone could be a fly on the wall during our IT-enabled pro-
ject selection committee meetings, they would not believe what they
saw. Powerful, sophisticated, knowledgeable women and men flying by the seat of their pants. Prejudice, bias, and just plain igno-
rance running rampant—mostly from those unaware it is even
happening. Beneath the surface of insightful questions and thought-
ful responses beats the soul of people who are confused, anxious,
and concerned. Often, a strong, passionate stand on a proposal
masks a deep anxiety and confusion. Out of this decision-making
process mysteriously evolve pronouncements concerning which
project proposals get the funding and which drop out.*

—An IT selection committee chairperson

*We seem to have good management folks on our project selection
team. However, how they make their decisions, and why, is a total
mystery to all of us. Thus, when our favorite, and seemingly enterprise irresistible, project proposal gets dumped, we tend to assume
the worst. Not knowing the selection team's criteria, their concerns,
or their objectives, it just looks like whoever had the most political sway got their project OK'd. As a result, we have people in our
department who are very disinclined to support project implementations that appear ill chosen. Why, they say, should we even try
to submit solid project proposals if they just disappear into a black
hole to be rejected?*

—A mid-level manager

Tolerating even a slightly flawed project selection process is a dangerous game to play in today's world of IT-enabled business strategies that
make or break entire firms (and industries). The cost of substandard selection processes is never small. For example:

- A budgeting project is selected instead of an e-mail enhancement proposal. Six months later, the e-mail proponents' warning of a major
  security exposure proves true, costing the firm millions to rectify.
- An inventory system with superior ROI is chosen, leaving unfunded a
  competitive analysis system whose "gut-feel" benefits from marketing
  were downplayed by the manufacturing-centric project selection committee. Twelve months later, the division is put up for sale, a victim of
  slow response to fundamental market changes evident to alert competitors for almost two years.
- While in the throes of recovering from the loss of business due to
  unforeseen major price cuts by key competitors, the chief executive

EXHIBIT 16.1 Why IT-Enabled Project Selection Processes Get Shortchanged

Factors

- Decision makers do not want the process discipline and/or exposure of their informal methods.
- Management is not aware that project prioritization and selection problems exist.
- Management is aware of problems, but mistakenly believes they are not a major issue.
- Management has higher priorities for process improvements other than IT investment selection.
- Consequences of faulty IT project selection methods are not well understood.
- Management decision making is considered "not amenable" to structure and procedures.
- There is a lack of management support and urgency.
- There is a lack of awareness of simple, effective methods for identifying the best-value project proposals.

officer (CEO) asks the manager of the pricing strategy group why he did not see this coming. The manager says that the group had had ideas on how to preempt competitor price cuts, but chose not to waste time by submitting project ideas. The group had been continually discouraged in the past by submitting proposals for IT-enabled projects that were rejected "for no good reason."

Given the seemingly "obvious" reasons for improving how IT projects get selected, why is progress so seemingly slow? Exhibit 16.1 recaps some reasons often encountered.

A Simple Project Prioritization Process

To help overcome anxieties and obstacles, such as those mentioned in Exhibit 16.1, this chapter describes a straightforward, reliable method identifying best-value projects. Known as the project prioritization process (P^3), it has four principles of operation:

1. Accuracy of identification of "best business value" of projects evaluated
2. Fairness of project selection
3. Enterprise visibility of selection criteria and methodology
4. Timely decisions

For all its power, P³ is designed to be simple, so that it might be:

- Easy to understand
- Easy to learn
- Ease to use
- Easy to explain

P³ is a weighting and scoring system. It is not the answer to every project selection issue. It does not, for instance, incorporate complicated mathematical analyses, such as Monte Carlo simulation, for risk analysis. Simulation methods can add another layer of sophistication to project selection. However, many firms feel they do not want to pay the price of extra complexity, training, and support that these approaches often bring.

However, in spite of this, P³ provides advantages such as:

- Ability to **clarify the differences** in both tangible and intangible value between seemingly dissimilar project proposals
- Ability to **install the process** with minimal time and effort investment
- **Minimal resistance to implementation** among those who must change their project proposal ways
- Sufficient **flexibility in design**, such that more sophisticated analytical methods can be attached to it later, if desired.

Given the advantages and caveats of P³, the key question to ask regarding its usefulness to a specific environment is, "Does P³ provide more accuracy, fairness, integrity, and usability to the project selection process currently being used?" If yes, then some or all of the methods, principles, and tools of P³ should be considered for adoption.

How Are We Doing? A Quick Project Selection Process Audit

Exhibits 16.2 and 16.3 provide a quick assessment tool for evaluating the extent to which an existing project investment selection method could benefit from approaches such as those found in P³.

The results of this type of audit can highlight areas potentially undermining the integrity of project selection. Examples of possible audit discoveries include:

- A lack of **management communication** to business case creators concerning what business issues management wants the project proposals to support most
  IMPACT: Mistargeted business case justifications, potentially lost project proposals of high value

EXHIBIT 16.2 Instructions: IT-Enabled Project Selection Process Audit Tool

---

INSTRUCTIONS

This IT-Enabled Project Selection Process Audit Tool provides a quick assessment of how well the organization uses a process that is simple, accurate, fair, timely, and open.

Note: This quality audit tool assumes that the individuals doing the scoring are familiar with the characteristics of high-quality business cases and related ROI activities outlined in this book.

Instructions below refer to the audit questions in Exhibit 16.3.

1. Complete heading information [business unit audited, date, person(s) doing audit].
2. Score each of the 17 Quality Factors as a 0 (little or none), 1 (some), or 2 (much), according to how well it accurately describes the audit question to the left of the scores.
3. If desired, add explanatory comments at the bottom of the sheet or on a separate sheet.
4. Upon completion of all scoring, total the score points as shown at the bottom of the sheet.
5. Use the Scoring Table below to assess the overall quality of and confidence in the selection process.

SCORING TABLE: IT-ENABLED PROJECT SELECTION PROCESS AUDIT
(maximum possible score = 34)

Over 26: High (Selection process contains most factors found in quality methods.)
17 to 26: Medium (Selection process is so-so. Use with caution.)
Under 17: Low (Selection process lacks quality to a serious degree. Improvement
   urged)

- An **underuse of intangible benefits** that, in fact, are central to the firm's ultimate business success
  IMPACT: Not funding the highest business value proposals
- Undetected frustration and **discouragement with the project selection process**
  IMPACT: Reduces employee morale, loss of worthwhile project proposals
- A strong desire to improve the project selection process, but **lack of dependable tools** to do so
  IMPACT: Employee frustration that further degrades opportunities for project value maximization

The three main components of the project prioritization process—the Project Prioritization Scoresheet, the Business Case Submittal Standards, and P³ Implementation Guidelines—are described next.

EXHIBIT 16.3 Scoresheet: IT-Enabled Project Selection Process Audit Tool

Business Unit Audited _____

Date of Audit _____

Person(s) Doing Audit _____

		SCORE		More
Quality Factors	*A*	*B*	*C*	*Information*
ACCURACY OF PROJECT SELECTION DECISIONS				
1. A clear set of decision criteria exists for comparing various projects.	0	1	2	Chapter 10
2. The decision criteria have intangible factors of importance to the firm's success.	0	1	2	Chapter 10
3. The decision criteria cover all relevant factors that influence the selections.	0	1	2	Chapter 10
4. The decision criteria are weighted according to importance to the final selection.	0	1	2	Chapter 10
5. Project selection decisions are made with a minimum of political bias.	0	1	2	Chapters 10, 11
6. The decision criteria address both benefits and risks.	0	1	2	Chapter 10
7. The decision criteria address the link of the project to major goals of the firm.	0	1	2	Chapters 10, 11
FAIRNESS OF PROJECT SELECTIONS				
8. A method exists for fairly comparing projects with different investment needs.	0	1	2	Chapters 8, 9, 10, 11, 12
9. A method exists for fairly comparing projects with different payback periods.	0	1	2	Chapters 8, 9, 10, 11, 12
10. Consistent financial formulas are used for all project candidates.	0	1	2	Chapter 11
11. Selection team members represent all units that are actively submitting projects.	0	1	2	Chapters 9, 10
VISIBILITY OF THE SELECTION PROCESS				
12. Project proposal submitters are aware of decision criteria used for selection.	0	1	2	Chapter 10
13. Stakeholders are notified about why a proposal was, or was not, accepted.	0	1	2	Chapter 12
SUPPORT FOR THE SELECTION PROCESS				
14. Senior executives believe the process to be simple, accurate, and fair.	0	1	2	Chapters 9, 16
15. Mid-level and operations people believe the process to be simple, accurate, and fair.	0	1	2	Chapters 9, 16
16. Members of the selection team believe the process to be simple, accurate, and fair.	0	1	2	Chapters 9, 16
17. Stakeholders of rejected projects believe the process to be simple, accurate, and fair.	0	1	2	Chapters 9, 16

Add the score for each column > > > ☐ + ☐ + ☐

Total audit score (Columns A + B + C) > > > ☐

Comments:

A Simple Project Prioritization Scoresheet

The Project Prioritization Scoresheet (PPS) is a one-page document outlining the relative appeal of competing IT projects, by scoring the characteristics of these projects against a common set of criteria. The PPS explained in this chapter in Exhibits 16.4 through 16.10 is an example. The contents of the PPS should be customized to each organization in order to reflect its strategy, culture, and values.

Uses

A PPS can help prioritize:

- Project funding proposals (go or not go)
- Vendor selections for a project already funded
- Implementation sequencing choices (e.g., should we roll out human resources (HR) to Europe first or start with Asia-Pacific? In what sequence should we install the new financial system's modules, such as budgeting, reporting, and general ledger?)
- Investments comparing IT-enabled projects to non-IT-enabled projects (e.g., should we invest in this IT project or a new fleet of trucks?)

PPS in Action: Three Worthwhile Projects, One Bag of Funds

Jerry Whitman, newly arrived chief financial officer (CFO) and head of ABC's IT Evaluation Committee (ITEC), was concerned. Historically, the firm had been able to make IT project funding decisions relatively informally. Today, they had a problem. Resentment had been growing among employees whose projects had not been funded. The chief executive officer (CEO) expressed concern and asked Jerry to find a way to solve this problem. As Jerry prepared for the ITEC meeting to be held the next day, he found that three very attractive proposals had been submitted for funding. He, however, knew that sufficient funds existed for only one of them.

The problem was that all three were deserving of funding. Not only did all have a financial attractiveness, but they were political hot potatoes. The executive sponsors of the individual projects had personally talked to Jerry to emphasize how important the funding of

(continued)

EXHIBIT 16.4 Project Candidates for ITEC Evaluation for Funding

Project ID#	A	B	C
Project name	Global KnowledgeBase (GKB)	Inventory Tracking System	Budget Forecasting System
Sponsor	Product Design Engineering	Manufacturing Department	Finance Department
Architecture	Intranet	LAN-based	Intranet
Initial cost	$1,000,000	$1,400,000	$500,000
ROI	125%	187%	210%
Payback period	12.5 months	18.1 months	24.3 months

their projects was to ABC, to each personally, and to their attitudes and support of the ITEC.

Jerry was anxious to have the ITEC viewed as an important contributor to ABC success, not as an impediment to strong executives who are under pressure to lead their groups to major business successes.

Jerry decided to construct a table (Exhibit 16.4) and use it for a discussion with his ITEC team at the next day's meeting. The task tomorrow: What type of process for evaluating these three projects would be best, given that the goal was to select the best business value project for ABC? Another goal was to be able to demonstrate to each project's sponsor that the project selection process was fair and understandable.

Attempt 1: All Tangibles All the Time

As Jerry pondered what approach to take, the mantra of the recently departed CFO, Fred Krelling, rang in his ears:

"Ultimately, business success comes down to cash. Keep enough of it coming in and you are fine. Let it get scarce and you are in trouble. Cash is king. That's the reason why all IT-enabled investment projects should be evaluated primarily on their ultimate impact on cash flow."

Since ABC had some major cash flow business challenges last year, Fred's preaching got a lot of play.

Keeping Fred's words fresh in his mind, and having done some research on scoring systems, Jerry decided to see if he could quantify the financial value of each project and then compare the outcomes.

EXHIBIT 16.5 Tangibles Grading Scale

ROI results	Grade
Under 0%	0
0 to 50%	1
51% to 100%	2
101% to 150%	3
151% to 200%	4
Over 200%	5

EXHIBIT 16.6 Ranking by Candidate: Tangible Factors

Type of Analysis	Project A: GKB	Project B: Inventory System	Project C: Budgeting System
Hard Money Factors Only			
ROI %	125%	167%	210%
Grade from grading scale	3	4	5
Weight given to tangibles	50	50	50
Score of tangibles	150	200	250
RANK	3	2	1

To do so, he constructed a grading scale (shown in Exhibit 16.5) to reflect the attractiveness of the return on investment (ROI) for each evaluated project proposal. Once calculated, the ROI was then matched to the scale in Exhibit 16.5 to see what grade each proposal would get. The higher the grade, the more attractive the ROI. The grade then would fit within the scoring system. This grading scale represented Jerry's understanding of the decision teams' opinions about what ROI percent constituted an excellent ROI (grade 5) versus poor (grade 1) ROI.

The scoring mechanism selected used the calculation of "weight (given to tangibles) multiplied by grade (from grading scale) equals score (of tangibles)." (See Exhibit 16.6.)

(continued)

After reviewing Exhibit 16.6 with the ITEC, the team members suggested they should proceed with the announcement that the Budgeting System was the funding winner. However, Jerry posed a question to the committee.

"How do we account for those things we cannot measure? What about the impact of these systems on management's top goals of revenue and profit increases? What about the issue of risk? Shouldn't intangible factors play some role here also?"

Clay Bell, vice president of Operations, countered that cash impact was all that was needed for a decision. Putting soft stuff into the decision analysis, such as intangibles, he argued, would unfairly muddy the water.

However, Eileen Whalen, vice president of Worldwide Sales, requested that the committee at least try an experiment using a scoring sheet that accounted for both tangibles and intangibles. After some discussion, the committee members agreed to do so.

Attempt 2: The Full Picture

The committee then did a scoring-based analysis of intangibles, then put the final scores side by side, as shown in Exhibit 16.7. When the committee did this, it noticed a curious thing. The top-ranked project when considering both tangibles and intangibles was the intranet-based Global KnowledgeBase. That project had ranked last when the tangible-only factors were considered (Exhibit 16.6). The difference was the intangibles. By using the PPS (Exhibit 16.8), the committee was able to see how combining both tangibles and intangibles reflected the needs of the enterprise more accurately.

EXHIBIT 16.7 Project Scores: Tangibles and Intangibles

Score	Project A: Intranet GKB	Project B: Inventory System	Project C: Budgeting System
Tangibles score	150	200	250
Intangibles score	153	47	2
Combined (grand totals) score	303	247	252
RANK	1	3	2

Understanding the Project Prioritization Scoresheet (PPS)

As mentioned earlier, the Project Prioritization Scoresheet is a device for weighting and scoring the characteristics of various IT investment candidates against a common set of criteria. Closely examine the PPS constructed by ABC Corporation in Exhibit 16.8. This PPS uses Balanced Scorecard decision categories, as first illustrated in Task 5 of Chapter 10 (Exhibit 10.6). (For any organization using the Balanced Scorecard, the acceptance of the PPS approach can come more readily since it embodies principles to which that organization has already committed.)

The PPS embodies several important principles for good project investment decision making. It:

- Uses **common decision criteria** when prioritizing competing project solutions
- Uses **business-issue criteria** that reflect business directions and factors at all relevant levels of the organization
- Accounts for both **tangible and intangible** issues
- Accounts for both **benefits and risks**
- Uses **weights** to identify the relative importance of each criterion
- Uses a **scoring system** incorporating hard-money and soft-money benefits and risks that reflect important issues throughout the firm
- Summarizes information within one page, for ease of seeing the "big picture"

SCORING PROCESS   Use the following procedures to complete the PPS:

1. **Name the levels**. Determine what each category of scoring represents. If a Balanced Scorecard method is used, then the four levels will be assigned names close to those shown in Exhibit 16.8 (i.e., Financial, Customer, Process, and Employee Learning and Growth).
2. **Select a numeric base** for the total of all weights.

Tip

Use 100 points as the base. This makes each weight similar to a percentage, which most people can easily understand.

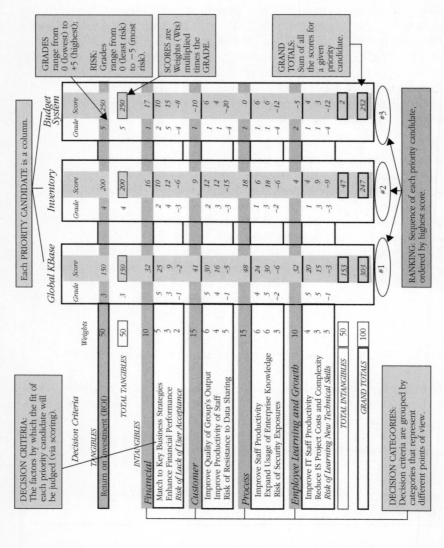

EXHIBIT 16.8 Explanation of ABC's Project Prioritization Scoresheet (Balanced Scorecard Categories)

3. Assign **weight totals ("points")** to each category.

Example

In Exhibit 16.8, the "Tangibles" section received 50 points and the "Intangibles" 50. The decision concerning how to divide the weights between these two groups was made by asking the decision participants or their representatives.

---

4. Assign **criteria weights ("points")**.

Example

In Exhibit 16.8, each category in the "Intangibles" section received from 2 to 6 points.

---

5. **Review weights** with decision participants. Allocate sufficient time for this step. Having the weights correctly allocated helps to ensure that subsequent research and analysis by the business case team is placed on the most important areas of value.

Note

Consider doing a preliminary weight assignment at the beginning of Task 5 ("Identify decision criteria" in Chapter 10). This often helps the effectiveness of the brainstorming by bringing focus to the areas with the greatest weight. The weights can then be reviewed at the Task 7 (Filter criteria) stage.

A Vendor Comparison Prioritization Scoresheet

After all discussion was concluded about the interpretation of the intranet GKB scoring results, ITEC leader Jerry Whitman called for a vote of the committee. Does the committee, he asked, wish to recommend to the decision team, the funding of the intranet GKB, as the

(continued)

project with the highest business value to ABC, of the three they compared? The committee voted unanimously "yes."

The committee immediately went into chatter mode as they congratulated themselves on completing the task at hand. As talk began to quiet somewhat, Jerry noticed that Sam White had a puzzled look on his face, and then raised his hand.

"Jerry," he stated, "the business case of the intranet GKB that we evaluated assumed a single vendor, Guidance Software. How do we know that is the best vendor for this major investment we are about to make? Why aren't we comparing multiple vendors for this task? We certainly wouldn't buy $1,000,000 of electronics for our test instruments without getting competing bids."

"Good point, Sam," Jerry replied. "I meant to mention that earlier, but forgot. The procedure we have set up is that once ITEC agrees to fund an IT project, then the vendor evaluation phase will begin with the business case team. Who ABC picks as the vendor, while extremely important to ABC overall, is not a task that ITEC has in its charter right now. We will be busy enough just focusing on funding issues. Thus, the vendor selection decision will be made by a team comprised of operational management and IT staff."

"Wouldn't this scoresheet approach work just as well with vendor comparisons as with project funding issues?" asked Sam, turning to the committee at large. Voices chimed in with general agreement.

"I'll make it a point," said Jerry, "to pass this suggestion on to Patti Perowski, our VP of Sales for Global Accounts, and the business case team's executive sponsor."

Prioritizing vendors involves many of the same "business value" principles as prioritizing projects for funding. For example, the following vendors could be compared, using the key parameters and computations shown in Exhibit 16.9. These financial characteristics, along with the intangible factors scores, are then factored into a slightly modified scoresheet as shown in Exhibit 16.10.

Notice the following differences between this "vendor comparison" scoresheet in Exhibit 16.10 versus the "project comparison" version in Exhibit 16.8.

- **Functional** comparison decision criteria have been added (see Lines A and C in Exhibit 16.10).
- The **weights have been adjusted** for individual criteria within the Process and the Employee Learning and Growth decision categories, to reflect the importance of the functional criteria.

EXHIBIT 16.9 Three Main Vendors Considered for the Intranet GKB System

Project ID#	A	B	C
Vendor Name	Guidance Software	Engineeristics	Rascale & Higgens
Vendor Product Name	Global Engineer Designer	EngineerONE	ProductPlace
Initial Costs	$900,000	$400,000	$250,000
5-Year Costs	$1,950,000	$1,500,000	$800,000
5-Year Payoff Total	$6,688,237	$4,718,887	$3,196,513
ROI	125%	181%	212%
Payback Period	12.5 months	9.1 months	7.6 months

- A new "**risk**" factor has also been added: "Risk of Vendor Viability Problems" (line B). Weights have been adjusted to handle it, also.
- The remainder of the decision criteria has **remained the same**, since these criteria are major factors in judging the true business value of any IT-enabled project to ABC.
- Although not explicitly shown in Exhibit 16.10, many of the functional differences among vendors can also be **reflected in the original decision criteria**. Thus, for example, "Improve Staff Productivity" under the Process category could have its grade impacted by how well the functionality of each vendor's solution helped support this specific criteria.

Guidance Software is the winner. Its higher costs and somewhat lower ROI, as compared to the other two vendors, are more than offset by Guidance's more favorable intangibles. This type of conclusion is not obvious, unless a scoresheet type of analysis is done. The scoresheet, provided all decision team members agree with its analysis, flushed out the true business value for ABC.

Business Case Submittal Standards

By the end of the ITEC meeting, Jerry and his entire committee were pleased with the use of the PPS to guide them in their decision to select the Global KnowledgeBase for funding. The selection of the decision categories, the weights, and finally the grades had given them an uncommon insight into what ABC needed from IT-enabled projects, and how well project candidates stack up against those criteria.

(continued)

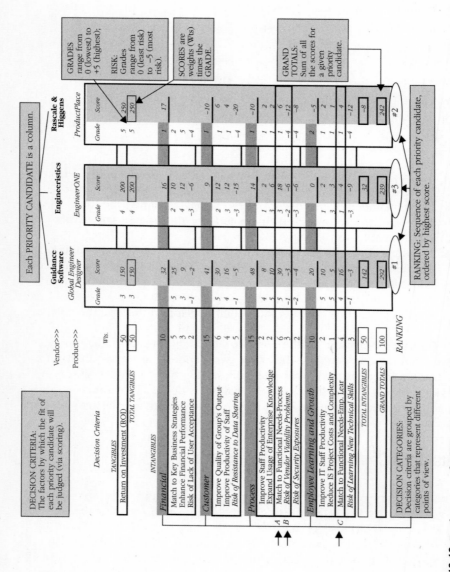

EXHIBIT 16.10 Explanation of ABC's Project Prioritization Scoresheet (Vendor Comparison)
Note: Arrows show vendor-comparison-specific criteria added to scoresheet shown in Exhibit 16.8.

Jerry wondered out loud to the committee if ABC should consider using the PPS approach to evaluate all future IT-enabled project proposals. If that made sense, he said, is there a way by which the submitters of the project proposals could incorporate in their business cases certain information that would (1) help each submitter understand how his or her proposal would be evaluated and (2) save ITEC time in recasting its business cases into a PPS format?

Helena Blackenberry, vice president of Manufacturing, urged caution. The last thing her busy business unit managers needed was more paperwork to fill out. If the whole process of project submissions looks like a big numbers game, she declared, then frankly, her people will figure out how to play it. But that might not be what ABC really needs to make the best business value decisions for the company overall.

Jerry countered by reminding Helena that the ITEC would always decide what weights and grades would be used, which ultimately would determine a proposal's outcome—high numbers that were submitted by a proposal team would not necessarily produce the winning investment. The business case submitters would simply suggest scores, accompanied by their reasoning.

After some additional ITEC discussion on the pros and cons of having a more standardized business case submittal process, the meeting was over. Due to the obvious interest by the committee in exploring this issue, Jerry asked Jose Morez if he would look into how ABC could institutionalize the PPS and then report back to ITEC at its meeting next month with his recommendation.

Using Standardized Decision Criteria

Exhibit 16.11 shows a very simple method for having business case submitters recast a small amount of their analysis into a format that would be compatible with a PPS, such as that used by ABC Corporation above. This PPS-for-all approach has four components, the design and content of which come from the central IT evaluation committee:

- Standardized decision criteria
- Standardized weights for each criterion
- Standardized rating scales for each criterion (similar in structure to Exhibit 16.5)
- Instructions to business case teams on how to apply these to individual business cases

Exhibit 16.11 shows two interesting aspects of the intranet GKB solution which would be of interest to the evaluation committee:

- The GKB payoff areas (called PayoffCards) cover 10 of the 12 standard categories in the PPS. This broad coverage bodes well for the GKB in the project selection process, since the PPS weights also reflect the desirability of a relatively even spread of decision factors.
- The two standard decision criteria areas not addressed by GKB are risk factors.

Notice the following aspects of the ITEC Criteria Match Worksheet shown in Exhibit 16.11.

- First column: ITEC's standardized decision criteria list
- Second column: ITEC's standardized weights
- Third column: GKB's grade (on a scale of 0 to 5) of the fit of the intranet GKB solution to this standard decision criteria on this row
- Fourth column: GKB's score (second column × third column)
- Fifth column: Listing of intranet GKB PayoffCard(s) that most closely match the standardized decision criteria on this row
- Sixth column: Abbreviation indicating if the PayoffCard on this row is an intangible (I), or a tangible (T)
- Seventh column: GKB team's reasons for the grade it selected for this row

The ITEC Criteria Match Worksheet is attached to the business case when submitted to ITEC. The time required for the GKB business case team to complete this form, assuming it had completed the rest of the business case, should be less than one hour.

P³ Implementation Guidelines for the Evaluation Team

To maximize the opportunity of the Project Prioritization Process, a number of management imperatives and actions are recommended.

- **Get the criteria right.** Invest time in making sure the standardized decision criteria are correct. The right criteria help ensure that top-ranked projects are truly the best for the organization. In addition, relevant criteria sell key people on the value of the prioritization approach.
- **Put consensus building on center stage.** Use criteria that appeal to all three types of decision makers: senior management (enterprise, strategic concerns), operations management (business unit/departmental strategies, tactics), and information systems (IS) management (data, systems issues).

Decision Criteria	Wts.	Global KBase	Grade	Score	Related PayoffCard(s): Intranet GKB Business Case	Type of PayoffCard	Reasons for Grade Selected
TANGIBLES							
Return on Investment (ROI)							
TOTAL TANGIBLES	50		3	150			
INTANGIBLES							
Financial	10			32			
Match to Key Business Strategies	5		5	25	Increase competitive advantage (Exh. A-3.1)	I	Directly contributes to revenue increases
Enhance Financial Performance	3		3	9	Increase profits from GKB cost savings /Reduce TCO (Exh. A-3.4, A-3.12)	I	Strong ROI (125%); short payback period (12.5 mo.)
Risk of Project Failure	2		-1	-2	Reduce the risk of GKB failure (Exh. A-3.10)	I	Low due to ABC technical skills and appl. maturity
Customer	15			41			
Improved Appeal of ABC Offerings	6		5	30	Make better new product decisions (Exh. A-3.5)	T	Better new products and better decisions about them
Increase Customer Loyalty	4		4	16	Reduce customer turnover (Exh. A-3.9)	T	Customers want more new products
Risk of Customer Dissatisfaction	5		-1	-5	NONE	N/A	NONE
Process	15			48			
Improve Timeliness	6		4	24	Increase enterprise flexibility (Exh. A-3.3)	T	Ability to fast more new products designed,
Improve Effectiveness and Efficiency	6		5	30	Reduce commo. and print costs (Exh. A-3.6)	T	Labor and material savings
Risk of Security Exposures	3		-2	-6	Reduce risk of security breaches (Exh. A-3.11)	T	Fewer breaches, less cost per breach
Employee Learning and Growth	10			32			
Improve Group/Individual Productivity	4		5	20	Increase engr. productivity/Reduce content mgr. skill requirements (Exh. A-3.2, A-3.7)	T	Make better use of available resources
Improve Employee Loyalty	3		5	15	Reduce engineer turnover (Exh. A-3.9)	T	Cut engineering turnover
Risk of Learning New Technical Skills	3		-1	-3	NONE	N/A	NONE
TOTAL INTANGIBLES	50			153			
GRAND TOTALS	100			303			

Legend: I = INTANGIBLE PAYOFF AREA   T = TANGIBLE PAYOFF AREA   N/A = Not Applicable   ( ) = Location in Appendix

EXHIBIT 16.11 ITEC Criteria Match Worksheet: GKB Business Case Team

EXHIBIT 16.12 Grading Scale Comparison for "Increase Customer Loyalty"

Generic Scale		Customized Scale	
Value	Definition	Value	Definition
5	Much	5	Improve customer retention rates by 5 percentage points
4	Some	4	Improve customer retention rates by 4 percentage points
3	Average	3	Improve customer retention rates by 3 percentage points
2	Little	2	Improve customer retention rates by 2 percentage points
1	Almost none	1	Improve customer retention rates by 1 percentage point
0	None	0	No improvement in customer retention rate

- **Balance the criteria.** General guidelines: Have at least 35 percent of your weights directly address senior management issues. At least 20 percent should specify risks. Tangible factors (hard-money factors) should range from 30 to 80 percent of the total weights.
- **Use customized grading scales.** Grading scales define the numeric value to assign for a given characteristic of a prioritization candidate. Customized grading scales are preferred to generic ones. Customization provides more precision when assigning grades. For example, for the prioritization decision criterion "Increase customer loyalty," the customized grading scale in Exhibit 16.12 could be used.
- **Keep criteria up to date.** Modify the criteria and weights from time to time, as market and business conditions change.
- **Clarify who assigns scores.** Make clear to business case teams that although they will be scoring their own projects, their score may, at the evaluation committee's discretion, be modified. The scorings by the teams are suggestions, not edicts.
- **Emphasize the reasoning.** Urge the teams to have strong rationale concerning why they chose the grades they did.
- **Do completeness checks.** Urge the teams to examine what percentage of the payoff areas that they list (the fifth column in Exhibit 16.11) are tangible versus intangible, benefits versus risks, business versus technical, and external versus internal. Generally, it is desirable to have a balance of all these types.

Other important guidelines include:

- Provide hurdle rates.
- Get key stakeholders involved in the establishment of the standardized decision criteria, weights, and so on.
- If the PPS is to be rolled out to the field, be sure to enforce its usage.
- Give feedback to submitters.
- Communicate senior management's vision, values, and goals to the business case teams.

Systematic project prioritization methods can bring consensus instead of division to the emotionally charged process of selecting projects for investment.

The next chapter discusses how to track the realization of the payoffs that were promised when the project was selected.

CHAPTER 17

Tracking: Making Sure Benefits Get Realized

How you measure the performance of your managers directly affects the way they act.

—John Dearden, Harvard Business School *Harvard Business Review*, September–October 1987

Theme

Benefits are more certain when management monitors value every step of the way, from project funding through system retirement.

Benefits Realization: Fantasy or Fact?

No one ever plans not to realize benefits from an IT-enabled investment. Yet surveys throughout the decades indicate that, more often than not, expected benefits never appear.

Forecasting benefits with a business case is one thing. Making them happen is another. Like many things in business life, making benefits become real requires a dedicated set of people, resources, and processes.

Why is realizing benefits from information technology (IT)-enabled investments so tough (even after eliminating those reasons related to system failures and resistance to change)? Some of the most frequently cited reasons are given in Exhibit 17.1.

EXHIBIT 17.1 Examples of Reasons Why IT Benefits Are Hard to Realize

- No one seems to care once the project is funded.
- No one seems to know how. The business case was shelved.
- The business case was built in la-la land. We operate in the real world.
- The implementation team never talked to the evaluation team, who never talked to the business team.
- Benefit shortfalls were not discovered until it was too late.
- Things change, externally and internally.
- We do not like formal stuff.

When all is said and done, however, the major reason why benefit hopes evaporate is that *no management process exists (or if it exists, it is ignored or flawed) to ensure ongoing project success is occurring.*

Benefits realization is a management process for ensuring that payoffs expected to happen from an IT investment do in fact occur. The setup and operation of a true benefits realization (BR) program is getting increasing respect and attention as the frequency and cost of IT investment shortfalls continue to hover at astonishing levels.

This chapter provides guidance to measure "How well are we doing?" and some tips addressing "How can we do better?" Specifically, it:

- Introduces a process **audit tool** for making a quick assessment of how effectively a firm's existing benefits realization process is pulling its weight in the battle to maximize IT project value.
- Identifies key **principles** of a sound benefits realization program.
- Shows how to **strengthen the business case** to better support BR.

The IT Benefits Realization Process Audit

Exhibits 17.2 and 17.3 provide a rapid method of assessing how seriously and effectively the enterprise is managing the realization of benefits by asking:

- Does a true benefits realization process actually exist?
- Is it sound?
- Is it used?
- Is it effective?
- Will it endure?

EXHIBIT 17.2   Instructions: IT Benefits Realization Process Audit Tool

---

INSTRUCTIONS

This IT Benefits Realization Process Audit Tool provides a quick assessment of how well the organization uses a process that is effective.

Note: This quality audit tool assumes that the individuals doing the scoring are familiar with the characteristics of high-quality business cases and related return-on-investment (ROI) activities outlined in this book.

Instructions below refer to the audit questions in Exhibit 17.3.

1. Complete heading information [business unit audited, date, person(s) doing audit].
2. Score each of the 20 Quality Factors as a 0 (little or none), 1 (some), or 2 (much), according to how well it accurately describes the audit question to the left of the scores.
3. If desired, add explanatory comments at the bottom of the sheet or on a separate sheet.
4. Upon completion of all scoring, total the score points as shown at the bottom of the sheet.
5. Use the Scoring Table below to assess the overall depth and quality of a benefits realization process.

SCORING TABLE IT BENEFITS REALIZATION PROCESS AUDIT
(maximum possible score = 40)

Over 30: Much strength (Process contributes much to benefits realization.)
20 to 30: Some strength (Process contributes some value to benefits realization.)
Under 20: Weak (Process contributes little or nothing to benefits realization.)

Upon completion of the scoring explained in Exhibits 17.2 and 17.3, the most needy action areas can be brainstormed and then put into play.

Principles of a Good IT Benefits Realization Process

A benefits realization process is an important activity because it provides:

- Early warning of **payoff shortfalls**, thus enabling remedies to be applied in time to reverse the course ("finger in the dike" principle)

EXHIBIT 17.3 Scoresheet: IT Benefits Realization Process Tool Audit

---

Business Unit Audited _____

Date of Audit _____

Person(s) Doing Audit _____

Quality Factors	Score A	B	C	More Information
CAPABILITIES AND USE OF THE PROCESS				
1. Formal benefits realization process exists in the organization.	0	1	2	Chapters 9, 17
2. Business case is a visible and active part of implementation project management.	0	1	2	Introduction, Chapter 17
3. Executive responsibility is assigned to the benefits realization process.	0	1	2	Chapter 17
4. Prior to implementation, business cases are reexamined for thoroughness.	0	1	2	Chapters 9, 17
5. Prior to implementation, business case assumptions are examined in more detail.	0	1	2	Chapters 9, 17
6. Sensitivity analysis is conducted to review exposure to hard-to-control events.	0	1	2	Appendix, Chapter 11
7. Both tangible and intangible payoff areas are tracked and evaluated.	0	1	2	Chapters 10, 11, 14
8. Aligns benefit forecasts among business case, vendor evaluation, and launch teams.	0	1	2	Chapters 8, 17
9. Actively reconciles business case forecasts to implementation variances.	0	1	2	Chapter 8, 17
10. Includes process for review if external factors change.	0	1	2	Chapter 17
11. Process clearly links new system capabilities to operations and senior-level benefits.	0	1	2	Chapters 8, 10, 17
12. Formal postimplementation benefit reviews are conducted.	0	1	2	Chapter 17
13. Uses a reliable system for metric data collection.	0	1	2	Chapters 5, 17
14. Reports benefits realization progress at least quarterly to stakeholders.	0	1	2	Chapter 17
INTEGRATION, EFFECTIVENESS, AND SUPPORT OF THE PROCESS				
15. Process is an integral part of organization's performance measure methods.	0	1	2	Chapter 17
16. Examples exist demonstrating the value of the benefits realization process.	0	1	2	Chapters 9, 17
17. Process is actively and visibly supported by senior management.	0	1	2	Chapter 17
18. Stakeholders in the new system's implementation are actively involved in process.	0	1	2	Chapter 17
19. Process is respected by both business and IT managers.	0	1	2	Chapter 17
20. Process is regularly reviewed for modifications to reflect new business realities.	0	1	2	Chapter 17

Add the score for each column >>> ☐ + ☐ + ☐

Total audit score (Columns A + B + C) >>> ☐

Comments:

_____

_____

_____

_____

- Alerts to **benefit assumption errors** in the business case, thus allowing management to alter implementation decisions
- **Guidance on implementation strategy** (e.g., should Module A be rolled out to Asia-Pacific or Europe first?)

Examples of management actions stimulated by good IT benefits realization methods include:

- **Correction of erroneous business case benefit assumptions**, thus resetting management expectations to a more realistic level
- **Resequence of implementation options**, to avoid or minimize benefits shortfall
- **Adjust implementation staffing levels and/or skills** to assure attainment of expected benefits

Effective benefits realization methods incorporate a number of key principles such as those outlined in Exhibit 17.4.

How Good Business Cases Contribute to the Successful Realization of IT Benefits

Numerous principles for building cases were described in Chapters 8 through 15 of this book. A number of these approaches directly support the goals of a benefits realization process and thus help make it successful. Exhibit 17.5 provides some examples.

EXHIBIT 17.4 Principles of a Good IT Benefits Realization Process

- Effective benefits realization is a formal, not an ad hoc, process.
- There is executive sponsorship of the BR process.
- Business case metrics, assumptions, and rationale set the bar for benefits success.
- The business case is the basis for the main tracking document.
- Tracking process focuses on highest priority benefits.
- Benefit forecasts are modified quickly if need be.
- Managers are accountable for the attainment of every key benefit.
- Benefits data collection system is reliable.
- Process identifies who is to act upon BR results.
- Regular review meetings are conducted to track BR progress.

EXHIBIT 17.5   IT Benefits Realization Principles and Related Construction Tools

Benefits Realization Principle	Business Case Creation Method	Reference
Use the business case as the foundation for the main tracking document	Principle supporting ROI computations	Tasks 14, 15, 16
Have reliable metrics	PayoffCards: Evidence and References	Task 11
Have metrics that address high-level business value	ValueBoard, Value Ladders, Payoff Alignment Test	Tasks 5, 8, 14, 15, 16
Determine the believability of business case metrics	PayoffCards: Evidence and References	Task 12
Determine the believability of business case assumptions	PayoffCards: Evidence and References	Tasks 1, 13
Determine the believability of business case rationale	PayoffCards: Business Importance: Evidence and References	Tasks 9, 12, 13
Make certain a manager is held accountable for the attainment of every key benefit	PayoffCards: Evidence and References	Tasks 11, 12, 13
Prioritize benefits, and manage them accordingly	Key themes, ValueBoard, Top Benefits Report	Tasks 5, 15
Confirm that the right benefits have been identified in the business case	Key themes, Value-Board, Payoff Alignment Test	Tasks 5, 8, 15

The Value Ladder: A Tool for Clarifying Benefits Realization Targets

If a benefits realization process is to succeed, it must identify, and then track, how the functions of the program being implemented will provide value all the way to the top of the enterprise. It is not enough for a program to promise, for example, to reduce the cost of purchase order processing from $125 each to $25. A true benefits realization process identifies and tracks how that benefit (e.g., reduction in purchase order processing cost) then drives business results such as increasing corporate revenue or increasing the firm's competitive advantage. Achieving higher level benefits is especially difficult if the business case has not mapped this linkage out at the time of program funding.

The Value Ladder is a straightforward tool for helping the benefits realization process identify this mapping, so that appropriate data collection and analysis methods can be built around it. As outlined earlier in this book (Task 8: Align Criteria in Chapter 10), the purpose of the Value Ladder is to graphically display how an investment option's features and/or functions impact the objectives and ultimately the business results of an enterprise.

The natural first step in the benefits realization process is to review a Value Ladder that depicts the primary theme of the business case for the program that is about to be implemented. (See the example in Exhibit 17.6, which comes from the Appendix.)

This Value Ladder is the visual equivalent of the following statement:

> *The intranet Global KnowledgeBase solution makes possible more productive and loyal design engineers. These engineers, in turn, will thus be able to more effectively contribute to the creation of*

EXHIBIT 17.6 Value Ladder Summary of Benefits to ABC Corp. of the Intranet GKB

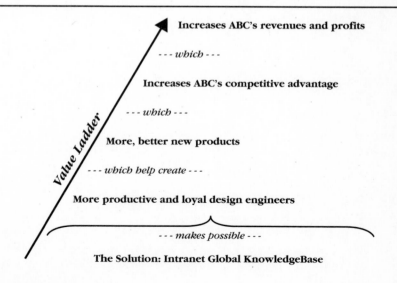

more, better new products. These new products will help enhance
ABC's competitive advantage, which in turn will help increase rev-
enues and profits (which is a key management goal for the year).

Because these benefits are at the heart of the GKB business case in the
Appendix, they should be at the heart of a benefits realization process
related to it. Once the BR team has validated this key theme, then data-
gathering and reporting methods can be designed for collecting the metrics needed to track these crucial benefit areas.

The Appendix that follows provides a comprehensive example of a
business case that employs the principles and methods outlined in this
book, including the highly visible usage of key metrics that form the basis
for the benefit realization process described above.

Sample Business Case

Theme

Complete example of a fictional business case that illustrates key principles and concepts outlined in the main body of the book.

Explanation of This Sample Business Case

This Appendix contains the complete business case for ABC Corporation's evaluation of an intranet-based Global KnowledgeBase (GKB) for use by the firm's product design engineers. While this business case is fictional, it is a composite of many real-life situations the author has encountered. As such, this sample illustrates many key principles and concepts discussed in the main chapters of this book.

This sample business case is included here to:

- Help the reader more quickly grasp how the book's techniques operate in real life.
- Show the reader a role model of a best-practice business case that deals with a situation where the investment is significant to the enterprise and where the decision of whether to invest is murky and politically controversial.
- Provide a template usable for development of other business cases the reader may wish to create.

By no means should all business cases contain this level of detail and reporting. However, the overall structure and topic contents of this sample are applicable to any size investment. The level of effort, as well as the page count, can simply be contracted or expanded to reflect the extent of analysis requested by the decision team. The author recommends that business cases be kept to a maximum page count (not including appendices) of 30 pages (for a highly complex and controversial investment), or preferably much less.

Memo

TO: IT Evaluation Committee, ABC Corporation

FROM: GKB Business Case Team

SUBJECT: Business Case for the Intranet Global KnowledgeBase (GKB) Initiative

DATE: November 19, 20X2

We are pleased to submit to the IT Evaluation Committee the attached document, "Business Case for ABC Corporation's Intranet Global KnowledgeBase Initiative."

This document has been developed in accordance with ABC Corporation's newly adopted "Business Case Design and Evaluation Guidelines." The purpose of these new guidelines is to both strengthen and streamline the manner in which ABC develops and evaluates business cases. This in turn becomes a major driver to maximize the business value from IT investments.

We understand that this business case is the first one submitted under these new guidelines. We wish to thank the committee for this opportunity.

As provided for in these new guidelines, a copy of this business case is being sent to ABC's value analysis repository for use, as needed, by future business case development teams.

The GKB business case team looks forward to feedback from the IT Evaluation Committee concerning the usefulness of this business case to the committee's decision, along with suggestions for future improvements to the process of business case development.

Respectfully submitted by:

Jerry Whitman,
Team Leader
GKB Business Case Team

Business Case for ABC Corporation's Intranet Global KnowledgeBase Initiative

Prepared for

The ABC IT Evaluation Committee

Prepared by:

Patti Perowski, VP Sales, Global Accounts, Team Executive Sponsor
Barry Williams, Director of Product Design, Evaluation Team Leader
Evelyn Chung, Systems Analyst
Mark Fabreney, Content Manager
Quita Ortega, Director of Finance
Shanti Wittcome, Product Design Engineer
Bryce Branson, Partner, ACME Consulting, Special Adviser

Delivered on:

November 19, 20X2

Preface

This document presents the research, findings, and recommendations of the business case team formed to assess the business value of the proposed Intranet Global KnowledgeBase for ABC Corporation's product design engineers.

Table of Contents

Appendices
Appendix A-1: People Contributing to This Business Case Analysis
Appendix A-2: Financial Results by Year (IRR, NPV, ROI)
Appendix A-3: PayoffCard Profiles (Discussion of Each
                 Payoff Area)
Appendix A-4: Business Case Analysis Process Used

List of Exhibits

Section I : Introduction

A. Business Drivers Triggering This Business Case

ABC Corporation, as a medium-sized manufacturer of specialized test equipment sold to electronic product manufacturers worldwide, has an annual revenue of $520 million. ABC ranks second in size to the leading competitor, Global Testing, Inc. Sixty percent of ABC's revenues are from North America, while 40 percent originate from Europe, South America, and Asia.

In recent years ABC has come under increasing market pressure from both global and regional competitors. Executives have determined that in order to reduce serious competitive inroads into key markets, the firm must increase revenues by 15 percent per year while simultaneously expanding the firm's ability to flexibly respond to new market developments. In order to achieve these two goals, the management committee has decided that ABC can best improve its competitive advantage by (1) winning more sales deals and (2) accelerating the introduction of more appealing new products.

For the past year ABC's globally scattered new-product design teams have emphasized the importance (to their productivity) of getting faster and more cost-effective access to the firm's Global KnowledgeBase (GKB) of best-practices product design information. The GKB currently resides on three server systems, located in Paris, France; Dallas, Texas; and Singapore. Approximately 30 engineers, researchers, and others currently have direct access to the GKB electronically, while 30 others have phone access to a central content research staff who inquire into the GKB for them and then e-mail, fax, or Express Mail the results.

In order to respond to management's call for rapid introduction of more successful new products (and also to assist sales in closing more deals by increasing the quality of customer proposals), Craig West, ABC's chief information officer (CIO), has recommended that management provide funds for upgrading and installing the Global KnowledgeBase onto an intranet. This would provide direct and easier access for more engineers, regardless of location, as well as reduce numerous costs.

ABC's senior management has expressed interest in the intranet suggestion, and has thus asked that a business case be constructed to provide more specifics on costs, savings, level of investment, and payback period. In response to this request, the Business Case Evaluation Team was formed. This document is the output of the team's efforts.

B. Scope of the Business Case Analysis

1. Purpose of This Business Case

   The purpose of this business case is to assess the business value of an investment in the acquisition and implementation of an intranet-based Global KnowledgeBase from Guidance Software during the next fiscal year.

2. Options Evaluated

   The two options considered were:
   - Contract for and install an intranet-based solution from Guidance Software called Global Engineer Designer,
   - Continue using the status quo (in-house-developed, client-server-based) solution, which has been installed and has been in operation at three product design locations of ABC (Dallas, Texas; Paris, France; and Singapore) for the past four years.

3. Decision Team Composition

Role in the Decision Process	Name, Responsibility/Title
Decision Makers	Jewel Weston, Chairman of the Board
	Ron Black, CEO
Decision Recommenders	Jerry Whitman, CFO
	Craig West, CIO
Decision Influencers	Clayton Bell, VP Operations
	Helena Blackenberry, VP Manufacturing
	Jose Morez, VP Marketing
	Eileen Whalen, VP Worldwide Sales
	Christine Woo, Director New Product Development
	Randy Zanlaski, Global Director, Engineering Design

   These people have been identified as the decision participants for the go/no-go decision concerning the Global KnowledgeBase opportunity. Members of the IT Evaluation Committee (ITEC) include those in the "Decision Recommenders" and "Decision Influencers" only. These decision participants are the audience for this business case.

4. Analysis Guidelines Received

The following analysis guidelines were received from the decision team:

Guideline Topic	Guideline Received
Time frame of analysis	5 years
Financial formulas (hurdle rates)*	Internal rate of return (IRR) (30%)
	Net present value (NPV) ($1 million)
	Return on investment (ROI) (25%)
	Payback period (payback) (24 months)
Duration of analysis	4 weeks
People resources of team	7 people; maximum of 15 person-weeks total to be expended
Format of deliverables	• Written report 35 pages or less (not including appendices)
	• 60-minute presentation to IT Evaluation Committee
Special factors	Assess risk of project problems, special risks unique to option selected
Due date of business case	November 19

Hurdle rates are the minimally acceptable financial results.

5. Business Case Team Members
   Business case team members are:

Team Leader	Barry Williams, Director of Product Design
Team Members	Evelyn Chung, Systems Analyst
	Mark Fabreney, Content Manager
	Quita Ortega, Director of Finance
	Shanti Wittcome, Product Design Engineer
Team Executive Sponsor	Patti Perowski, VP Sales, Global Accounts
Special Adviser	Bryce Branson, Partner, ACME Consulting

6. Business Case Analysis Process and Resources
   The people consulted and process used for this business case development are outlined in Appendices A-1 and A-4, respectively.

Section II: Executive Summary

A. Recommendation

ABC Corporation should immediately install the intranet GKB. It has an IRR of 109 percent, an NPV of over $3 million, an ROI of 125 percent, and a payback period of 12.5 months—all much better than ABC's hurdle rates. Intangible advantages include enhancing ABC's competitive advantage via more, better new products, thus increasing revenues and profits.

B. Summary of Value Results

Improving engineering productivity and loyalty are the main, core advantages of the intranet GKB solution. These benefits translate into improving the quality and quantity of new products, a key for enhancing ABC's competitive advantage and thus its revenue. This crucial cause and effect is illustrated in Exhibit A.1.

One of ABC's largest customers, Jose Whittenstein, chief executive officer (CEO) of Allied Manufacturers, said it best: "I prefer doing business with ABC, but I won't accept late, second-rate product designs. Get me better new products, faster, and we'll double our business with you."[1]

1. Financial (Tangible Factors)
   For the five-year period, the intranet-based GKB solution's IRR is 109 percent, ROI is 125 percent, NPV is over $3 million, and the payback

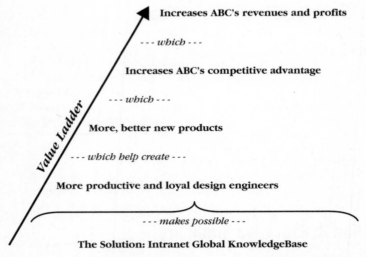

EXHIBIT A.1 Summary of Intranet GKB Business Value to ABC Corporation

---

1. Quote during ABC's annual Client Conclave, Brussels, Belgium, August 10.

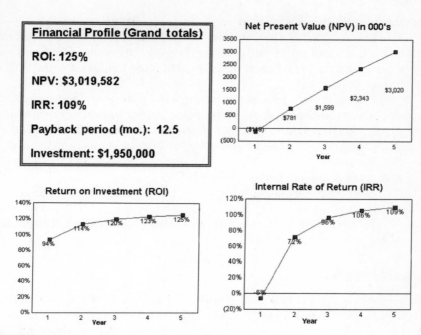

EXHIBIT A.2 Executive Summary of Tangible Benefits

EXHIBIT A.3 Financial Comparison: GKB versus ABC Hurdle Rates

Factor	Business Case Result	Hurdle Rate	Intranet GKB is ...
IRR	109%	30%	Over three times greater than the hurdle rate
NPV	$3,019,582	$1,000,000	Triple the hurdle rate NPV
Payback period	12.5 months	24 months	One-half faster than the hurdle rate
ROI	125%	25%	Five times greater than the hurdle rate

period is 12.5 months. The financial results in Exhibit A.2 show that cumulative value continues to increase for each year of the five-year period. Financial results from the intranet GKB greatly exceed all hurdle rates. (See Exhibit A.3.)

2. Match to Balanced Scorecard

The 12 payoff areas discussed in this business case have an excellent match to all four levels of the Balanced Scorecard[2] strategy and performance measurement system in use by ABC (see Exhibits A.6 and A.7).

3. Intangible Factors

One of senior management's most emphatic goals is to increase ABC's competitive advantage in the marketplace. A large number of quantified payoff areas directly support this intangible (nonquantified) goal. For more detail, see the ValueBoard and Value Map (Sections III.B.3 and 4).

4. Risk Analysis

Risk A (GKB project failure or shortfall) = medium

Risk B (security breaches) = low

5. Sensitivity Analysis

This business case is considered "moderately" sensitive to changes in assumptions.

C. Next Actions

Management is urged to make this GKB decision within the next 30 days. The direct cost of decision delay exceeds $50,000 monthly, due to postponement of benefits. A key payoff area, "Increasing competitive advantage," is also negatively impacted, thus delaying revenue and profit increases, one of management's top goals.

Section III: Analysis

A. Key Assumptions of Analysis

- All costs and benefits are incremental to the option of continuing with the existing client-server system.
- The new intranet GKB is to be installed the second quarter of ABC's next fiscal year. Thus, all payoff area calculations reflect 75 percent of full-year benefits for Year 1 of this analysis, rather than 100 percent. The remainder of Years 2 through 5 reflects 100 percent.
- Only high-level costs are shown in this business case. Detailed cost calculations can be obtained by requesting the document "Detailed Cost Analysis of Intranet versus Client Server-Based Global KnowledgeBase" from the finance department.

---

2. ABC's Balanced Scorecard initiative conforms to the methods as outlined in Robert Kaplan and David Norton's seminal books on this topic.

B. Value Analysis Results

1. Top Benefits (See Exhibit A.4)
   - Almost one-half of all savings come from the top three payoff areas.
   - One-third of the benefits come from the top two payoff areas related to engineering savings ("Increase engineering productivity" and "Reduce engineer turnover").
   - The top five payoff areas are relatively close to each other in size of savings.

2. Key Metrics Improvements/Key Intangibles
   The forecast for base-period-to-target improvements per payoff area, shown in Exhibit A.5, requires relatively small increases. The two largest savings areas, "Increase engineering productivity" and "Reduce engineer turnover" (shown in Exhibit A.4) for example, only require a four-percentage-point improvement. Details on these numbers are contained in Appendix A-1 (PayoffCard Profiles).

3. ValueBoard/Balanced Scorecard View
   The 12 payoff areas of this business case are shown below in Exhibit A.6, aligned in a Balanced Scorecard format. Each payoff area is

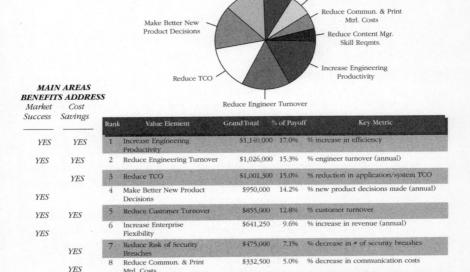

MAIN AREAS BENEFITS ADDRESS						
Market Success	*Cost Savings*	Rank	Value Element	Grand Total	% of Payoff	Key Metric
YES	YES	1	Increase Engineering Productivity	$1,140,000	17.0%	% increase in efficiency
YES	YES	2	Reduce Engineering Turnover	$1,026,000	15.3%	% engineer turnover (annual)
	YES	3	Reduce TCO	$1,001,300	15.0%	% reduction in application/system TCO
YES		4	Make Better New Product Decisions	$950,000	14.2%	% new product decisions made (annual)
YES	YES	5	Reduce Customer Turnover	$855,000	12.8%	% customer turnover
YES		6	Increase Enterprise Flexibility	$641,250	9.6%	% increase in revenue (annual)
	YES	7	Reduce Risk of Security Breaches	$475,000	7.1%	% decrease in # of security breaches
	YES	8	Reduce Commun. & Print Mtrl. Costs	$332,500	5.0%	% decrease in communication costs
	YES	9	Reduce Cotent Mgr. Skil Reqmts.	$267,188	4.0%	% decrease in compensation per content manager

EXHIBIT A.4 Top Benefits Ranked by Payoff Amounts

EXHIBIT A.5 Key Metric Improvements/Key Intangibles

Value Element Name/Key Metric	Base Period	Target	Units of Improvements
Increase engineering productivity % increase in efficiency	0%	4%	4%
Increase enterprise flexibility % increase in revenue (annual)	0.0%	0.5%	0.5%
Make better new product decisions # of new product decisions made (annual)	4	4	0
Reduce commun. & print material costs % decrease in communications costs	0%	20%	20%
Reduce content manager skill requirements % decrease in compensation per content manager	0%	15%	15%
Reduce customer turnover % customer turnover	15%	14%	–1%
Reduce engineer turnover % engineer turnover (annual)	15.0%	11.0%	–4.0%
Reduce risk of security breaches % decrease in # of security breaches	0%	20%	20%
Reduce TCO % reduction in application/system TCO	0.0%	7.0%	7.0%
Increase competitive advantage	Medium		
Increase profit via GKB cost savings	Medium		
Reduce risk of GKB project failure	High		

positioned on the Balanced Scorecard level ("Financial," "Customer," "Process," and "Employee Learning and Growth") that most represents its focus.

Note that the payoff areas are relatively well balanced among the four Balanced Scorecard levels, as well as between "Market Success" (left side of the ValueBoard) and "Cost Savings (right side of the ValueBoard). Also note that:

- Three payoff areas have an exclusive Market Success focus ("Increase enterprise flexibility," "Make better product decisions," and "Increase competitive advantage").

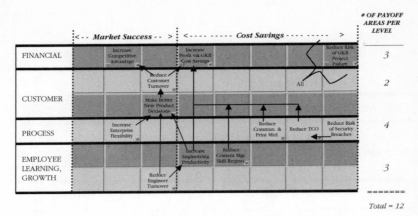

EXHIBIT A.6 Balanced Scorecard ValueBoard of Key Payoff Areas

- Four have an exclusive Cost Savings focus ("Reduce content manager skill requirements," "Reduce communications and print material costs," "Reduce TCO," and "Reduce risk of security breaches").
- Three payoff areas have both a Market Success and Cost Savings focus ("Reduce engineering turnover," "Increase engineering productivity," and "Reduce customer turnover").
- "Reduce risk of GKB project failure" applies to the entire set of payoff areas on the ValueBoard.

For details concerning the calculations, assumptions, and rationale behind each payoff area, see Appendix A-3 (PayoffCard Profiles).

4. Value Ladders/Balanced Scorecard View

The Value Map shown in Exhibit A.7 is a visual display of the primary value theme of this business case, which is:

The main advantage of the GKB solution is that it significantly improves engineering productivity and loyalty. This, in turn, helps to improve the quality and quantity of new-product designs, a factor ABC executives have identified as crucial for enhancing ABC's competitive advantage and thus its revenues and profits.

5. Tangibles Worksheet

The primary costs and benefits that constitute the financial results of this business case are shown in the Tangibles Worksheet in Exhibit A.8. In addition to a summary of the financial results, this document shows that the intranet GKB option has a total five-year cost of

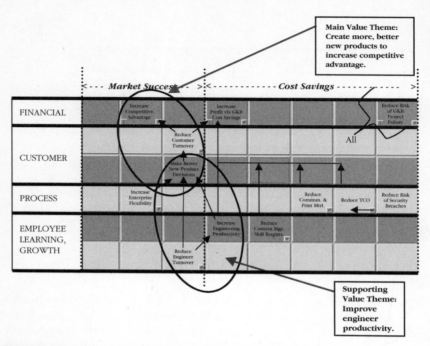

EXHIBIT A.7 Balanced Scorecard ValueBoard with Value Ladders

$1,950,000. Total net benefits during this time frame are $5,638,237, yielding a total net cash-flow result of $4,738,237.

Each line item in the "Payoff" section is the summary of the calculations presented in the corresponding PayoffCard shown in Appendix A-3.

6. Risk Analysis

Two types of risks were evaluated at management's request. More sophisticated risk analyses were deemed by management as not necessary.

The primary risk is considered to be GKB project failure or shortfall. It is judged to be a medium risk. Any systems project has an inherent risk factor due to the nature of its complexity and demands for change within an organization. Since the client-server option evaluated involves no change from current operation, the intranet solution has a relatively higher risk. However, this risk is reduced significantly due to the IT department's recently enhanced intranet skills, plus the maturity of the Global Engineer Designer application software.

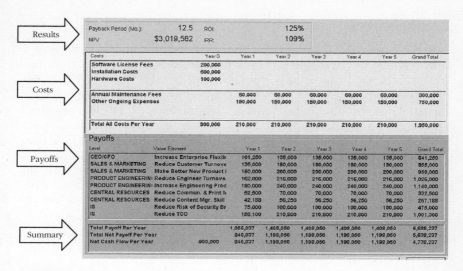

EXHIBIT A.8 Tangibles Worksheet for ABC Corporation's Global KnowledgeBase Business Case

A secondary risk is security breaches. It is considered to be a low risk with the intranet GKB option. Although intranet solutions are generally considered more prone to such breaches than client-server, the architectural design of the Global Engineer Designer includes many state-of-the-art security features that reduce these risks significantly.

For details see the discussion of these two risks in Appendix A-3 (PayoffCard Profiles).

7. Sensitivity Analysis

This business case is considered "moderately" sensitive to changes in data assumptions. For example, "Improving engineering productivity" constitutes 17 percent of all monetary benefits, based on a 4 percent improvement in efficiency. Varying this efficiency improvement factor, plus or minus 2 percentage points, moves the payback period down to 11.5 or up to 13.5 months, respectively. This 4 percent improvement factor is considered conservative.

In addition, as shown on the Executive Summary report, the IRR, NPV, and ROI improve for each additional year of this cost-benefit analysis. For example, returns on these financial parameters on the basis of a five-year analysis period are greater than if the analysis were done on a four-year basis. The same is true for a three-year or two-year analysis.

C. Next Actions

It is recommended that management select the intranet GKB investment option within the next 30 days. The direct decision delay cost is more than $50,000 monthly in terms of postponement of benefits. [NPV of $3,019,582/ time period of analysis of five years (i.e., 60 months).] In addition, a key intangible factor, "Increasing competitive advantage," is also negatively impacted by a decision delay.

It is also recommended that this business case document should form the basis for the project management system for tracking and reporting the actual realization of benefits from whichever option selected from this business case.

Appendices

Appendix A-1

People Contributing to This Business Case Analysis

(in addition to the Business Case Team)

Name	Group	Business Case Role
Doris Andersen	Product Design	Reviewer
Lester Anzivino	Information Technology	Research: Intranet software users
Kirsten Argo	Information Technology	Reviewer
Kellie Brown	Finance and Administration	Data Contributor
Walter Cannara	Finance and Administration	Data Contributor
Geraldine Careman	Executive Staff	Reviewer
Amanda Crossman	New Product Development	Reviewer
Mike Cummington	Sales and Marketing	Research: Customer impacts
Scott Danneska	Logistics	Research: Supply chain impacts
Lenny Deal	Executive Staff	Reviewer
David DeAngeles	New Product Development	Research: Market directions
Francesca Farrell	Marketing Research	Research: Third-party citations
Martha Hanson	Engineering	Researcher: Solution drivers
Kayla Hopman	Information Technology	Researcher: Vendor due diligence
Dawn Landing	International Operations	Research: People impacts
Judy Livingston	Marketing	Research: Market
Alice Longview	Marketing	Reviewer
John Mac	Information Technology	Reviewer
Matt Mayerton	Headquarters	Reviewer
Bill Morrison	Customer Services	Reviewer: Customer impacts
Kevin Rushman	Field Operations	Reviewer
Herb Shipman	Sales	Data Contributor

(continued)

Name	Group	Business Case Role
Kevin Sumatra, Jr.	Finance and Administration	Data Contributor
Suzanne Triggerson	Accounting	Research: Financial impacts
Chris Waleski	Headquarters	Reviewer
Dorthea Wang	Headquarters	Reviewer
Yvette Waters	Product Design	Research: Evidence
Martin Watkins	Human Resources	Data Contributor, Reviewer
Yolanda Whittenberg	Human Resources	Data Contributor

Appendix A-2

Financial Results by Year

Internal Rate of Return (IRR)

Year 0	Year 1	Year 2	Year 3	Year 4	Year 5	Total
Total all costs per year:						
$900,000	$210,000	$210,000	$210,000	$210,000	$210,000	$1,950,000
Total payoff per year:						
	$1,056,037	$1,408,050	$1,408,050	$1,408,050	$1,408,050	$6,688,237
Net cash flow per year:						
−$900,000	$846,037	$1,198,050	$1,198,050	$1,198,050	$1,198,050	$4,738,237
IRR	−6%	72%	96%	106%	109%	***

Net Present Value (NPV)

Year 0	Year 1	Year 2	Year 3	Year 4	Year 5	Total
Total all costs per year:						
$900,000	$210,000	$210,000	$210,000	$210,000	$210,000	$1,950,000
Total payoff per year:						
	$1,056,037	$1,408,050	$1,408,050	$1,408,050	$1,408,050	$6,688,237
Net cash flow per year:						
$2900,000	$846,037	$1,198,050	$1,198,050	$1,198,050	$1,198,050	$4,738,237
NPV	$−118,977	$781,135	$1,599,420	$2,343,314	$3,019,582	

Return on Investment (ROI)

Year 0	Year 1	Year 2	Year 3	Year 4	Year 5	Total
Total all costs per year:						
$900,000	$210,000	$210,000	$210,000	$210,000	$210,000	$1,950,000
Total payoff per year:						
	$1,056,037	$1,408,050	$1,408,050	$1,408,050	$1,408,050	$6,688,237
Net cash flow per year:						
$−900,000	$846,037	$1,198,050	$1,198,050	$1,198,050	$1,198,050	$4,738,237
ROI	94%	114%	120%	123%	125%	

Appendix A-3

PayoffCard Profiles

(alphabetical by title)

PayoffCard Profiles

EXHIBIT A-3.1 "Increase Competitive Advantage"

FINDINGS

Better proposals and better selling new products increase our competitive advantage and thus ABC revenue and profits.

Definition:
Competitive advantage is the value-based uniqueness a firm achieves versus its competitors. Competitive advantage has "three generic strategies: cost leadership, differentiation, and focus." Ref. 1. ABC uses a differentiation strategy of creating a steady stream of innovative new products.

Business Importance:
In recent years ABC has come under increasing market pressure from highly innovative global and regional competitors. In response, ABC executives wish to improve the firm's competitive advantage and thus its revenue by launching more new products.

Solution Driver:
The intranet platform, due to quick access to a single, more accurate, unified database, allows engineers to provide faster and better response to sales needs for more competitive proposals and to design better-selling new products.

Evidence:
- "Competitive advantage is at the heart of a firm's performance in competitive markets." Ref. 2.
- "One of our key strategic goals is differentiation. We plan to achieve this goal by introducing newer, better products faster. Any ABC initiative that enables product development is likely to be an initiative that management can get behind." Ref. 3.

References:
- Refs. 1, 2: *Competitive Advantage: Creating and Sustaining Superior Performance*, Michael Porter, Free Press, New York, 1985, pp. xvi, xv.
- Ref. 3: M. Powers, CEO of ABC Corp. at the annual companywide meeting, October 2002.

Comments:

Intangible PayoffCard
Key assumption: An improvement in competitive advantage proportionally increases the firm's contribution (i.e., its operating margin). "Other factors" include contribution from internal groups such as F&A, HR, IT, and so on.

EXHIBIT A-3.2 "Increase Engineering Productivity"

FINDINGS

By increasing engineering efficiency by 4 percent, over $1 million can be saved.

Definition:
Improvement in productivity of design engineers so they have time to do more new-product designs.

Business Importance:
More productive engineers increase the opportunity to use their highly valued design skills in ways most useful to ABC Corp.

(continued)

EXHIBIT A-3.2 (Continued)

Solution Driver:
Collaborative features of an intranet solution allow for engineers to reduce
(1) training time away from the job and (2) time to acquire knowledge. The
solution also allows new hires to learn faster.

Calculations:

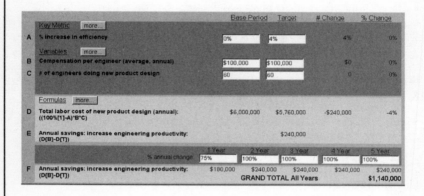

	Key Metric more...	Base Period	Target	# Change	% Change
A	% increase in efficiency	0%	4%	4%	0%
	Variables more...				
B	Compensation per engineer (average, annual)	$100,000	$100,000	$0	0%
C	# of engineers doing new product design	60	60	0	0%
	Formulas more...				
D	Total labor cost of new product design (annual): ((100%[1]-A)*B*C)	$6,000,000	$5,760,000	-$240,000	-4%
E	Annual savings: increase engineering productivity: (D[B]-D[T])		$240,000		

		1 Year	2 Year	3 Year	4 Year	5 Year
	% annual change	75%	100%	100%	100%	100%
F	Annual savings: increase engineering productivity: (D[B]-D[T])	$180,000	$240,000	$240,000	$240,000	$240,000
	GRAND TOTAL All Years					$1,140,000

Evidence:
- "The valuation of companies has changed . . . , putting a-higher value on
  . . . knowledge, competence, brands, and systems. . . . It is the . . .
  people alone—the 'human capital'—who build the value." Ref. 1.
- "Efficiency of engineers increases significantly when they are given
  access to collaborative tools that make their jobs easier to learn and
  do." Ref. 2.

References:
- Ref. 1: *The Human Value of the Enterprise: Valuing PEOPLE as Assets—
  Monitoring, Measuring, Managing*, Andrew Mayo, 2001, p. 2.
- Ref. 2: 2001: *Survey of Mid-Sized Engineering Firms*, ABC Staff Survey,
  2002, Fall p. 22.

Notes:
"% increase in efficiency" in calculations derived from the following
assumptions: (1) Current training costs can be cut by 25 percent from avg. of
training 10 engineers/yr @ $10,000 per engineer; (2) engineers can save an
avg. of 1 hour/access/month per engineer.

EXHIBIT A-3.3 "Increase Enterprise Flexibility"

FINDINGS

The ability to more quickly respond to market changes will yield an additional $600,000 savings.

Definition:
Ability of organizations to quickly and economically change strategy, structure, and/or resources in response to market changes. ABC executives' goal is to flexibly respond to new market developments.

Business:
Uncommon business flexibility is a critical success factor for organizations facing major changes in demand, supply, market reach, customer expectations, entry of new competitors, and so on.

Solution Driver:
The intranet platform will allow engineers instant worldwide access to higher-quality and more frequently updated information, thereby accelerating new-product creation more closely attuned to market needs.

Calculations:

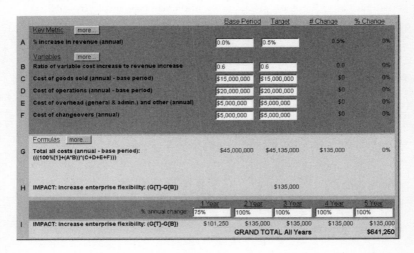

		Base Period	Target	# Change	% Change
	Key Metric more...				
A	% increase in revenue (annual)	0.0%	0.5%	0.5%	0%
	Variables more...				
B	Ratio of variable cost increase to revenue increase	0.6	0.6	0.0	0%
C	Cost of goods sold (annual - base period)	$15,000,000	$15,000,000	$0	0%
D	Cost of operations (annual - base period)	$20,000,000	$20,000,000	$0	0%
E	Cost of overhead (general & admin.) and other (annual)	$5,000,000	$5,000,000	$0	0%
F	Cost of changeovers (annual)	$5,000,000	$5,000,000	$0	0%
	Formulas more...				
G	Total all costs (annual - base period): (((100%*[1]+(A*B))*(C+D+E+F)))	$45,000,000	$45,135,000	$135,000	0%
H	IMPACT: increase enterprise flexibility: (G{T}-G{B})		$135,000		

		1 Year	2 Year	3 Year	4 Year	5 Year
	% annual change:	75%	100%	100%	100%	100%
I	IMPACT: increase enterprise flexibility: (G{T}-G{B})	$101,250	$135,000	$135,000	$135,000	$135,000
			GRAND TOTAL All Years			**$641,250**

Evidence:
- "To be industry leaders, they must be adaptive, flexible, and quick to respond to change." Ref. 1.

(continued)

EXHIBIT A-3.3 (Continued)

- ". . . an entire organization is an ongoing balancing act (of) . . . setting direction, linking processes and systems and making CONSTANT adjustments." Ref. 2.
- "As markets change, so too must an engineering firm quickly adjust or be left behind as an also-ran. Technology systems are critical for these firms to adapt to new market needs." Ref. 3.

References:
- Refs. 1, 2: *The Power of Alignment*, George Labovitz & Victor Rosansky, 1997, pp. 14, 15.
- Ref. 3: *Critical Success Factors for Engineering Firms in the New Economy*, S. Ericks, ABC research staff, 2001, p. 36.

EXHIBIT A-3.4   "Increase Profit via GKB Cost Savings"

FINDINGS

An additional $3.9 million profit contribution will be realized from all cost savings payoff areas outlined in this business case.

Definition:
Cost savings at ABC Corp. which improve profits include (1) reducing engineering, content management, sales, and IS labor costs and (2) decreasing the use of communication and print materials.

Business Importance:
Bottom-line cost savings are a crucial metric for measuring the effectiveness of management actions, as well as for reporting business results to both internal and external stakeholders.

Solution Driver:
The following intranet-based GKB features contribute to ABC cost savings: common look and feel, consistency of operation, unified view, low skill demands on users, ease of learning, and personal computer independence.

Evidence:
- "Engineering firms are notorious for having some of the highest cost structures in the world. Prime areas for shaving costs include: labor and goods/services." Ref. 1.

Reference:
- Ref. 1: *How ABC Corp. Can Thrive in an Increasingly Competitive Landscape*, B. Keller, COO, ABC Corp., Employee Meeting, Jan. 8, 2002.

Comments:
Five payoff areas contribute to this PayoffCard: "Reduce customer turnover," "Reduce engineering turnover," "Increase engineering productivity," "Reduce content manager skill requirements," "Reduce communications and print material costs," and "Reduce TCO." All calculations for these payoff areas are contained on their individual PayoffCards.

EXHIBIT A-3.5 "Make Better New Product Decisions"

FINDINGS

More timely and accurate new-product decisions will bring in an additional $950,000.

Definition:
Senior management has a greater likelihood of choosing the most profitable new products to launch from a variety of candidates.

Business Importance:
An organization's success is, ultimately, the sum total of the impact of its series of management decisions. This is especially true of a firm such as ABC that uses product innovation as a key competitive differentiator.

Solution Driver:
Due to the comprehensive, accurate, and easily accessible nature of the GKB, managers can better assess the validity and viability of proposed new-product designs.

Calculations:

		Base Period	Target	# Change	% Change
	Key Metric more...				
A	# of new product decisions made (annual)	4	4	0	0%
	Variables more...				
B	Payoff per new product decision from current decision process (annual)	$3,000,000	$3,000,000	$0	0%
C	% of new product decisions to be improved	0%	5%	5%	0%
D	Extra payoff per new product decision: more timely decisions	$500,000	$500,000	$0	0%
E	Extra payoff per new product decision: more accurate decisions	$500,000	$500,000	$0	0%
	Formulas more...				
F	Payoff from new prod. decisions made with current decision process (annual): (A*B)	$12,000,000	$12,000,000	$0	0%
G	Payoffs from better new product decisions (annual): (C*A)*(D+E)	$0	$200,000	$200,000	0%
H	Total payoffs from better new product decisions: (F+G)	$12,000,000	$12,200,000	$200,000	2%
I	Annual Savings: make better new product decisions: (F(B)-F(B))+(G(B)-G(B))+(H(T)-H(B))		$200,000		

		1 Year	2 Year	3 Year	4 Year	5 Year
	% annual change:	75%	100%	100%	100%	100%
J	Annual Savings: make better new product decisions: (F(B)-F(B))+(G(B)-G(B))+(H(T)-H(B))	$150,000	$200,000	$200,000	$200,000	$200,000
			GRAND TOTAL All Years			$950,000

(continued)

EXHIBIT A-3.5 (Continued)

Evidence:

- "Decision making is arguably the most important job of the senior executive and one of the easiest to get wrong." Ref. 1.
- "In our survey, those firms that were able to utilize a global database of product information were able to improve decision making (e.g., more accurate and more timely decisions) by almost 25%." Ref. 2.

References:

- Ref. 1: "What You Don't Know about Making Decisions," David Garvin & Michael Roberto, *Harvard Business Review*, September 2001, p. 108.
- Ref. 2: 2001: *Survey of Mid-Sized Engineering Firms*, ABC Research Group, Fall 2001, p. 18.

EXHIBIT A-3.6 "Reduce Communication and Print Material Costs"

FINDINGS

A lesser consumption of services and supplies adds up to a savings of over $300,000.

Definition:
A decrease in the consumption of services and supplies related to global product design. Examples are (1) communication: phone, fax, overnight mail, and (2) print materials: paper, binding costs of engineering drawings and specs.

Business Importance:
The reduced cost of these goods and services contributes directly to improved profits.

Solution Driver:
Many pieces of physical information are available in soft copy via the GKB, thus decreasing communications, mailing, and print materials costs.

Calculations:

		Base Period	Target	# Change	% Change
	Key Metric more...				
A	% decrease in communications costs	0%	20%	20%	0%
	Variables more...				
B	Communications costs (annual)	$50,000	$50,000	$0	0%
C	% decrease in print materials costs	0%	50%	50%	0%
D	Print materials costs (annual)	$120,000	$120,000	$0	0%
	Formulas more...				
E	Total savings on communications and print materials costs (annual): (F+G)	$170,000	$100,000	-$70,000	-41%
F	Total communications costs (annual): ((100%[1]-A)*B)	$50,000	$40,000	-$10,000	-20%
G	Total print materials costs: ((100%[1]-C)*D)	$120,000	$60,000	-$60,000	-50%
H	Annual savings: reduce commun. and print materials costs: (E(B)-E(T))		$70,000		

		1 Year	2 Year	3 Year	4 Year	5 Year
	% annual change	75%	100%	100%	100%	100%
I	Annual savings: reduce commun. and print materials costs: (E(B)-E(T))	$52,500	$70,000	$70,000	$70,000	$70,000
			GRAND TOTAL All Years			$332,500

Evidence:
- "Those firms that wisely utilize intranet-based systems can lower costs of communications and print materials by at least 20%." Ref. 1.

Reference:
- Ref. 1: *How ABC Corp. Can Thrive in an Increasingly Competitive Landscape*, B. Keller, COO, ABC Corp. Employee Meeting, Jan. 8, 2000, p. 7.

EXHIBIT A-3.7 "Reduce Content Manager Skill Requirements"

FINDINGS

The GKB's intranet-based architecture can be effectively used by lesser-skilled content managers at compensation levels 15 percent below those being used today, which will lower labor costs by over $250,000.

Definition:
Decrease the skill level required for content managers to be effective.

(continued)

EXHIBIT A-3.7 (Continued)

Business Importance:

For ABC, content management historically has been an expensive, labor-intensive process. Being able to use lower cost employees, while still maintaining quality, is highly desirable.

Solution Driver:

Via an intranet architecture, content creation and maintenance can be simplified, thus enabling lesser-skilled (and more readily available in the labor market) content managers to be used.

Calculations:

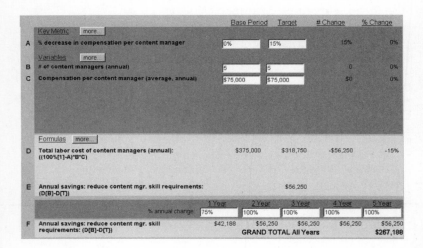

	Key Metric more...	Base Period	Target	# Change	% Change
A	% decrease in compensation per content manager	0%	15%	15%	0%
	Variables more...				
B	# of content managers (annual)	5	5	0	0%
C	Compensation per content manager (average, annual)	$75,000	$75,000	$0	0%

	Formulas more...				
D	Total labor cost of content managers (annual): ((100%[1]-A)*B*C)	$375,000	$318,750	-$56,250	-15%
E	Annual savings: reduce content mgr. skill requirements: (D(B)-D(T))		$56,250		

		1 Year	2 Year	3 Year	4 Year	5 Year
	% annual change:	75%	100%	100%	100%	100%
F	Annual savings: reduce content mgr. skill requirements: (D(B)-D(T))	$42,188	$56,250	$56,250	$56,250	$56,250
		GRAND TOTAL All Years				$267,188

Evidence:
- ". . . there has evolved a large pool of highly qualified managers skilled in Internet-based data retrieval who can be hired at up to 30% of the cost of traditional content managers." Ref. 1.

Reference:
- Ref. 1: Interview with C. Haines, ABC Corp. HR Manager Aug. 28, 2002.

EXHIBIT A-3.8 "Reduce Customer Turnover"

FINDINGS

Faster, better new products cut customer turnover by 1 percentage point; saves $855,000.

Definition:

Customer turnover: Ratio of those who leave during a given period of time to total customers at the beginning.

Business Importance:

Losing customers is not only expensive from a cost and profit margin point of view, but also risks negatively impacting the employees' morale and ABC's market image.

Solution Driver:

GKB enables product design engineers to respond faster to proposal requests. The proposals can be sent faster to existing customers with demanding time frames, who then experience "great service" that assists retention. Better new products with high appeal to existing customers can also be developed quickly.

Calculations:

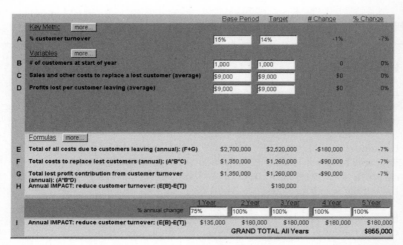

		Base Period	Target	# Change	% Change
	Key Metric more...				
A	% customer turnover	15%	14%	-1%	-7%
	Variables more...				
B	# of customers at start of year	1,000	1,000	0	0%
C	Sales and other costs to replace a lost customer (average)	$9,000	$9,000	$0	0%
D	Profits lost per customer leaving (average)	$9,000	$9,000	$0	0%
	Formulas more...				
E	Total of all costs due to customers leaving (annual): (F+G)	$2,700,000	$2,520,000	-$180,000	-7%
F	Total costs to replace lost customers (annual): (A*B*C)	$1,350,000	$1,260,000	-$90,000	-7%
G	Total lost profit contribution from customer turnover (annual): (A*B*D)	$1,350,000	$1,260,000	-$90,000	-7%
H	Annual IMPACT: reduce customer turnover: (E(B)-E(T))		$180,000		

		1 Year	2 Year	3 Year	4 Year	5 Year
	% annual change	75%	100%	100%	100%	100%
I	Annual IMPACT: reduce customer turnover: (E(B)-E(T))	$135,000	$180,000	$180,000	$180,000	$180,000
			GRAND TOTAL All Years			$855,000

(continued)

EXHIBIT A-3.8 (Continued)

Evidence:
- "An increase in customer retention rates of 5 percent increases profits by 25% to 95%." Ref. 1.
- "Decreasing customer turnover is one of the effective ways for us to increase profits." Ref. 2.
- ". . . research . . . by James Heskett at the Harvard Business School . . . holds that the endgame of business is growth and profit, which are tied to the ability . . . to create customer loyalty & retention." Ref. 3.

References:
- Ref. 1: *Loyalty Rules, How Today's Leaders Build Lasting Relationships*, F. F. Reichheld, 2001, p. 10.
- Ref. 2: Ron Black, CEO ABC Corp. at annual companywide meeting, October 2002.
- Ref. 3. *The Power of Alignment*, George Labovitz & Victor Rosansky, 1997, p. 15.

Notes:
"Cost to replace each customer leaving" includes expenses to find a replacement customer and the annual profit contribution lost from sales the departed customer did not generate.

EXHIBIT A-3.9 "Reduce Engineer Turnover"

FINDINGS

Engineers will experience higher productivity and morale due to the GKB, which will lead to a decrease of 4 percentage points in turnover, thus saving over $1 million.

Definition:
Engineer turnover is the ratio of product design engineers leaving a company in a given period of time to total product design engineers at the beginning of that period.

Business Importance:
Cutting the rate of turnover of product design engineers not only saves the cost of recruiting, hiring, and training replacements, but also reduces the drain of key design engineers whose senior level of experience is needed for innovative new-product designs.

Solution Driver:
The existence of an innovative, state-of-the-art GKB enhances the productivity and morale of the engineering staff.

Calculations:

Key Metric	more		Base Period	Target	# Change	% Change
A	% engineer turnover (annual)		15%	11%	-4%	-27%
	Variables	more				
B	Hiring costs per new engineer		$20,000	$20,000	$0	0%
C	Training costs per new engineer		$20,000	$20,000	$0	0%
D	Learning curve costs per new engineer		$10,000	$10,000	$0	0%
E	Compensation per new engineer (average, annual)		$80,000	$80,000	$0	0%
F	Job vacancy duration (months)		6	6	0	0%
G	# of engineers at start of year		60	60	0	0%
	Formulas	more				
H	Total engineer turnover costs (annual): (((B+C+D)+(E*(F\12[12])))*I)		$810,000	$594,000	-$216,000	-27%
I	Engineers needed to fill vacancies from turnover (annual): (A*G)		9	7	-2	-27%
J	Annual savings: reduce engineer turnover: (H(B)-H(T))			$216,000		

		1 Year	2 Year	3 Year	4 Year	5 Year
	% annual change	75%	100%	100%	100%	100%
K	Annual savings: reduce engineer turnover: (H(B)-H(T))	$162,000	$216,000	$216,000	$216,000	$216,000
			GRAND TOTAL All Years			$1,026,000

Evidence:
- "It takes a typical Silicon Valley firm only two years to lose half its employees." Ref. 1.
- "The costs to replace a top-notch engineer (to include: hiring, training, learning curve costs, etc.) can far exceed most of the other avoidable costs of an enterprise." Ref. 2.

References:
- Ref. 1: Loyalty Rules, *How Today's Leaders Build Lasting Relationships*, F. F. Reichheld, 2001, p. 1.
- Ref. 2: *Critical Success Factors for Engineering Firms in the New Economy*, S. Ericks, ABC research staff, 2001, p. 15.

EXHIBIT A-3.10 "Reduce Risk of GKB Project Failure"

FINDINGS

Proven GKB architecture combined with experienced ABC personnel significantly reduces the likelihood of project problems.

Definition:
Project failure is (1) the inability to implement the project on time and on budget or (2) the project never getting implemented. Risk is defined in terms of the likelihood of this failure happening as well as its magnitude.

(continued)

EXHIBIT A-3.10 (Continued)

Business Importance:
Reducing risk is especially important since penalties of failure are high:
(1) Project funds are lost, (2) opportunity costs are significant (a failed GKB
could threaten ABC's revenue goals), and (3) there is a negative impact on
the morale of hard-to-replace engineers.

Solution Driver
ABC has a higher degree of technical skills for an intranet project option
than a client-server option. In addition, the proven success of the intranet
GKB application in similar companies helps reduce the risk of engineers not
actively embracing the system.

Evidence:
- "A big impact on the success of a knowledge repository project is the
  reliability of the technical architecture and the availability of skilled
  technical personnel." Ref. 1.

References:
- Ref. 1: "How to Make Sure That Knowledge Repository Projects Succeed,"
  David Delaney, ABC IT Advisor, white paper Sept. 30, 2002. *Data
  Warehousing Journal*, June 2001, p. 20.

Notes:
Intangible PayoffCard.

EXHIBIT A-3.11 "Reduce Risk of Security Breaches"

FINDINGS

A 20 percent decrease in security breaches saves almost $500,000.

Definition:
Security breaches include events and activities such as virus attacks, hacker
penetration, and competitive espionage. "Reducing the risk" means
decreasing the frequency as well as the severity of the occurrences.

Business Importance:
Consequences of security breaches include loss of intellectual property,
productivity penalties from the reduction of the uptime reliability of the
GKB, as well as the cost to find the breach and repair it.

Solution Driver:

The architectural design of the GKB inherently provides an unusually high level of security protection.

Calculations:

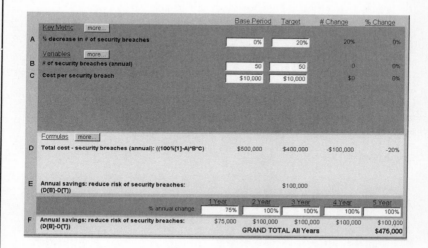

Evidence:

- "We believe that security breaches of all types cost enterprises in excess of $70 billion per year. In other terms, finding, locating and fixing security breaches can add as much as 1% to an enterprise's already stretched IT budget." Ref. 1.

Reference:

- Ref. 1: *The High Cost of Overlooking Security*, interview with J. Prince, Discovery Research Group, Oct. 2, 2002.

EXHIBIT A-3.12 "Reduce Total Cost of Ownership"

FINDINGS

Lower maintenance and expansion costs of an intranet-based GKB save over $1 million in total cost of ownership (TCO) of systems and software.

(continued)

EXHIBIT A-3.12 (Continued)

Definition:
Total cost of ownership of the GKB includes hardware, software, communications, training, and other related IT support costs that are incurred over its lifetime.

Business Importance:
Understanding and realizing a lower GKB TCO will save ABC money as well as reduce its reliance on hard-to-find, geographically dispersed technical personnel.

Solution Driver:
Inherent in the architectural design, the cost is less to maintain or expand one master GKB than multiple, dispersed product design databases, such as now exist with ABC's client-server knowledge bases.

Calculations:

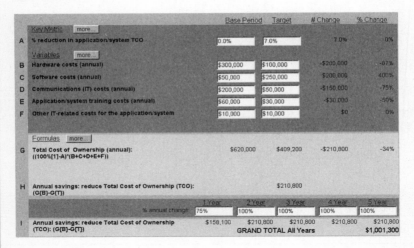

		Base Period	Target	# Change	% Change
	Key Metric more...				
A	% reduction in application/system TCO	0.0%	7.0%	7.0%	0%
	Variables more...				
B	Hardware costs (annual)	$300,000	$100,000	-$200,000	-67%
C	Software costs (annual)	$50,000	$250,000	$200,000	400%
D	Communications (IT) costs (annual)	$200,000	$50,000	-$150,000	-75%
E	Application/system training costs (annual)	$60,000	$30,000	-$30,000	-50%
F	Other IT-related costs for the application/system	$10,000	$10,000	$0	0%
	Formulas more...				
G	Total Cost of Ownership (annual): ((100%-[1]-A)*(B+C+D+E+F))		$620,000	$409,200	-$210,800	-34%
H	Annual savings: reduce Total Cost of Ownership (TCO): (G(B)-G(T))			$210,800		

		1 Year	2 Year	3 Year	4 Year	5 Year
	% annual change:	75%	100%	100%	100%	100%
I	Annual savings: reduce Total Cost of Ownership (TCO): (G(B)-G(T))	$158,100	$210,800	$210,800	$210,800	$210,800
			GRAND TOTAL All Years			**$1,001,300**

Evidence:
- "Well-managed worldwide corporate intranet-based databases have at least 20% less TCO than comparable client-server systems." Ref. 1.

Reference:
- Ref. 1: *Why Use an Intranet-Based Platform?*, Interview with D. Johnson, ML Research, Nov. 4, 2002

Appendix A-4

Business Case Analysis Process Used

In order to accurately, yet quickly, research, develop, and communicate this business case, the team used the VALUE-on-Demand methodology outlined in the book, *Making Technology Investments Profitable: ROI Road Map from Business Case to Value Realization (Second Edition),* by Jack M. Keen, John Wiley & Sons, Hoboken, New Jersey, 2011. This process, data flow, description of tools, and activities of the business case team are outlined in Exhibit A-4.1.

The Process

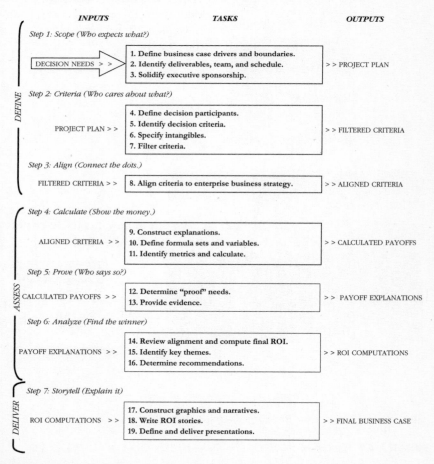

EXHIBIT A-4.1 Seven-Step Method for Building Successful Business Cases

Select a Business Case Project

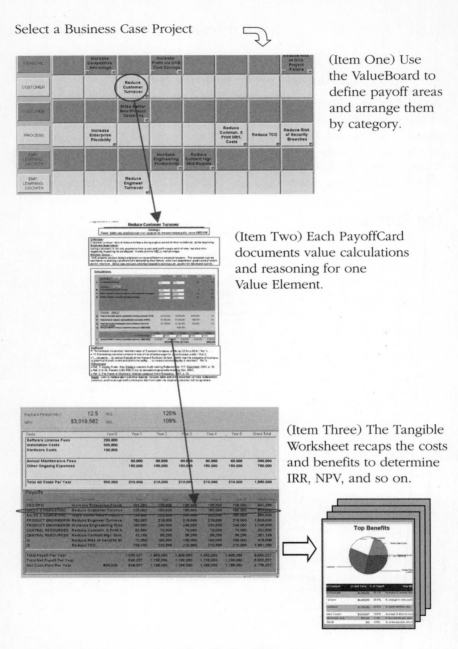

(Item One) Use the ValueBoard to define payoff areas and arrange them by category.

(Item Two) Each PayoffCard documents value calculations and reasoning for one Value Element.

(Item Three) The Tangible Worksheet recaps the costs and benefits to determine IRR, NPV, and so on.

(Item Four) Executive Reports visually show findings.

EXHIBIT A-4.2 Data Flow for VALUE-on-Demand Business Case Development

Data Flow

Exhibit A-4.2 shows how value calculation data flow from the initial identification of a payoff area—shown as a value element on the ValueBoard (Item One)—onto a PayoffCard, which recaps the definition, rationale, calculations, and evidence related to that value element. From there the Tangibles Worksheet (Item Three) is constructed, showing the IRR, NPV, ROI, and payback period. From that information, the executive and detail reports are created for the business case document.

Description of Tools

ValueBoard: A visual mapping business-to-technology road map that helps maximize the alignment between the investment and business goals of the firm.

PayoffCard: A benefit profile method of organization that helps focus on the contribution of a specific payoff area.

Value Ladder: A visual tool for exploring the cause-and-effect relationships among specific payoff areas addressed by the business case.

Tangibles Worksheet: A structured analysis and documentation of all monetary factors.

Executive Report: A summary of key findings of importance to the decision team.

Activities of the Business Case Team

- After the business case team was appointed by executive management, it had a one-day organization and brainstorming session. The purpose of the meeting was to scope (Step 1), identify criteria (Step 2), and align (Step 3).
- During this session the team identified 30 to 40 management concerns (cost and benefit issues) to help evaluate the proposed systems investment, and then placed them on the ValueBoard.
- These first-pass 30 to 40 management concerns on the ValueBoard were then culled down to the top 12 for inclusion in the final cost-benefit analysis (Item One in Exhibit A-4.2). This was done after interviewing executives, managers, and end users as well as researching secondary research sources. Appendix A-1 lists major contributors.
- Supporting data were then researched (Step 4—calculate) for the definition, business importance, solution drivers, and evidence/support

(Step 5—prove) of each of the 12 key payoff areas, and then they were documented on the PayoffCards (Item Two in Exhibit A-4.2).

- Formula sets were created for the key issues that could have quantifiable benefits.
- Data were gathered and applied to the calculations for the final end analysis of options (Step 6—analyze). The Tangibles Worksheet (Item Three in Exhibit A-4.2) and the Executive Reports (Item Four) showed the results.
- Validation of the analysis was conducted with the business case team executive sponsor as well as with people identified in Appendix A-1. After this was completed, the final GKB business case was written and presented to the decision team (Step 7—storytell).

Glossary

Base period The foundation period from which the ROI analysis is computed. This is often the status quo in many business cases. Considered as "Year 0" by the VALUE-on-Demand ROI methodology. The formulas calculate the differences between the base period and the target period and assign this value to the period Year 1.

Business case An analysis describing the business reasons *why* specific investment options should or should not be selected. A business case identifies the most relevant decision factors associated with a proposed investment, assesses their likelihood, and computes their value. Value includes both quantifiable and nonquantifiable considerations. The findings of the business case are then presented to the decision makers for their selection or rejection of the-recommendations developed by the business case authors. The premise of a business case is that the investment option with-the best cost-benefit payoff, related to all alternatives, should be selected. Also called "cost-benefit analysis."

Cash flow Net value of the ongoing inflows and outflows of cash for each period of the analysis. Does *not* include initial investment costs. "Net cash flow," which is defined in this glossary, *does* include initial investment costs.

Cost-benefit analysis See "Business case."

Cost elements Items of cost, which are included in the VALUE-on-Demand ROI methodology.

Decision criteria Factors by which the investment options will be evaluated by the decision team. Often called "benefits," "payoff areas," "value elements," or "risks" when used in the context of a business case.

Decision participants Individuals who will influence, recommend, or make the buying decision. As a group, they are often called the "decision team."

Decision team   The group of decision participants involved in the analysis and final selection of the investment under consideration.

Discounted cash flow (DCF)   See "Internal rate of return."

Discounted rate of return   See "Internal rate of return."

Expenses, ongoing   Costs associated with an investment option, which reoccur across multiple periods used in the ROI analysis.

Financial formula   Common indicator of financial attractiveness of an investment option. Key financial formulas are internal rate of return (IRR), net present value (NPV), payback period (PP), and return on investment (ROI). Often organizations use two or more of these financial formulas. Also, an enterprise may develop its own financial calculations to supplement or even substitute for these four typical financial formulas used in VALUE-on-Demand.

Grand total   The sum of all annual periods included in the ROI analysis.

Hurdle rate   The minimally acceptable financial results for a given financial calculation. For example, "the payback period must be four years or less."

Intangible   A Value Element that is *not* being expressed in monetary terms for the project under consideration. Value Elements can often be changed from tangible to intangible (or vice versa) depending upon the decision team's perspective. Intangibles are sometimes called "soft benefits."

Internal rate of return (IRR)   That rate of return that makes equivalent the positive cash flow from savings with the negative cash flow created by the investment itself. Stated another way, IRR is the discount rate at which the cash inflows are exactly equal to the cash outflows. Stated in financial terms, IRR is the interest rate at which the present value of cash inflows equals the present value of cash outflows. Stated another way, the combined discounted cash flow (DCF) equals zero. (Book reference: *Techniques of Financial Analysis*, by Eric Helfert.)

Investment, initial   Costs associated with acquiring and implementing a solution. For example, software license fees.

IRR   See "Internal rate of return."

Key metric   The primary variable that the user could change that would most impact the grand total calculated in a PayoffCard. The key metric may also be the variable that is most controllable by management. Thus, for example, "fuel costs" for an airline, while a significant variable impacting profitability, might not be a key metric for a profitability calculation. However, "revenue per seat mile" might be the key metric, since airline management can most influence this variable.

Level Roughly analogous to organizational levels in an enterprise. A level is the name given to any one of the six or so rows on a ValueBoard. Each level defines a different stakeholder group. Typically Level 1 (the top row) represents the point of view of the final decision makers (often senior management). The second level represents those stakeholders who often report to Level 1 managers. In general, levels closest to the top of the ValueBoard represent managers and staff more senior than those represented in levels further down the ValueBoard.

Metric A measurement used to guage a quantifiable aspect of a firm's performance. It consists of a variable and a variable value.

Net cash flow Net value of the inflows and outflows of cash for each period of the analysis, including initial investment costs. Differs from "cash flow" in that net cash flow includes initial investment costs.

Net present value (NPV) "Present value" is the value today of a future amount of cash invested at a specified interest rate. For example, the present value of $110 received a year from now, assuming 10 percent interest, is $100. In other words, $100 today is equivalent to $110 a year from now, providing the money can be invested successfully at 10 percent interest per year. Net present value is defined as the present value of all future cash flows, at a given interest rate.

NPV See "Net present value."

Option An investment being evaluated for a specific ROI analysis project.

Payback period (PP) Payback period is defined as the period of time needed to recover the investment for the option being evaluated. The formula for the payback period is not as standardized as the IRR and NPV formulas. A typical payback period algorithm might be:

1. If the initial investment is less than or equal to the total net payoff for Year 1, then the payback period is computed by dividing the initial investment by the total net payoff for Year 1. That percentage is then

multiplied by 12 to give the number of months for the initial investment to equal the net payoff. This answer will be 12.0 months or less.

2. If the initial investment is greater than the total net payoff for Year 1,
   then VoD tests to see if the initial investment is less than or equal to
   the cumulative total net payoff for Year 1 + Year 2. If yes, then the
   PP is calculated as 12 months plus the number of months between
   Month 13 and Month 24 where the initial investment equals the
   cumulative value of total net payoff for Year 1 + Year 2. This answer
   will be between 12.1 and 24.0 months.

3. If the initial investment is greater than the cumulative total net payoff
   for Year 1 + Year 2, then make a similar test as outlined in paragraph
   2 to see if the breakeven is within Year 3. If yes, then the calculations
   are similar to paragraph 2, except using total net payoff for Year 1 +
   Year 2 + Year 3. The answer will be between 24.1 and 36.0 months.

Tests and calculations similar to paragraph 3 above are made to see if the
breakeven is within Year 4 or Year 5 and so on.

Payoff area   See "Value Element."

PayoffCard   A concise collection of factors that describe, quantify, and
justify the value of a specific management issue, for an investment option
under consideration. In the VALUE-on-Demand ROI methodology terms,
a PayoffCard is a summary of all value-related factors for a given Value
Element.

PayoffCards typically have three uses:

1. To **define and document** specific factors that are to be included
   in the value ROI analysis being created
2. To **communicate** these factors, in a succinct format, to decision
   participants
3. To be **reapplied** for future business cases, if relevant

PP   See "Payback period."

Position   Location on the ValueBoard of a specific Value Element. For
example, Position 1–2 is at the intersection of the first level and second
column. Position 4–8 is at the intersection of the fourth level and
eighth column.

Present value   See "Net present value."

Project template An ROI model that has been predeveloped as a standard starting point for developing business cases for specific types of investment opportunities. For example, a project template might be created for all users who wish to develop a business case for customer relationship management (CRM) applications on the Internet. Users wishing to create an ROI analysis for a specific CRM could begin with the CRM Project Template and then modify it to account for the specifics of the investment option being considered. Using a project template, with its predefined Value Elements, calculations, and rationale, can help guide a user who perhaps has less time or less experience in developing business cases of the type included in the project template.

Return on investment (ROI) In the context of VALUE-on-Demand, ROI is used in two ways:

1. As a generic term meaning an investment analysis typically identified as a business case. When used in this context, "ROI" is a shortened version of the expression "ROI analysis."
2. As a specific method of calculation related to the net financial impact of a set of costs and benefits. Unlike NPV, IRR, and payback period, which use formulas generally agreed to by industry, ROI is calculated in different ways by different organizations. The VALUE-on-Demand method uses the calculation where the ROI numerator is the average annual value of the total net benefits less expenses for the total period being analyzed. The denominator is the total initial investment. Specifically, in VALUE-on-Demand terminology for a five-year analysis, the numerator of the ROI formula is the grand total of the total net cash flow per year divided by 5. The denominator is the total of all costs per year for Year 0.

Solution Drivers The characteristics of the solution provided by-the investment being analyzed which helps make possible the payoff described in the calculation section of the PayoffCard.

Stakeholder A person, or group of persons, who has a vested interest in the impact of the investment being considered. Typically stakeholders are the evaluators, recommenders, and decision makers of the investment under consideration, or future users of the investment.

Tangible The characteristic of a Value Element that indicates that its contribution to the ROI analysis can be expressed and measured on a monetary basis. For example, "Reduce expenses by $50,000" is a tangible Value Element because it has a specific monetary basis. A Value Element called "Improve profits" is tangible only if monetary "profits" generated by the investment under consideration can be calculated. Otherwise it is considered intangible.

Tangibles Worksheet   A VALUE-on-Demand ROI methodology screen and report that recaps the specific monetary expenses and benefits of an investment option. The Tangibles Worksheet shows four financial formula results of ROI, NPV, IRR, and payback period.

Tangibility   The extent that a Value Element can be quantified in monetary terms for a given ROI analysis. Value Elements are either tangible (i.e., a monetary value is currently being assigned) or intangible (a monetary value is not currently being assigned).

Target period   Value of a variable or formula by the end of Year 1.

Total net payoff per year   The ongoing net value of payoffs less ongoing expenses for a year shown, *including* Year zero.

Total payoff per year   The ongoing net value of payoffs less ongoing expenses for a year shown. *Excludes* Year zero.

ValueBoard   A visual mapping tool within the VALUE-on-Demand ROI methodology for improving the quality of the business case. The ValueBoard enhances the strength of the ROI analysis by visually signaling if the Value Elements at different levels of the organization are appropriately aligned, and if they have a strong appeal for each different type of decision team member crucial to the investment decision for which the business case is being constructed.

The ValueBoard show two types of crucial relationships between payoff opportunities and investment functionality that will make the payoff possible:

- *Who cares about what?*   This is the link of potential payoff areas to the interests of different types of decision participants involved in the investment decision. A CEO concerned with enterprise strategy and operations is more likely interested in different types of benefits than an accounting manager responsible for invoicing customers.
- *What causes what?*   This is the cause-and-effect link between pay-offs of interest and different types of stakeholders. For example, the billing manager may be excited about reducing invoice errors, but the CEO is not. However, if fewer invoice errors could improve customer satisfaction, thereby increasing repeat sales and thus enterprise profits, then the CEO might be extremely interested. The visual layout of the ValueBoard clarifies these key cause-and-effect linkages.

Value Element   A VALUE-on-Demand ROI methodology term representing a business issue of high concern to management. When this issue is profiled from a value-focused point of view in the VALUE-on-Demand ROI methodology, it is called a Value Element. Examples include "Reduce employee turnover," "Increase customer satisfaction," and "Improve labor productivity." Value Elements may be categorized as either "universal" or "project." Also called a "payoff area" or "benefit" when used in the business case."

Value Ladder   A graphical depiction of the cause-and-effect relationship between an investment option's features and/or functions and the objectives and the business results of an enterprise. More specifically, a Value Ladder is the name given to the relationship between two or more Value Elements. For example, a Value Element called "Increase labor productivity" could be defined as *making possible* (or *driving*) a higher-level Value Element called "Improve employee morale." This, in turn, could drive a higher-level payoff called "Reduce employee turnover." This series of three cause-and-effect Value Elements is called a Value Ladder, since each Value Element either drives or is driven by another.

Values   Quantities that are assigned to variables used within formulas. Also called "variable values" or "metrics."

Variable   An entity used as a component for calculating the results of a formula. A variable's value is the quantity chosen to represent the worth of that variable. Formulas, by definition, are a set of one or more variables. Variables are often called "metrics."

Variable values   Quantities that are assigned by the user to variables used within formulas. Sometimes called "values" or "metrics."

Bibliography

Bernstein, Peter L. (1998). *Against the Gods—The Remarkable Story of Risk*. New York: John Wiley & Sons.

Blond, Neil C., et al. (1994). *Blond's Evidence*. New York: Sulzburger & Graham Publishing.

Drucker, Peter F. (2002). *Managing in the Next Society*. New York: Truman Talley Books.

Friedlob, George, & Plewa, Jr., Franklin. (1996). *Understanding Return on Investment*. New York: John Wiley & Sons.

Goldberg, Natalie. (1986). *Writing Down the Bones*. Boston: Shambhala Publications.

Hammond, John S., Keeney, Ralph L., & Raiffa, Howard. (1999). *Smart Choices—A Practical Guide to Making Better Decisions*. Boston: Harvard Business School Press.

Harvard Business School Press. (2001). *Harvard Business Review on Decision Making*. Boston: Harvard Business School Publishing.

Haskins, Mark E., & Makela, Benjamin. (1997). *The CFO Handbook* (rev. ed.). New York: McGraw-Hill.

Hayashi, Alden (2001). *When to Trust Your Gut*. Boston: Harvard Business Review.

Helfert, Erich A. (1987). *Techniques of Financial Analysis*. New York: Richard D. Irwin.

Helfert, Erich A. (2001). *Financial Analysis Tools and Techniques— A Guide for Managers*. New York: McGraw-Hill.

Heller, Robert. (1998). *Making Decisions*. New York: DK Publishing.

Horn, Robert E. (1989). *Mapping Hypertext: Analysis, Linkages and Displays of Knowledge for Next Generation of On-Line Text and Graphics*. Lexington, MA: The Lexington Institute.

Horn, Robert E. (1998). *Visual Language: Global Communciations for the 21st Century*. Brainbridge Island, WA: MacroVU, Inc.

Kaplan, Robert S., & Norton, David P. (1996). *The Balanced Scorecard: Translating Strategy into Action*. Boston: Harvard Business School Press.

Kaplan, Robert S., & Norton, David P. (2001). *The Strategy-Focused Organization: How Balanced Scorecard Companies Thrive in the New Business Environment*. Boston: Harvard Business School, Publishing Corp.

Lamott, Anne. (1994). *Bird by Bird: Some Instructions on Writing and Life*. New York: Anchor Books.

Leigh, Andrew. (1993). *Perfect Decisions*. London: Arrow Books, Ltd.

Maital, Shlomo. (1994). *Executive Economics—Ten Essential Tools for Managers*. New York: Free Press.

Marchand, Donald, Kettinger, William, & Rollins, John. (2001). *Making the Invisible Visible—How Companies Win with the Right Information, People and IT*. West Sussex, England: John Wiley & Sons.

McFarlan, F. Warren, Applegate, Lynda M., & McKenney, James L. (1999). *Corporate Information Systems Management: The Challenge of Managing in an Information Age, 5th edition*. Irwin/McGraw-Hill.

McFarlan, F. Warren, Applegate, Lynda M., & McKenney, James L. (1996). *Corporate Information Systems Management: The Issues Facing Senior Executives, 4th edition*. Irwin.

McKee, Robert. (1997). *Story: Substance Structure, Style, and the Principles of Screen Writing*. New York: HarperCollins Publishers.

Montague, Read. (2006). *Why Choose This Book?* New York: Penguin Group.

Niven, Paul R. (2002). *Balanced Scorecard Step-by-Step: Maximizing Performance and Maintaining Results*. New York: John Wiley & Sons.

Olve, Nils-Goran, Roy, Jan, & Wetter, Magnus. (1999). *Performance Drivers—A Practical Guide to Using the Balanced Scorecard*. West Sussex, England: John Wiley & Sons.

Parker, Marilyn, & Benson, Robert. (1988). *Information Economics—Linking Business Performance to Information Technology*. Englewood Cliffs, NJ: Prentice-Hall.

Parker, Marilyn, Benson, Robert, & Trainor, H. E. (1989). *Information Strategy and Economics*. Englewood Cliffs, NJ: Prentice-Hall.

Reichheld, Frederick F. (Bain & Co. Inc.). (1996). *The Loyalty Effect—The Hidden Force behind Growth, Profits, and Lasting Value*. Boston: Harvard Business School Press.

Reichheld, Frederick F. (2001). *Loyalty Rules, How Today's Leaders Build Lasting Relationships*. Boston: Harvard Business School Press.

Russo, J. Edward, & Schoemaker, Paul J. M. (2002). *Winning Decisions: Getting It Right the First Time*. New York: Doubleday.

Schwarts, Barry. (2004). *The Paradox of Choice*. New York: HarperCollins.

Steps to Success. (2007). *Make Effective Decisions*. London: A & C Black.

About the Author

Jack M. Keen is the Value Analytics Leader for Infosys Consulting, the strategic consulting unit of Infosys Technologies, Ltd., a leading global player in IT services. Jack's 25-plus years of computer industry experience include serving as a management consultant to executives of leading organizations as well as being a Fortune 500 division manager, executive trainer, sales manager, and systems analyst.

For the past 19 years, Jack has focused full-time on advising leaders of major enterprises on best practices for justifying and prioritizing technology-based investments, and then managing programs so their full value is achieved. He is recognized worldwide as a thought leader in creating and delivering high-impact value realization approaches. He serves as a charter member of Infosys's global value realization thought leadership team, responsible for guiding the continuous evolution of best practices for business case, stakeholder accountability, metrics management, decision support for prioritization and customization, and benefits tracking.

More than 200 organizations (public and private, profit and nonprofit) in 15 countries on four continents have embraced the concepts and principles Jack advocates. Over 7,000 professionals worldwide have been trained on many of these techniques. Favorable commentary on these approaches has appeared in major trade media, including *CFO* and *CIO* magazines. Jack is a frequent conference guest speaker and workshop facilitator, and has authored more than 40 articles, including monthly columns for *CIO* magazine (www.cio.com) and datamation.com.

Jack has an MBA from Harvard Business School and a Bachelor of Science in Industrial Engineering from Stanford University. He has served as vice president of the International Board of Directors for the 61,000-member Harvard Business School Alumni Association.

He can be reached at JackMKeen@gmail.com.

279

Index